PICK:™
The Easy Way

Volume I
Database and Word Processing for the New User

MATTHEW H. STERN
BETSY POLLACK

Comprehensive Information Sciences Inc.

Every effort has been made to provide the reader with complete and accurate information. However, the authors and publisher assume no responsibility for error or omission, suitability for any use or purpose, damages resulting from the use of the information contained herein, or infringements of patents or other rights.

Copyright (c) August 1987 Comprehensive Information Sciences Inc., all rights reserved. No part of this book may be reprinted, reproduced, stored in a retrieval system, or utilized or transmitted in any form or by any means without the prior written approval of the copyright owner.

Library of Congress Cataloging-in-Publication Data:

Stern, Matthew H.
  PICK: The Easy Way.

  Includes indexes.
  Contents: v. 1. Database and word processing for the new user --
  v. 2. Expanded theory and operation.
  1. PICK (Computer operating system) I. Pollack, Betsy
  II. Title
QA76.76.063S74   1986   005.4'46   86-2586
ISBN 0-936477-01-6 (pbk. : v. 1)

Printed in the United States of America by Arcata Graphics

1 2 3 4 5 6 7 8 9

87 88 89 90 91 92 93 94 95

Comprehensive Information Sciences Inc.
P. O. Box 622
Huntington, New York 11743
U. S. A.

FOREWORD

In an increasingly competitive marketplace for computer systems and software products, the Pick System continues to grow in popularity and acceptance. The remarkable worldwide growth of the Pick System in recent years can be attributed to an expanding awareness of the importance to business of an operating system that was designed for data management.

The Pick System is much more than a traditional operating system. Even to use the words "operating system" is to limit its potential. This is rather like referring to the space shuttle as a motor vehicle. The Pick System is, fundamentally, a "data management environment" that brings to the user a consistent, powerful, adaptive, and practical means for running his business.

This excellent series by Matt Stern serves as an overview of this data management environment. Tailored for the new user, Volume I concentrates on basic system concepts, laying the foundation for the other volumes in the series.

We at Pick Systems commend Mr. Stern for increasing the awareness and education of those interested in exploring the Pick System with these books.

So now throw away any preconceived ideas that you may have of an "operating system" and welcome to *PICK: The Easy Way*.

>   Jeffrey Hunt
>   Director of Product Support
>   Pick Systems, Irvine California

PREFACE

This book was written for the new user - new to computers and/or new to the Pick Operating System. The only requirement is a desire to learn; previous knowledge of computers or a programming language is not necessary.

The unique capabilities of Pick enable even the beginner to harness a wide range of built-in functions. In everyday language the text takes the reader step-by-step from an overview of computers and file concepts into simple procedures which gradually become more complex. You will find the Glondex at the back of the book a practical and innovative reference for definitions of common terms combined with an index for page numbers.

Although not a part of the Pick Operating System, some version of the JET word processor is included as standard equipment on most systems. JET I or II is the common name; examples of other names are the Microdata *Wordmate*, the Ultimate *Ulti-word*, and the ADDS Mentor *Documentor*.

Every effort has been made to enable the new user to work as independently as possible. However, given the number of keys on a keyboard, there may be times when a key is pressed in error and the help of a more experienced person will be needed.

Entering the world of computers is challenging and rewarding. We hope you enjoy it and continue your exploration.

This book applies to the generic Pick system found on the following manufacturers' trademarked products:

COMPANY	PRODUCT NAME/FAMILY
Altos Computer Systems	586, 3068
Applied Digital Data Systems (ADDS)	Mentor
Archford Computer International	M-68000, M-68020
Aston Technology Ltd.	MC68000

CDI Information Systems, Inc.	IBM Series/1, RT/6150
CIE Systems/Bonneco	680
Concurrent Operating Systems Technology	Sequoia
Datamedia Corporation	932
Electronique Serge Dassault	68000
Fujitsu Espana	80286/386
Fujitsu Microsystems of America, Inc.	2020
General Automation, Inc.	Zebra
IBC Technologies, Inc.	MC 68010
Icon Systems & Software, Inc.	MPS 0202
Intertechnique (IN-2)	Multi-6
McDonnell Douglas (Microdata)	Reality, Spirit, Sequel
Nixdorf Computer Corporation	8890 VM
Pick Systems	PC/XT, PC/AT
Rexon Business Machines	80286/80386
Scan Optics (formerly Pertec)	Sabre
STC Business Communication System	5/32, 6/32
Systems Management, Inc. (SMI)	IBM CS 9000
Tau/Nippon Steel, Inc.	M-68000
Toltec Computer	Edge
The Ultimate Corporation	Honeywell Level 6, DEC LSI 11 and VAX, IBM 4300
Wicat Computer of Australia Pty.	M-68000
Xmark Corporation	Turbo Tower Series

Note that the McDonnell Douglas and Ultimate systems vary somewhat from generic Pick.

The vendors listed below are related licensees and their products are quite similar to Pick and have moderate compatibility:

Cosmos Inc.	Revelation
Prime Computer Inc.	Information
Vmark Computer Inc.	UniVerse

Because of the diversity of systems using Pick, you may discover slight differences between examples in this book and your particular system. When this occurs, consult the user's reference manual that came with your computer.

ACKNOWLEDGEMENTS

The authors are most grateful to the following people for their invaluable assistance on this project:

Charles and Janice Josephson, Joel Nirenberg, Keith Richman, Peter Stern, Robert Sivori, and Randy Thomas.

Thanks are also due:

Mike and Peter Schellenbach of AccuSoft Enterprises for their assistance and use of the ACCU/PLOT-II utility for the graphics.

Jackie Bahr and Gary Schneider of the Hewlett-Packard Corporation for their assistance with the Laser-Jet Series II printer for typesetting and graphics.

John E. Treankler of JET Software Inc. for the JET Word Processor which was used for the manuscript and for writing the foreword to the chapter on JET.

Dave Royston and Tony Speed of Mainstream Technologies for Mainlink which was used for communicating between our word processing systems.

Philip Earl; Jeffrey Hunt, author of the Foreword; and Frank Petyak of Pick Systems for their help, enthusiasm, and use of the Pick Operating System for the PC/XT. Special thanks to Dick Pick for developing this remarkable Operating System in the first place.

To friendship and the completion of an exciting project

CONTENTS

1 INTRODUCTION TO THE COMPUTER
- 1.1 WHAT IS A COMPUTER? 1
- 1.2 WHAT A COMPUTER CAN (AND CANNOT) DO 2
- 1.3 COMPUTER EVOLUTION 5
- 1.4 ABOUT HARDWARE 7
- 1.5 ABOUT SOFTWARE 8
- 1.6 THE PICK OPERATING SYSTEM 9
- 1.7 REVIEW QUESTIONS 10

2 ORGANIZING THE FACTS: FILES
- 2.1 INTRODUCTION 13
- 2.2 ARRANGE THE DATA: LOGICAL FILE STRUCTURE 15
- 2.3 ASSIGN THE DATA: TABLES AND DATABASE 17
- 2.4 THE FILE ON THE DISK: PHYSICAL FILE STRUCTURE 22
- 2.5 FILES IN THE PICK SYSTEM 24
- 2.6 REVIEW QUESTIONS 26

3 GETTING STARTED: HANDS ON
- 3.1 INTRODUCTION 27
- 3.2 THE TERMINAL 27
- 3.2.1 THE KEYBOARD 27
- 3.2.2 THE SCREEN 28
- 3.3 LOGON 29
- 3.3.1 CREATE AN ACCOUNT 29
- 3.3.2 LOGGING ON 31
- 3.4 THE DICTIONARY AND THE DATA FILE 33
- 3.5 CREATE THE DICTIONARY 34
- 3.6 CREATE THE DATA FILE 55
- 3.7 LOGGING OFF 61
- 3.8 ERROR EXAMPLES 61
- 3.9 REVIEW QUESTIONS 63

4 KEEPING THE FILE CURRENT: UPDATE
    4.1 OVERVIEW   65
    4.2 WHAT IS IN THE FILE? THE LIST COMMANDS   65
    4.3 INTRODUCTION TO UPDATING   74
    4.4 INPUT NEW DATA: ADD   76
    4.5 REPLACE DATA: CHANGE   88
    4.6 REMOVE DATA: DELETE   91
    4.7 FINAL STEPS OF UPDATE   103
    4.8 ERROR EXAMPLES   108
    4.9 REVIEW QUESTIONS   110

5 PRODUCING INFORMATION FROM THE DATA
    5.1 WHAT IS ACCESS?   111
    5.2 EXTRACT DATA: LIST WITH SELECTION CRITERIA   112
    5.3 THE VERBS COUNT, SUM, STAT   117
    5.4 MORE SELECTION CRITERIA   126
    5.5 JUSTIFICATION   129
    5.6 REARRANGE OUTPUT: THE SORT VERB   132
    5.7 STRING SEARCHES   143
    5.8 ERROR EXAMPLES   148
    5.9 REVIEW QUESTIONS   151

6 OUTPUTTING FAMILIAR DATA IN NEW WAYS
    6.1 OVERVIEW   153
    6.2 HEADINGS AND FOOTINGS   153
    6.3 TOTALS   162
    6.4 SUBTOTALS VIA CONTROL BREAKS   165
    6.5 IMPLICIT ATTRIBUTE LISTS   179
    6.6 ERROR EXAMPLES   183
    6.7 REVIEW QUESTIONS   188

7 CHANGING THE OUTPUT VIA THE DESCRIPTOR
    7.1 DESCRIPTOR REVIEW AND LINE 10: LENGTH   189
    7.2 LINE 9: JUSTIFICATION   192
    7.3 LINE 3: TAG   197
    7.4 LINES 7 AND 8: CONVERSIONS AND CORRELATIVES   200
    7.4.1 MASK CHARACTER: MC   203

    7.4.2   PATTERN: P   209
    7.4.3   GROUP EXTRACTION: G   212
    7.4.4   TEXT EXTRACTION OR TEXTRACT: T   215
    7.4.5   CONCATENATION: C   220
    7.4.6   RANGE: R   229
    7.4.7   PUNCTUATE NUMERIC DATA: MR   233
    7.4.8   ARITHMETIC: A   239
    7.4.9   TRANSLATION: TFILE   253
    7.4.10 DATE: D   258
    7.4.11 PROCESSING WITH SELECTION CRITERIA   264
    7.5   ERROR EXAMPLES   279
    7.6   REVIEW QUESTIONS   281

8 WORD PROCESSING WITH JET
    FOREWORD   283
    8.1   WHAT IS JET?   283
    8.2   BEGIN THE ITEM   286
    8.3   CURSOR POSITIONING   292
    8.4   EDIT THE TEXT: INSERT, CHANGE, AND DELETE   295
    8.5   ALIGN THE TEXT: RULERS   304
    8.5.1   OVERVIEW   304
    8.5.2   CURSOR POSITIONING   307
    8.5.3   ALIGNMENT CHARACTERS   307
    8.5.4   DELETE   311
    8.5.5   SAVE AND GET A RULER   311
    8.5.6   LEAVE RULER MODE   313
    8.5.7   APPLICATIONS   315
    8.6   ADVANCED EDITING   317
    8.6.1   ABOUT FILES AND ITEMS   317
    8.6.2   THE SPELLING CHECKER   322
    8.6.3   INSERT ON A NEW LINE   325
    8.6.4   MERGE   326
    8.6.5   SEARCH (AND REPLACE)   331
    8.6.6   CUT AND PASTE   338
    8.7   SUMMARY GUIDES   346
    8.7.1   THE JET MODES   346
    8.7.2   FUNCTIONS OF THE KEYS IN JET   351
    8.8   FINISHING TOUCHES   353
    8.8.1   OVERVIEW   353

8.8.2   HEADINGS AND FOOTINGS   354
8.8.3   NEW PAGE   359
8.8.4   SPACING   359
8.8.5   JUSTIFICATION   360
8.8.6   INDENT   361
8.8.7   HILITE   363
8.8.8   UNDERLINE   365
8.8.9   BOLDFACE   368
8.9   PRINT THE ITEM   370
8.10   JOIN THE DATABASE WITH THE ITEM   373
8.11   ERROR EXAMPLES   381
8.12   REVIEW QUESTIONS   383

Glossary/Index (Glondex)   385

Additional Trademarks   397

Chapter 1

Introduction to the Computer

1.1 WHAT IS A COMPUTER?

"Someday I'd like to learn about computers."
"I'm afraid of computers."
"The computer goofed."
"Computers are taking over our lives."

Whenever the conversation turns to the subject of computers these comments are typical of what we hear.

You are reading this book because "someday" is here and you are ready to enter the fascinating computer world. There is nothing to be afraid of; you can master other electronic labor-saving devices like calculators, microwave ovens, and VCRs, and the computer is no different. As for "goofs" the computer is incredibly accurate; usually it is the operator who makes the mistakes.

"Taking over our lives" is an exaggeration but the presence of computers is obvious, whether they are seen in banks, gas stations, and at cash registers or unseen by the public as in an insurance company's headquarters or the IRS. This machine that seems to be everywhere, does nothing that people cannot do, only the computer does it faster and much more accurately. It has been designed to store data - the "facts" given to the computer whether they are true or false - and process them according to stored instructions to produce the information wanted by the user.

A typical business application is the record keeping necessary to process a customer's order: enter all customer information along with product identification, quantity, and price; have the computer check the credit rating; update inventory control; and calculate and print the invoice. The same organization can use a different procedure for its payroll operation.

There are only two requirements to understand a computer: common sense and patience. Follow the operating instructions as you would with any new appliance. When you start to drive a car you are probably more interested in getting behind the wheel than learning to be a mechanic but it helps to know the fundamentals to get the most out of the machine; the same is true here. And so before focusing on the Pick Operating System let us take a brief look at computers in general.

The computer is powered by electricity and most of those in use today are the *digital* type which work by sensing the presence or absence of very small amounts of electrical current. Thus we have a two state or *binary* (consisting of two things) system where ON is represented by 1 and OFF by 0. 1 and 0 are called *bits*, a contraction of binary digits; all data is expressed in this form. As beginners we do not use actual binary representation. It is enough to know that this is the basis of the whole complex operation of a computer.

Bits are combined - usually 8 - into a *byte* in order to create a character code. The bit is the smallest part of the computer's language just as one character is the smallest part of ours. Each letter, number, and most of the symbols on a typewriter has its own pattern of 1's and 0's. One of the standard codes is *ASCII* (American Standard Code for Information Interchange). In it for example, capital letter A corresponds to 0100 0001 in binary.

The conversion to binary is done automatically for us. All that the user has to remember is that the computer has been manufactured to work in a particular way. When it "understands" what you want it to do, it performs with great speed and accuracy. If the instructions are not in the format acceptable to your system, you will be frustrated at not getting the results you expect. Whatever you do the computer never gets annoyed or laughs at your mistakes; instead it tries to help by means of a message. It never gets bored with the most tedious tasks or waits for thanks for a job well done. It is truly a unique slave.

1.2 WHAT A COMPUTER CAN (AND CANNOT) DO

It is important to realize that a human brain and a computer do not work in the same way. People can think intuitively and also do more than one thing at a time. The computer can do neither; it blindly follows instructions, one at a time, sequentially (except for some highly specialized systems). If the sequence is altered the outcome will be different.

The computer performs three basic functions:

1. Arithmetic: add, subtract, multiply, and divide
2. Comparisons using logical operators such as equal, greater than, and less than; logical operations with AND and OR.
3. Storage and retrieval of data.

These operations are performed with unbelievable speed - millions per second - and remarkable accuracy by all types of computers although speed and accuracy vary with the physical capabilities of the system.

The computer is ready, willing, and able to get busy but cannot start without help. It must be given facts in a form it can accept and then be told exactly what to do with them in terms it has been set up to follow. Our first responsibility is to analyze the project. What information do we want the computer to produce or *output*? What data - *input* - is necessary to generate this output? And finally what processing steps will transform the data into the output? These three steps are referred to as the data processing cycle but as you can see it is more like a flow pattern.

The operations which the computer does so well are not limited to mathematical calculations. A small sample of some of the thousands of applications includes:

Aviation: airline reservations; pilot records; history of repairs; replacement of components.

Bridal Registry: a store's listing of a bride's preferences for wedding gifts. When an item is purchased for the bride it is removed from the list to avoid duplication.

Cemetery: sales; interment records; space inventory.

Engineering: CAD (Computer Aided Design) to produce designs in a fraction of the time formerly required.

Factories: computers with and without vision (robots) to perform tedious or hazardous work.

Medicine: Hospitals - patient master index, administration, laboratory management, dietary control. Handicapped - aid to those with impaired hearing, sight, or speech, and motor disabilities. Pharmacy - Rx records, drug interaction, patient profiles.

Real Estate: multiple listing; mortgage information; prospect matching; searches.

Religious Organizations: membership and contribution records.

Restaurants: portion control; recipe costing.

Security: sort, respond to and report on signals.

Veterinary: animal ancestry; breeder, owner, and medical records; print registration certificates.

Zoo: attendance; animal medical and geneology records; payroll and personnel.

The list seems endless yet it keeps expanding.

Growth has been hampered by the computer's inability to "think." A human brain can sift the information it receives: absorb it and at the same time draw conclusions from it based on prior experience. For example, when a person sees a tree he knows from childhood to walk around the tree and not into it. The sight of the tree is visual input and the computer will always walk into the tree unless it has been given specific instructions to avoid a collision.

The computer also has difficulties dealing with words. When people read or hear a word that has several meanings they understand through the context in which the word is used. But how do you explain to a computer which meaning to choose for a word such as "arm" ? Is it the upper limb of a human? A branch of a tree? The elbow support on a chair or sofa? Nautically, the end of a yard or section of an anchor? Arms could be weapons (a noun) or furnish with weapons (a verb). When it comes to figurative expressions extracting the meaning becomes even harder: "at arm's length" is a good distance off; "in the arms of Morpheus" means sleeping; power is implied in "the arm of the law"; and "with open arms" is cordially. This is the kind of problem faced by researchers in AI (*Artificial Intelligence*) who explore ways to make computers "think".

Expert systems are one practical application of AI. A skilled programmer learns from an expert in a particular field the deductive reasoning based on experience that produces the answers to problems. A computer program is written to duplicate the logic used by a human brain. The result is an Expert or Knowledge Based system which, for example, can perform medical diagnoses or pinpoint car malfunctions.

The goal is to analyze human intelligence and duplicate it to the degree possible in order to build computers with greater powers. *Artificial* is the key word here. No matter how powerful the computer it remains a machine without imagination and without perception. *Real intelligence* is in the human mind with insight and common sense, and the inspiration to create true wonders like symphonies, great paintings, philosophical theories, and only incidentally devices to produce information.

1.3 COMPUTER EVOLUTION

Today's computer did not suddenly emerge in its present form. Throughout history inventors have looked for ways to solve problems with more speed and accuracy. The roots of the computer start with the abacus, a calculating device with sliding counters that has been in use for thousands of years.

Not until the 17th century does the next stage appear when two philosopher-mathematicians created calculating machines. First was Blaise Pascal (1623-62) a Frenchman whose name was given to a modern computer language and later the German Baron G. W. von Leibnitz (1646-1716). There is another gap until the early 19th century when Joseph Marie Jacquard, (1752-1834) a French inventor, devised a method of using holes on punched cards to control weaving color patterns on a loom. This was a radical innovation in the textile industry.

Charles Babbage (1792-1871), English mathematician, is named as the father of the modern computer. His designs culminated in 1833 with the Analytical Machine which was never built because the technology of his day could not produce the precision parts that were required. It took over 100 years and the impetus of World War II to develop recognizable ancestors of the modern computer. Along the way Herman Hollerith (1860-1929), a statistician, used punched cards for the first time to automate data processing of the 1890 census.

More recent pioneers include Allan Turing best known for his work in cracking German military codes in England during WW II; John von Neumann who introduced the concept of the stored program; and John W. Mauchly and J. Presper Eckert. Working for the U.S. Army, in 1946

Mauchly and Eckert completed *ENIAC* (Electronic Numerical Integrator And Calculator) the first large scale electronic computer. It was powered by 18,000 vacuum tubes which were slow by today's standards and frequently failed; it occupied 1,500 square feet of space and weighed 30 tons.

Subsequent development (broken into "generations" of less than a decade each) progressed from this huge, slow, expensive machine. Tubes were later replaced by transistors which in turn gave way to integrated circuits. Now a tiny chip of silicon about 1/8th of an inch square holds thousands of circuits. Each improvement resulted in greatly reduced size and cost along with increased processing speeds, capabilities, and accuracy. As we enter the fifth computer generation the search continues for more advanced technology and how to give computers more "effective" intelligence.

The evolution of computer languages runs parallel to the physical improvements. In the beginning (first generation), the user had to write out possibly thousands of lengthy commands in the machine's binary language of 0's and 1's: one instruction for each machine level instruction.

Afterward (second generation) came Assembler languages consisting of codes more easily understood and written than binary. However there was still the one-to-one correlation. A processor in the computer translates Assembler language into machine language. The goal has always been toward languages closer to English - *high level* - where one command generates many at the machine level. This makes it easier for the user to give instructions to the computer. A compiler automatically changes the high level language into machine level language which is the only one that the computer "understands."

The first high level language (third generation) was *BASIC* (Beginners All-Purpose Symbolic Instruction Code) developed by John Kemeney and Thomas Kurtz at Dartmouth College in the early 1960's. It is still widely used and an expanded version is currently provided with the Pick Operating System. Other languages have been created for specific areas such as *COBOL* (Common Business Oriented Language) for business, and *FORTRAN* (Formula Translator) for science. Computer terminology has spawned many acronyms - pronounceable words made up of the first letter(s) of a series of words - such as these names of languages.

The distinctions between types of computers have become blurred but the general categories are the mainframe, the largest, most complex and costly; the mini(computer) which is less powerful and expensive yet well suited to many purposes; and the smallest, the micro(computer), introduced in 1971 as a result of the development of the smaller and cheaper chip. Home computers and PCs (Personal Computers) are classified as micros.

There are also special purpose computers that are embedded in machines and "dedicated" to a special task such as controlling a washing machine or microwave oven.

According to the late Kenneth O. May, Professor of Mathematics at the University of Toronto, the development of the electronic computer is one of the major events in world history; it penetrates everywhere at every level.

And so computers are not the "coming" thing, they are already here to stay and we can be sure of continued changes in design and broader applications.

1.4 ABOUT HARDWARE

Hardware refers to all the physical parts of a computer. Every system consists of three major components: a *CPU* (Central Processing Unit), *Memory*, and *I/O* (In/Out) *devices*.

The CPU is the heart of the system; it controls all computer activities and performs calculations, comparisons, and logical operations.

(Main) Memory or *RAM* (Random Access Memory) is a work area. Like a scratchpad it holds currently used data and instructions. The contents of RAM are described as *volatile* which means that they are in it only temporarily and erased when the system is turned off. Memory size is measured in units of K from kilo meaning one thousand, but 1K is actually 1024 bytes. Systems are described as having 64K, 256K, and 512K up to several megabytes (one megabyte equals a binary million bytes) for a large mini or mainframe.

I/O devices, also called *peripherals*, allow the computer to have contact with the outside world. They bring data and instructions to the CPU and take the output from it. For example, the terminal keyboard for entering data is an input device; the TV-like screen shows input as it is typed and also displays output. The optical scanner that reads bar price codes and the joystick of a computer game are also input devices that make it possible for the user to *interface* or communicate with the computer. In addition to the terminal screen some other output devices are printers which produce *hard copy* - written reports usually on paper - and voice synthesizers which convert output into pseudo speech. The user has the choices of directing output for immediate inspection as mentioned or storing it for the future or both.

Some peripherals also make it possible to store data and instructions outside the computer and bring them in as necessary for processing. This *auxiliary* or *secondary* storage greatly expands the potential capacity of Memory.

The information transferred by the peripherals must be stored on some kind of medium. Most common are the *disk* - a round flat plate - and *tape* - similar to recording tape. Both have magnetized particles on their surfaces for the pulses of electricity which are the bits of the binary code. Data, instructions, and output can be stored on disk or tape. One important application is to duplicate records, usually on tape, for *backup* in case of a malfunction that results in the loss of data. Here the term "data" includes instructions. The backup tape is then used as input to recover the lost data.

The disk drive is the peripheral device that transfers data between computer and disk; the tape drive does the same for tape.

All of these hardware elements are useless on their own; they can do nothing until software takes over to manage them.

1.5 ABOUT SOFTWARE

Software, generally called *programs*, makes it possible to use the hardware. All programs consist of a sequence of instructions that perform a specific task. They can be divided into programs supplied by the manufacturer and already in the computer when it is purchased, or application programs furnished by the user which are equivalent to the processing steps in the data processing cycle. The data that is required for input should also be included with the software. Although programs and data are described as non-physical computer elements they are physically represented in the form of magnetized bits on a medium. Hardware and software work together to make the computer useable; neither is capable of accomplishing anything alone. The combination of the hardware's power and how the software utilizes it determine the effectiveness of the system.

Before shipping the hardware, the computer vendor must install an *operating system* (OS), the series of programs that make the system operable. The OS coordinates I/O functions, data flow, memory management, and many other highly complex tasks to ensure the greatest operating efficiency. Since the OS resides on the disk, the parts must be brought into memory as they are needed.

Although not actually part of the Pick Operating System, all Pick-based systems include resident hardware known as *ROM* (Read Only Memory) to *boot* or start up the OS. ROM is non-volatile; it does not lose its contents when the power is turned off. A small program in the ROM starts the booting (bootstrap) process by fetching a few instructions from the disk (the *boot record*) into memory. The boot record contains additional instructions to bring in more of the OS and the snowballing continues until the system is "up" and ready to use; ROM is not active until the next time the machine is powered on. Once the OS is operational it continues until the machine is turned off.

Another type of program - the utility - is supplied with the computer and performs of a standardized operation such as sorting data.

Application programs are procedures for solving particular problems like computing a payroll or updating charge account records. Here the choice is up to the user. He/she can write a program in a programming language acceptable to the system or purchase one or more related programs in a ready-to-use software package compatible with the system to do the special job. Most of the examples of uses for the computer in Section 1.2 were taken from a directory of software with over 800 entries available for Pick-based systems.

1.6 THE PICK OPERATING SYSTEM

The Pick Operating System is like other operating systems in that it controls the computer, but unlike the others because of its broader scope. Some of its many unique capabilities permit a person with no prior knowledge of computers or programming languages to utilize a wide range of built-in functions. Therefore, a new user can tap directly into the computer system instead of being limited to a software package that may or may not suit his needs. In 1965 Richard (Dick) Pick met Don

Nelson and the result of their association was the first commercial version of the Pick Operating System marketed in 1973. Currently almost 30 manufacturers incorporate the Pick OS in their computers. All of the work of the OS is done for us and we need not be concerned with problems such as scheduling tasks, managing memory, and sorting files. The Pick System was designed to provide business and management applications with an efficient and flexible system that is at the same time user friendly (easily used by non-experts).

The parts of the OS with which we deal are several different processors each with its own particular function. The processor in charge is TCL (Terminal Control Language). It invokes whichever specialized processor is needed, turns control over to it, and then resumes control after the work segment is completed. This is like a contractor who calls in subcontractors for various parts of a project but eventually takes charge again. In addition to TCL we shall be using two of the standard Pick processors: the EDITOR which creates and modifies text, and ACCESS which retrieves and manipulates data. JET, the word processor, is not actually part of the Pick OS. Since most manufacturers include a version of JET, it is also covered in this book.

Some of the other Pick processors are the SPOOLER which manages output to be printed, PROC which executes stored procedures, and PICK/BASIC for BASIC programs. The SPOOLER is mentioned briefly in Chapter 8 in regard to JET output; the other processors are not suited to the beginner's level and therefore are not discussed.

This text addresses the generic Pick system but, because of the diversity of manufacturers, procedures may vary slightly. If a question arises consult your user reference manual.

1.7 REVIEW QUESTIONS

1. *Is it necessary to know a programming language to use the Pick Operating System? Why?*
2. *Describe the range of applications for the use of computers.*
3. *Give 5 examples of I/O devices.*
4. *What is the difference between Hardware and Software? In which category is an operating system?*
5. *What is a high level computer language? Give an example.*
6. *How is a computer different from a human brain?*
7. *Give the steps of the data processing cycle in their practical se-*

quence.
8. *What is the difference between RAM and ROM?*
9. *What is the heart of a computer system? What does it do?*
10. *Describe several stages in the development of the computer up to the present.*
11. *What is machine level language?*
12. *What is a bit? What is its purpose?*

Chapter 2

Organizing the facts: Files

2.1 INTRODUCTION

The world constantly bombards us with all kinds of unrelated facts, yet the human brain can absorb and later retrieve much of the jumble stored in its memory. The computer is more accurate and faster than a brain but cannot cope with unorganized facts. The raw material or data must be organized in some way before processing can be done. Therefore it is up to us to analyze the facts with the aim of arranging them best for the computer.

The first step is to place similar items together into a group. Whether it is a collection of stamps, a bunch of wildflowers, a squadron of planes, or a class of students, each group is a collection of related items. This collection is called a *file* for computer purposes; it reflects a small part of the real world.

You probably never thought of a telephone book as a file but it is a common example. Each subscriber has a unique telephone number which means that there are no two alike. In the company records the telephone number is used as a key to the customer's account. The key makes it possible to locate or recover the facts about the individual account such as name and address. All the customers in an area make up a file of facts that are stored together in the telephone directory.

The most efficient way to organize the file for the phone company office is to arrange or *sort* the telephone numbers in sequence. The telephone number is used as the key on which the file is sorted. Find the key in its place in the file and you have all the facts about that particular subscriber. This arrangement is fine when you know the number but no help at all if you know the subscriber's name but not the number. Therefore, the file has been rearranged to meet the user's needs: it is now sorted using the name as the key and you can easily retrieve the telephone number (and address if wanted). Note that although it is possible to have more than one subscriber with the same name, you are still able to get to the needed information.

Another common example of a file is the card catalog in the library: the related items in the file are books. For this example consider that each book has a title, author, subject, and call number (the identifying number given to each book before it is shelved) which here is assumed to be unique. Just as the telephone company employee retrieves facts about the account by means of the phone number, you can get to the book on the library shelf because the books are lined up in the order of their call numbers. But how do you pick out the book without knowing the call number? The card catalog must be arranged so that the call number is shown. One borrower knows the name of the author and therefore chooses the file that is sorted on the key of author. He looks up the call number and finds the book easily whether the library (the file) is small or enormous. Another reader knows only the title of the book and goes to the card catalog where the books are sorted with the title as the key. The call number is taken from the title card and then the book can be located in the stacks. A third copy of the library file is lined up by subject matter for those who want to use it as the key. Thus the file has been ordered in three different ways yet each arrangement contains the same data about every book and you merely use one key or another to retrieve the information. Without this kind of system you would have to go through all of the books until you found the particular one that you wanted.

The concept of organizing data into a file and then using one property as the key on which the file is sorted is also suited to computer processing. The approach is the same whatever the kind of facts: employee personnel records, stock inventory, or second-hand bathtub dealers.

Before doing anything else, decide what information you want from the computer because the nature of the output determines the way the raw data is organized. Then you can get started. The goal is to set up the data in a form easy to use and understand. It is possible that in spite of taking great care in the first steps you will find areas for improvement later on. Take the time to make the changes - you are not chiseling in stone. The examples in the text are exactly what they are called: 'examples' and have been chosen as common situations for most users. After reading each chapter consider how best you can apply the procedures to your individual needs.

2.2 ARRANGE THE DATA: LOGICAL FILE STRUCTURE

Each subscriber in the phone book and each book in the library is described as an *item* in its particular file. An item is defined as one object in a group of related objects; every item has a unique key such as the customer's phone number, the book's call number, or the employee's social security number. This unique key is never altered because it identifies the item and provides the path to all the other facts about the item. A person's address or marital status, the quantity of stock on hand, and a bank balance all change, some more often than others, but the key is never altered.

In addition to the key, which is called the *item-id*, the item usually has other properties or characteristics that are associated with it. Because the file is made up of similar items, each item has the same features: every employee has a name, an address, a pay rate, and a gender. These properties are referred to as the *attributes* of the item. All of the items have the same properties but each item has its own particular values for each attribute. The diagram represents the structure of the employee file for The Coriander Company.

The CORIANDER File Structure

	attribute1	attribute2	attribute3
item-id	NAME	JOB	ADDRESS

The items in the file are related because all are employees. Each item has a unique identifier - the item-id - which is the employee number, and three attributes: name, job description, and address. Usually the address is broken into separate attributes, one each for street, city, state, and zip. For simplification, here we use only the first part.

See Figure 2.1 on page 16.

The first item in the table is item-id 61. Read across for the other facts or data about this item. Attribute1 for all the items is NAME; the value for NAME in item 61 is BOB BLUE. Attribute2 is called JOB; the value here is SALES. Attribute3 is ADDRESS; the value is 123 HICKORY ST.. In this way the structure of the file provides a logical framework for the data it holds.

```
                    attribute1   attribute2   attribute3
        item-id      NAME         JOB          ADDRESS
Item->  | 61   Bob Blue    Sales      123 Hickory St. |
Item->  | 8    Jo Green    Sales      17 Elm Avenue   |
Item->  | 73   Pat Brown   Typist     22 Maple Lane   |
```

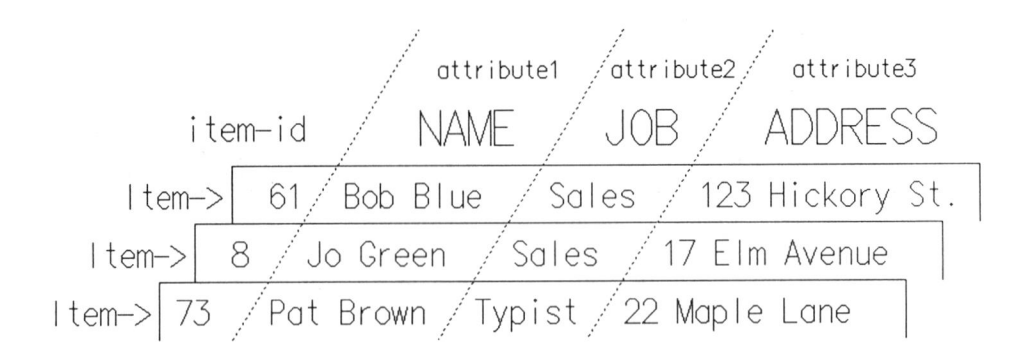

FIGURE 2.1: THE CORIANDER FILE WITH DATA VALUES

Explore the possibilities before making the final decision when creating your files. Storing the facts about an item as separate attributes is like putting each property into an individual compartment. This makes it easy for us to instruct the computer to retrieve one or more attribute values. You can combine or separate the data depending on your needs. For example, item 61 has BOB BLUE as the value for NAME. It is possible to store the name in two attributes by using attribute1 for FIRSTNAME and attribute2 for LASTNAME. They can be put together later if necessary. Now attribute3 becomes JOB and attribute4 becomes ADDRESS. Note that the contents of the file have not changed in any way, only the structure. All the items in the file must conform to the new scheme.

The Revised CORIANDER File Structure

```
            attribute1   attribute2   attribute3  attribute4
item-id     FIRSTNAME    LASTNAME     JOB         ADDRESS
```

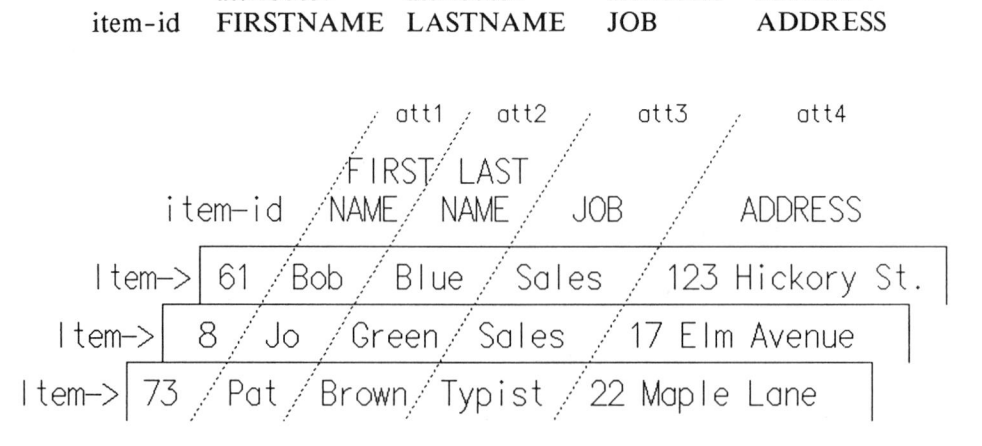

```
              att1   att2    att3       att4
              FIRST  LAST
    item-id   NAME   NAME    JOB        ADDRESS
Item-> | 61   Bob    Blue    Sales      123 Hickory St. |
Item-> | 8    Jo     Green   Sales      17 Elm Avenue   |
Item-> | 73   Pat    Brown   Typist     22 Maple Lane   |
```

FIGURE 2.2: THE REVISED CORIANDER FILE WITH DATA VALUES

Choose names for the attributes that are clearly understood by all who use the file. Is PRICE cost or selling? Is DIAMETER inside or outside? Is WEIGHT gross or net? Where values such as these are expressed in numbers, the same units must always be used: dollars or cents, feet or inches, pounds or ounces. Analyze the requirements of your data and create the appropriate architecture. This is the structure to hold the data. Then you can transform the raw facts into a file made up of items which can be read by the computer. As you can see, the main ingredient is common sense applied to individual needs.

2.3 ASSIGN THE DATA: TABLES AND DATABASE

Although the ultimate purpose of organizing facts is to create a usable format for the computer, we are at the same time making it easy for ourselves. Once we conceptualize the structure for the data we can easily assign places for all the facts to stored in it. We are so used to retrieving data that has been arranged within a framework that we are barely aware of it. Everyone is familiar with material set up in table form. The space for the facts is divided into rows that extend across and columns that go up and down. Because there are two directions to read - horizontally and vertically - the table is described as two dimensional.

One such example is Baseball Standings. Each item (team) occupies a line across the table. The first column holds the unique identifier or item-id which here is the name of the team. As you read across the row you find that each column contains one attribute or property associated with that particular team. Each column on the chart represents an attribute in the file. The name of the attribute acts as the column heading and defines the type of data in the column. Because the facts are organized but separated, each in its own compartment, you can either find the team (item-id) and read across the row to get all the facts about that team or find an attribute and then go across the row in the other direction to get the item-id.

GALACTIC LEAGUE WEST

TEAM	WON	LOST	PCT.
MARS	41	30	.577
EARTH	38	30	.559
JUPITER	35	32	.522
NEPTUNE	23	44	.343

Suppose you want the facts about the MARS team. Find the item-id MARS and read across. Perhaps you want to know what team has won 52.2% of its games. Go to the column marked PCT. and read down until you find your target of .522. Then read across to learn the item-id or team to which .522 belongs; here it is a value for JUPITER. Return to the column PCT. and repeat the search for any other item with .522. We all do this kind of thinking so fast and so automatically that it seems unnecessary to analyze how we do it. However we must be aware of the steps involved in order to prepare facts for processing. After data has been structured as in the Baseball Table, it is possible for the computer to retrieve data much as we have done. Do you realize that the League Standings can be called a file? It is certainly a collection of related items (teams) and their properties. For computer purposes it is ideal although the fans may not see it quite that way.

The file is the framework for all stored data and provides the raw material for subsequent manipulation. As previously recommended, first decide what information you want to get out of the file and then determine what facts are necessary to produce that kind of information. For learning the procedures we shall work with a test data file. You *must* use data especially created for experimenting.

When setting up the table for your data file use pencil, paper, and eraser. The more carefully you think the design through, the fewer problems you will have later on. Also remember the KISS principle: Keep It Simple, Stupid. As you develop your plans label the columns (attributes) and enter enough sample data to reflect a representative assortment of what will eventually be in the file. In this way you can see if the structure is suited to the data. It may be better to divide the facts into more than one file; the clue lies in the nature of the data itself. The table as a structure is not only convenient for people but also the most frequently used format for computer output.

You must select a unique name for the file by which it will be recognized. Since we shall be using capital letters when we type into the computer, we use upper case for these words in the text. Choose a descriptive title that will be easy to associate with the file, such as INVENTORY or PARTS, yet one that is not cumbersome because you must type it in whenever you work with the file. The range of possibilities is almost limitless within these few constraints:

The system allows a maximum length of fifty characters (bytes) for the name. It may consist of numbers (numeric data), letters (alphabetic data), or a combination (alphanumeric), and any punctuation marks or symbols with the exception of comma, semicolon, single and double quotes, backslash, and parentheses. Do not use spaces between words (embedded blanks). Remember that each non-letter counts as a character when checking the total length of the name. In short, each key on the keyboard equals one character.

SUMMARY: NAME of the FILE

NAME: must be unique

LENGTH: maximum 50 characters

CONTENTS: numeric or non-numeric characters or a combination
    EXCEPT , ; ' " \ ( ) embedded blanks

Sample File Names

   Correct
      1910-COINS
      EMPLOYEES:CASHIERS
      STORAGE

   Incorrect
      APPLES;BUSHELS
         ERROR No Semicolons ; Allowed

      FLORIDA SHELLS
         ERROR Embedded Blank

      HIPPOPOTAMI/GIRAFFES*INDIGENOUS-TO-THE-SERENGETI-PLAINS
         ERROR Too Long

When you see the word *filename* throughout this book it is a reminder that embedded blanks are not permitted in the name of a file.

Suppose we have a housewares store that sells kitchen gadgets and we need a file for all the gadgets we stock. The logical name for the file is GADGETS and it meets the criteria. Each gadget in the store has a unique code number which is ideal for the item-id because no two are alike. The constraints on the item-id are the same as for the filename. However when a combination of characters is used all item-ids must have the same pattern. For example, letters, a period, and two numbers; or numbers, a dash, and one letter. Whatever the format use it consistently for every item-id.

Next come the names for the attributes or the column headings. The first column is always reserved for the item-id. What other properties do the GADGETs have in common? Every GADGET or item in the file has a name e.g. spoon, ladle, fork etc.. We choose NAME as the first attribute. All the GADGETs also have some quantity on hand; let us shorten this to QTY for the second attribute. After a bit more thinking, we decide to add one more attribute for COLOR. Each of these attribute names becomes the heading for its own column. Always choose names that are easy to remember and also define the facts in the column. Do not change the name after it is assigned. When the table is designed, the attribute columns can be in any order.

This is the file structure:

The GADGETS file

	attribute1	attribute2	attribute3
item-id	NAME	QTY	COLOR

Before continuing we must check if the names we have chosen are permitted. The constraints for attribute names are the same as those for filenames:

SUMMARY: NAME of the ATTRIBUTE

NAME: must be unique within the attribute names in this file; it can start with a letter or a number

LENGTH: maximum 50 characters

CONTENTS: numeric or nonnumeric characters or a combination EXCEPT , ; ' " \ ( ) embedded blanks

The names we selected are legal. If you wondered why words like attribute1 were written without a space, it is a reminder that no embedded blanks are allowed in an attribute name.

The total of all the characters in the item-id and the attributes equal the length of the item. The maximum allowed for one item is 32,267. As new users we can stay well below the limit.

The next step is to put the data values for each gadget into the table. The order in which the items are entered does not matter; each item is retrieved by its item-id and not by its row in the table. The item-id always goes in the first column. When it comes to the data values, avoid extra blanks. For example you might start with a RED SPOON, item-id 8, and quantity 12. Be very careful to enter the value for each attribute in the proper column. Once the computer has been told that attribute1 is the NAME of the item, it takes whatever appears in that position to be the NAME. If the data for item 8 is entered as RED for attribute1 NAME, and SPOON for attribute3 COLOR, there is no way for the system to figure out that you made a mistake and transposed the two values. The computer does not know what you meant to enter and merrily processes a GADGET named RED with the color SPOON. You are not looking for this kind of humor in your output. Stay alert.

The data values for the first row of the table look like this:

The GADGETS file with one data item

item-id	NAME	QTY	COLOR
8	SPOON	12	RED

Each item in the file is entered, one row at a time, until all the items are in the table. The following is the complete file:

FILENAME: GADGETS

GADGETS

item-id	NAME	QTY	COLOR
8	SPOON	12	RED
9	SPOON	10	YELLOW
20	LADLE	19	TAN
30	WHISK	8	BLUE
7	SPOON	1	BROWN
21	LADLE	4	RED
50	FORK	23	TAN
42	SPATULA	17	RED
49	SPATULA	35	AVOCADO

In brief thus far, facts have been organized into a file and then the file was arranged in a two dimensional table. One or more files can further be organized into what is called a *database* that reflects the needs of its users. For example, when each department in a company maintains its own records there is bound to be duplication such as in personnel and payroll. Consolidation of the facts results in an integrated database which eliminates redundant data, requires less storage space, and permits faster data retrieval and update. In addition more usable information can be produced from the raw data. Most databases include security measures to control the operations permitted each user by assigning a *privilege level* or limit to the kinds of manipulation that can be done.

Since the table illustrates the relations of the items it contains, it is termed a *relational database*. Simply described, the table provides a method of getting to each compartment containing a fact. This idea is better expressed as the computer's ability to retrieve an item via either the item-id or one of its attributes.

There are other types of databases such as hierarchical and network which use different structures and are more complex. Since the Pick system uses the relational database, other architectures are not covered in this book.

You have just designed the beginning of a database by using ordinary language and everyday concepts. Would you have believed that a person new to computers could accomplish this? Once the database has been created you will be surprised how much can be done with it. The built-in capabilities of Pick make it possible for a beginner to perform a wide range of operations without learning anything about programming. Be patient, we shall go through the steps together.

2.4 THE FILE ON THE DISK: PHYSICAL FILE STRUCTURE

The emphasis has been on organizing the data into a structure that can be handled by the computer and makes sense to the user. The concept of the two dimensional table is an example of a *logical* file structure. How the computer stores the data on a medium such as magnetic tape or disk is known as *physical* file structure.

The type of storage medium determines the way in which the computer gets to the data. When the file is on tape, the computer must read through the entire file from beginning to end, sequentially. This is no problem unless only a small part of the file is wanted, then the user must wait

Organizing the facts: Files 23

for the whole file to be processed. However, when the file is stored on disk, it can be read through sequentially like tape but it is also possible for the computer to go more or less directly to an individual item and ignore everything else. This fast method of data retrieval is called *direct* or *random* access and is the one used here. The operator does not have to worry about the physical file structure; all the work is done automatically by the computer. This is described as *transparent* to the user.

The item-id is not only the identifier by which the item is found but also the basis of its storage location. Transparent to the user, the system applies a formula to the item-id and uses the results to assign the storage address for the item. This is known as *hashing* and is not one of our responsibilities.

The following explanation of file storage is conceptual rather than technical. A disk is made up of units of storage space or *frames*. Each data frame is like a sheet of paper and has a fixed capacity of 512 bytes (on most versions of Pick). Visualize the frames as sheets of paper laid out on the floor. The file will be written on these sheets. The smallest possible space for a file is one frame; a huge file may require a block of several thousand frames. The frames are spaced out in two directions. The horizontal dimension is the number of frames or groups from one side of the layout to the other; it is called the *modulo*. The vertical dimension is the number of frames from top to bottom; it is the *separation*.

Each frame has an address by which it can be located and also a *pointer* that gives the location of the frame containing the next part of the file. A pointer is address information that enables the system to link data. The result is that the file always appears to the user to be in order although physically it may be in different locations.

Whenever a file is to be entered in the system, space must first be reserved on the disk. This will be shown in the next chapter. After the original space allocation is filled, the file can expand into *overflow space*: unused space currently available on the disk.

Once the computer has set aside the frames for the file, it has places to put the facts about the structure of the data and also the data values. The entire physical operation results in the most efficient utilization of disk space. Not only is direct access possible but also the automatic expansion and contraction of file space as requirements change.

2.5 FILES IN THE PICK SYSTEM

Before the computer can process any of the data we have so carefully organized, it must be informed of certain essentials. The Pick system must know: Who is allowed to use the computer? How much is this user permitted to do? What files belong to each authorized user? How is each Data File structured? Where is each file stored? What are the actual values in the Data File? All of this and more must be given to the computer - but do not worry, very little is the beginner's responsibility. The enormous range of required information can be broken roughly into two broad categories: 1. the data itself, and 2. all the other essentials that are not data.

When creating the GADGETS Data File you saw how a file is constructed and given its own name by which it is accessed. Pick uses files to store every piece of information in the computer. Since there are two general types of facts, there are two types of files to hold them. The Data File is already familiar; it contains data elements such as item 8, a red spoon, and there are 12 on hand. The other kind of file is called *Dictionary*, but it is not like a conventional dictionary of word definitions. Here the Dictionary serves as a directory or table of contents that includes the storage location of the file and the organization of the data. In this way all facts can be stored in the type of file that suits them - either a Dictionary or a Data File.

For a conceptualized view of the relationship of these files imagine a hierarchy of four levels with the Data Files at the bottom on level 4. This is where the GADGETS Data File would be placed.

On level 3 just above the Data Files are the File Dictionaries referred to as Dictionaries. For our purposes a Data File is associated with its own Dictionary and they have the same name. Thus the GADGETS Dictionary holds the structure and location, by way of a pointer, for the GADGETS Data File below.

An account is an authorized name for logging on to the system. One user may have more than one account, and one account may have more than one user. Each account on the system has a *Master Dictionary* at level 2. The Master Dictionary stores the facts about that account, such as the commands (vocabulary) allowed to it, and the names and addresses of the account's Dictionaries at level 3.

Organizing the facts: Files

At the top on level 1 there is one System Dictionary, the directory of all authorized account names. Here are the particulars about each account including a pointer to the account's Master Dictionary at level 2.

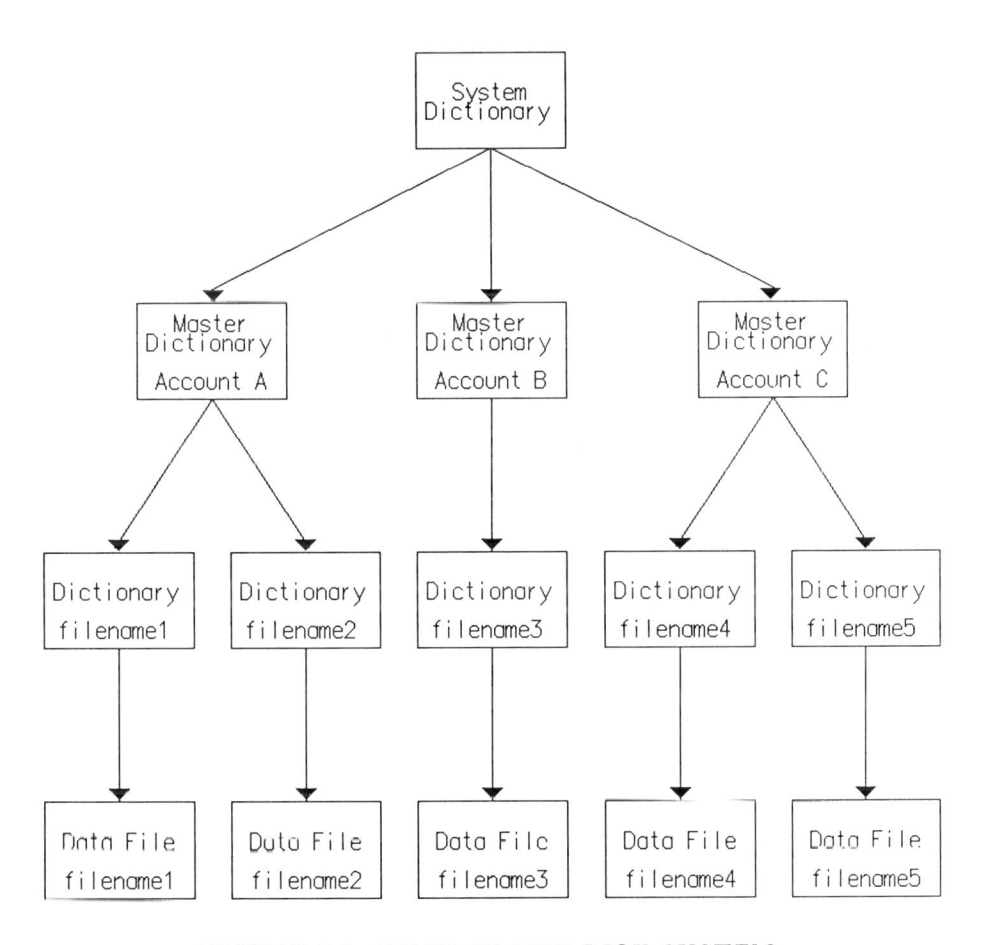

FIGURE 2.3: FILES IN THE PICK SYSTEM

This scheme designed for the Pick Operating System provides fast retrieval of any data element and also great flexibility to make changes as they are required. The system can accommodate any number of files and each file can contain any number of items (depending on disk space). Each item can vary in length up to a maximum of just over 32 thousand bytes (32,267 characters); each item and thus a file can shrink or expand automatically as necessary. Many systems impose multiple restrictions on file contents; but here there are virtually none.

2.6 REVIEW QUESTIONS

1. What is an item in a file?
2. Is it essential to use test data for experimenting? Why?
3. What is the main difference between a Dictionary and a Data File?
4. Why must data be organized for the computer?
5. What is the difference between logical and physical file structure?
6. What is the function of a key when a file is sorted?
7. Are there any constraints in choosing a filename?
8. In the Pick system many procedures are transparent to the user. Explain.
9. Give an example of an attribute.
10. How is data arranged in a two dimensional table?
11. What effect do tape and disk storage have on data retrieval?
12. What is a file?
13. What is a frame? How is it found?
14. Are embedded blanks permitted in the name of an attribute?
15. Can the key (item-id) of an item be altered? Why?

Chapter 3

Getting Started: Hands On

3.1 INTRODUCTION

Before starting to use the computer we must become acquainted with a few essentials - the equipment and how to operate it. Although progress may seem slow, by going through each step carefully you will gradually gain expertise. Questions may arise as you encounter these new procedures. Rather than overwhelm you at the beginning of each step, we have inserted explanations where most appropriate. Continue to read and follow each instruction as it is given; the meaning will become clearer as you go along.

3.2 THE TERMINAL

3.2.1 THE KEYBOARD

All instructions and user-supplied information are entered into the system via the keyboard. At first glance the terminal keyboard looks like that of a typewriter. You find the familiar keys for letters and numbers as well as the conventional symbols and punctuation marks plus keys with new functions that will be explained as they are needed. On the typewriter you have the choice of using upper or lower case letters. At this time you must enter only in upper case (caps). This is the form the letters must take to be accepted by the system; in Chapter 7 we cover how to change case for output.

The numeric keys must be used when numbers are typed in. Although zero 0 and the letter O may seem alike on the printed page there is a slight difference in their shapes and on the screen the zero will probably be displayed with a line through it; the system cannot accept one for the other. Do not confuse the number 1 and lower case letter l. Always use the proper keys for letters and numbers.

The keyboards of different terminals vary slightly in appearance, but they perform in essentially the same way. As text is typed in, it appears on the screen. After the line is typed in, the computer cannot act upon it until you indicate that the line is complete. Depending on the model of your keyboard, the key that shows completion of the line will probably be marked either ENTER, RETURN, SEND LINE, NEWLINE, or an arrow pointing down and left. To find out which key performs this function on your keyboard ask an associate or refer to the manual supplied by the manufacturer of the terminal. In the instructions given in this text, we shall indicate completing a line by <return> an abbreviation for Carriage Return.

3.2.2 THE SCREEN

On the screen you will see a rectangular block or underline that may or may not blink. This is the *cursor* and indicates the position that the next typed character will occupy. As you type in text, the cursor moves along from left to right. After you complete the line, the cursor reappears on the left end of the next line.

Mistakes are most easily corrected while the text is on the screen and before the line is completed. Get into the habit of taking a moment to check the line before you press <return>. When you notice an error, use the back space key to move the cursor from right to left to get to the problem. As the cursor travels across the line it erases whatever it passes over. Type in the correct characters and continue. Note that this can be done only on the current line. A different procedure must be followed to correct errors in a line after it has been completed; this will be explained in Chapter 4. Do not be upset if you find a mistake in a completed line; continue reading and work to whatever extent is possible. Make the correction later.

When you press <return> you give the computer a chance to act on what you have entered. The response on the screen is an appropriate answer followed by a character called a *prompt*. The prompt character varies with the system processor being used, but all indicate the computer's readiness to accept input. As we use a processor we shall identify its prompt. The prompt is generated by the system; never try to type one in yourself because it cannot work that way.

The dialogue between the user and the computer is somewhat like two CB radio operators conversing. One speaks and, when finished, gives the other an opportunity to talk. The prompt means that the system is ready to accept your next instruction. Just as you imply "over" by using the completion key, the system says "over" by displaying the prompt.

3.3 LOGON

You have been waiting patiently for the moment to put your "hands on" the terminal. Before you can start, obviously the system must be "up" and ready. Just like a bank the computer has many accounts. Every user on the system has an individual account name which should be unique and follow the same rules as for a filename. The first step of each session is always *logging on* or identifying yourself as a valid user. Since you have no experience yet, someone has probably created your account and entered all the information necessary for you to operate the computer. From now on samples of output on the screen are shown. There may be slight variations among installations although all have the Pick Operating System. The meanings are essentially the same.

Throughout the text the lines to be typed in are underlined and end with the instruction to press the <return> key. Although system words are in uppercase and user supplied words are in lower case letters in the examples, we enter everything in caps as a convention. The responses are also shown in caps as they appear on the screen.

3.3.1 CREATE AN ACCOUNT

Your company may have special policies and security restrictions that must be adhered to and so you should not create your own account. See the person who is responsible for giving you your account name and skip to Section 3.3.2. If someone is using the terminal wait until he or she has logged off and it is available for you.

If you are in charge of the computer system continue with the steps below.

The screen displays a LOGON message similar to

```
PLEASE ENTER ACCOUNT NAME:
```

or

```
Logon
```

or

```
LOGON PLEASE
```

Use the following procedure to create a new account. Type in

    SYSPROG <return>

As with all commands some of the responses vary from system to system. Do not be surprised if your message is not the same as shown here. The response is the TCL prompt

    >

or

    :

Some systems have a *menu* (a list of available procedures) and do not take you directly to TCL therefore choose the appropriate option. If you are not sure press the <return> key. At TCL enter

    >CREATE-ACCOUNT <return>

Response

    ACCOUNT NAME?

The account name must be unique; last names are recommended. If there are duplicates combine the last name with a period and an initial or the first name such as GRAY.J or GREEN.WILLIAM. Avoid general terms like CLASS or TUTORIAL. Enter the name of the account in caps next to the question mark and complete the line with <return> for example

    ACCOUNT NAME? STERN <return>

Each of the following responses appears one at a time. On several of the lines no information is required at this time and only <return> is necessary.

    L/RET-CODE(S)? <return>
    L/UPD-CODE(S)? <return>
    PRIVILEGES? SYS2 <return>
    MOD,SEP? <return>

The response for the example is

Getting Started: Hands On

```
CREATE-FILE (DICT STERN 29,1)
[417] FILE 'STERN' CREATED
```

Other system information is displayed on the next several lines.

We are not using a password now and so when you see

    PASSWORD?   press <return>

Response

    FINISHED
    >

or

    ACCOUNT STERN CREATED
    >

You have now authorized yourself to use the system. Enter

    >OFF <return>

3.3.2 LOGGING ON

The screen displays a LOGON message such as

    PLEASE ENTER ACCOUNT NAME:

or

    logon

or

    LOGON PLEASE

Type in

    your.account.name <return>

If the computer rejects the account name check the spelling. Remember that the system cannot assume that J.BLUE and JANE.BLUE are the same person. It has no way of knowing that RICH.GREEN is RICHARD. GREEN. Spell the name exactly as it was originally given to the system. If you are not a valid user or you do not spell your valid name correctly, you will get this answer

```
USER-ID?
PLEASE ENTER ACCOUNT NAME:
```

For example, suppose you typed in GRAY instead of GREY. The screen displays

```
PLEASE ENTER ACCOUNT NAME: GRAY
USER-ID?
PLEASE ENTER ACCOUNT NAME:
```

Start again and enter the name as it should be spelled.

The computer vocabulary is made up of two kinds of words: those with specific functions and meanings built into the system, and those chosen by the user for file and attribute names, and data values. The latter are called *user supplied* words.

We cannot overemphasize the importance of consistency. Whether giving names or commands, you must use the form exactly as it is expected. Intuition is not an available option on any machine. As long as you remember this requirement you will spare yourself a great deal of frustration.

After LOGON, the screen display varies with the manufacturer. The general format of the response is

```
<<< a code number, the computer manufacturer's name >>>
<<< time product name date >>>

>
```

such as

```
<<<--------------THE PICK SYSTEM--------------->>>
<<<--14:10:12--PC-XT Version 1.3--09 JAN 1987--->>>

>
```

The > symbol above (or : the colon) is the prompt character for the Terminal Control Language (TCL) Processor. This is the Processor automatically entered after LOGON.

Time is expressed in twenty-four hour format using two digits each for hour, minute, and second. Midnight is 0:00. The hours from 1 A.M. to noon are 1 to 12. From 1 P.M. to 11 P.M. 12 is added to the hour. For example, 10:15 A.M. becomes 10:15:12 (seconds can be omitted); 2:37 P.M. is 14:37.

The date is expressed in the format

```
date month year
```

such as

```
09 JAN 1987
```

The computer is not ready to function until the Operating System is ready. Before you started to work someone had already taken care of this and also entered the date and time which initiated the system's clock. If you are the system manager refer to the reference material on how to boot the system.

3.4 THE DICTIONARY AND THE DATA FILE

In Chapter 2 you made up a Data File consisting of related items. Each item has a unique identifier and common properties such as a name, a quantity, and a color as its attributes. The structure of these attributes must be described before the system can handle the data for you. Every Operating System has its own way of providing this information. It is recorded in the Pick system by a Dictionary as discussed in Chapter 2. Here the Dictionary contains the location of the Data File (a pointer generated automatically by the system) and the construction of the Data File (supplied by the user).

It is somewhat like searching for the furniture in a particular apartment within a huge apartment complex. First you need the address of the building and then the apartment number. Assume that every apartment has the same layout. If you know that there is an entrance hall just inside the door with the living room on the right and the kitchen on the left, you can easily find the contents of each room in a particular apartment.

This is the kind of guide service that the Dictionary provides for the computer. The filename is like the building address; the item-id is like the apartment number. When you are looking for the furniture in the living room, you can easily find it in any apartment because all the apartments are constructed on the same plan. There are two different concepts involved: first, the specific location and its configuration; and second, whatever occupies the site. The location and configuration of the related Data File are contained in the Dictionary; the actual items of data make up the Data File associated with the Dictionary. Knowing this, you can understand the next tasks which are to create the Dictionary and its Data File.

Keep in mind that data entry becomes tedious and errors easily occur but it is vital to be aware of the consequences of mistakes. The acronym "GIGO" stands for "garbage in / garbage out" and means exactly what it says. The computer will process whatever is supplied to it. If the information is not correct, the results cannot be of any value. The importance of accurate data entry cannot be overemphasized. Always check your text and correct errors using the back space key <u>before</u> pressing the <return> key. If you notice a mistake after you have pressed <return> continue reading in order to familiarize yourself with the procedures that follow. We shall cover the steps for correcting data entry errors in Chapter 4.

On some terminals you may look up and notice that the screen has become blank and yet the system is on; this happens whenever there is a period of no activity. Press <control> and R together and whatever was on the screen will reappear.

3.5 CREATE THE DICTIONARY

You must create the Dictionary and its associated Data File more or less concurrently. Of course the two jobs cannot be done simultaneously.

The prompt on the screen is > as you have already seen and indicates that we are at TCL (Terminal Control Language). This Processor executes our first command to allocate space for both the Dictionary and the Data File.

The procedures that follow consist of steps which must be performed in the sequence specified. Computers are very fussy about the order in which instructions are given. The sample data has been kept simple. After you have walked through the operation until it becomes familiar, you

Getting Started: Hands On

will be able to apply the method to your own needs. Therefore, for your first time, we suggest you go along with the text and perform each instruction as it is given.

The first step is to tell the computer what to do. The general command format is

>CREATE-FILE yourfilename dictmod datamod

The prompt is on the screen; for our sample enter

>CREATE-FILE GADGETS 3 17 <return>

Note that the syntax is different on the Microdata system; enter

:CREATE-FILE (GADGETS 3,1 17,1) <return>

It is essential to use the precise form required by the system. "Almost the same" will not work. Note the hyphen in CREATE-FILE and the spaces between the information in the line. At this time you need not be concerned with the two numbers; they indicate the beginning sizes of the Dictionary and the Data File respectively. In this way the system can reserve space for what we intend to create but this is not a size limitation since both areas can be enlarged later if necessary. You will not always use 3 and 17; these are recommended choices for this exercise.

The sample response is

[417] FILE 'GADGETS' CREATED; BASE = 22886, MODULO = 3, SEPAR = 1
[417] FILE 'GADGETS' CREATED; BASE = 49735, MODULO = 17, SEPAR = 1

Note that your BASE numbers may not be the same as in the example. The response confirms that the system is reserving space for the two separate entities - the Dictionary and the Data File.

The new user may be curious about what is being done and what appears on the screen and so simplified explanations are included below. In the response the first line of the message refers to the Dictionary; the second line is for the Data File.

[417] is an internal code for the type of message sent from the system. The code number always appears in brackets and for now can be ignored.

FILE, as you know, is the format in which all information is contained.

'GADGETS' is the file name. It is in quotes because the name is user-supplied.

BASE is the location on the disk where the reserved block of space starts, or the first frame of the file; BASE is automatically assigned by the system. It is just like having the address of that apartment complex in order to find the furniture.

MODULO is the number of frames horizontally. The first number in the CREATE-FILE command is the modulo for the Dictionary. We used 3 and it appears on the first line of the response. The second number in the command applies to the Data File, therefore 17 is on the second line of the response.

SEPAR (for SEPARation) is the number of frames vertically. Since no separation was given in the first sample command, the system automatically assigns the number 1 to the Dictionary and also to the Data File. Whenever the system proceeds to take some understood action, unless otherwise directed, it is called *defaulting*. Here it *defaults* to a separation of 1 because no number was given.

The second line gives the corresponding reply for the Data File.

The system has reserved two blocks of space via the CREATE-FILE command.

Before starting the Dictionary, let us review: Pick stores all data in the format of a file which has been defined as a collection of related elements called items.

The GADGETS Data File has been laid out as a 2-dimensional table; we decided what properties the data items would have and designed the columns accordingly, choosing the number of columns and the headings: NAME, QTY, and COLOR. Each line across the table represents one item in the GADGETS Data File. As noted in Chapter 2 the order of the items in the table does not matter.

```
              MODULO
              < = 3 >
              □ □ □   ↑ SEPAR = 1

       BASE ↑
```

Space Reserved for the Dictionary

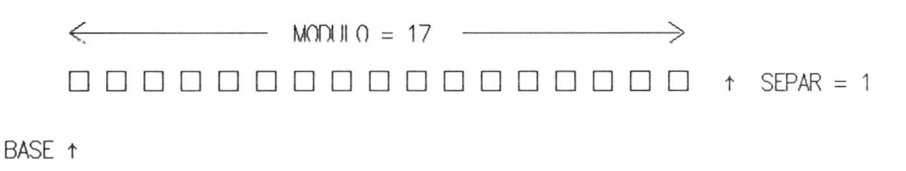

```
     ←————— MODULO = 17 —————→
     □ □ □ □ □ □ □ □ □ □ □ □ □ □   ↑ SEPAR = 1

BASE ↑
```

Space Reserved for the Data File

FIGURE 3.1: BASE, MODULO, AND SEPARATION

FILE NAME: GADGETS

GADGETS item-id	NAME	QTY	COLOR
8	SPOON	12	RED
9	SPOON	10	YELLOW
20	LADLE	19	TAN
30	WHISK	8	BLUE
7	SPOON	1	BROWN
21	LADLE	4	RED
50	FORK	23	TAN
42	SPATULA	17	RED
49	SPATULA	35	AVOCADO

Now we are about to make another type of file with a different kind of information. To distinguish this type from a Data File it is called a **File Dictionary** which is shortened to Dictionary, and each item in it is referred to as a *Descriptor*.

The group of related items in the Dictionary is the attribute names from the Data File. Each attribute name is developed into a separate Descriptor with its individual item-id and certain properties. The unique names of the attributes - NAME, QTY, and COLOR - become the item-ids. But unlike the Data File the user cannot choose the number or the names of the properties. Here the system calls for specific information about the structure of each attribute and the facts must be in a conventional order. In this way the two files work together: the Dictionary is like a guide to its associated Data File. As mentioned in Chapter 2 the Dictionary for the GADGETS file has the facts about the Data File and the GADGETS Data File contains the actual data values.

Since a 2-dimensional table is already a familiar structure for holding information, start by seeing how the Dictionary looks when set up as a table. The leftmost column is for the item-id and the columns across are numbered from 1 to 10. Using the test data so far we have

column →	1	2	3	4	5	6	7	8	9	10
item-id										
NAME										
QTY										
COLOR										

FIGURE 3.2: THE DESCRIPTORS IN TABLE FORMAT

Each column requires a particular fact about the attribute:

1. What type of item is this? In a Dictionary all of the items are Descriptors which are called Attribute Definition Items.

2. What is the position of the attribute here being described (what attribute number is it) ? The proper term is the Attribute Mark Count or AMC.

3. through
8. Are not being used at the present time but will be reserved for the future.

9. What is the justification of the values for this attribute? *Justification* means the starting point from which the characters proceed. Think about the two kinds of text: numbers and letters, and you realize that each advances from a different direction. Numbers start at the right and continue to the left; they are called *right justified*. Letters are the opposite: they start at the left and continue to the right and thus are described as *left justified*. Numbers may be embedded within a field of letters but the field is still considered to be left justified.

10. How many characters (length) will this attribute need for output? The figure is for output only and is in no way a constraint on the data to be carried in the file.

The headings for the columns can now be added to the table:

column →	1	2	3 4 5 6 7 8	9	10
			Reserve for future use	Justi-fica-tion	
item-id	Type	AMC			Length
NAME					
QTY					
COLOR					

FIGURE 3.3: THE DESCRIPTORS WITH COLUMN HEADINGS

The next step is to fill in the facts across each line starting with item-id NAME. An Attribute Definition Item is abbreviated to A which goes in the first column. Continue along the NAME line. NAME is attribute 1 therefore its AMC is 1. To reserve columns 3 through 8 for future use we enter a . period in each column. The data values for NAME are made up of letters in our test data and so are left justified. L goes in column 9. The last column is for output length. The longest name so far in the Data File is SPATULA with seven characters; figure that a length of 10 should be enough for any items to be added later. The line for NAME is complete. Next fill in the facts for QTY.

As with NAME, this is an Attribute Definition Item and therefore column 1 is A. QTY is attribute2 thus its AMC is 2. Columns 3 through 8 are handled as before. The data values for QTY are expressed as numbers which are right justified or R. Since we do not expect to have more than 999 pieces of any GADGET on hand the output length is 3 (for 3 characters).

The last line is for item-id COLOR. Moving across we have A (as before). COLOR is attribute3 and so its AMC is 3. Again columns 3 through 8 each get a period. Values for COLOR are alphabetic characters (letters) and left justified or L. An output length of 15 should be enough for a COLOR.

The diagram for the Dictionary of the GADGETS file is filled in as below. Each line represents one Descriptor in the Dictionary.

column →	1	2	3	4	5	6	7	8	9	10
item-id	Type	AMC	\multicolumn{6}{c}{Reserve for future use}	Justi-fica-tion	Length
NAME	A	1	.	.	.	.	.	.	L	10
QTY	A	2	.	.	.	.	.	.	R	3
COLOR	A	3	.	.	.	.	.	.	L	15

FIGURE 3.4: THE DATA FOR EACH DESCRIPTOR

This table format is used only to show how the Descriptors are constructed. Normally you do not see a Descriptor displayed horizontally.

If you are not using the GADGETS Data File substitute the facts about your item-ids and attributes for those above.

Once the facts have been organized we are ready to type them in. We next create individual Descriptors - one at a time - for NAME, QTY, and COLOR.

After you logged on you saw the TCL prompt > or : which means that the system is waiting for your instruction at Terminal Command Language level. In Chapter 1 the role of TCL was explained as that of the user's command interpreter. Up to this point TCL was able to perform the function we wanted with the CREATE-FILE command. Now, to create the Descriptors for the GADGETS Dictionary we call on the EDITOR, the processor that handles all text within the system. When TCL receives the EDIT command it turns control over to the EDITOR. The verb that starts the command is either EDIT or its short form ED. A verb is the action to be performed and almost always requires the name of the file and of the item(s) upon which it is to act. The general command format to EDit a Dictionary is

```
>ED DICT filename item-id1 item-id2 .....
```

As seen from the Dictionary layout, the same name, e.g. QTY, is the item-id of the Descriptor and also the name of the attribute. For our example we must create three Descriptors and so place all of the item-ids in the command, enter

```
>ED DICT GADGETS NAME QTY COLOR <return>
```

The Editor responds with

```
NAME
NEW ITEM
TOP
```

Each item is presented on the screen in the same order as in the command. Therefore we start with NAME as shown on the first line of the response. This is a NEW ITEM; the system has not been given any facts about it prior to this. TOP means that we are at the beginning of the item. Note that the EDITOR processor has its own prompt, a period, which replaces the TCL prompt. The EDITOR works in two different modes: Command for most operations and Input which specializes in accepting new text. The . prompt indicates that the EDITOR is waiting for a command (generally they are one or two characters). We want to Input data therefore call for Input mode by entering

```
I <return>
```

I is the abbreviation for Input.

Input mode automatically provides a line number on the left side of the screen: we see 001+. The plus sign + indicates Input mode and the cursor next to it shows where the next typed character will appear. Each line number comes up in turn and must be given specific information about the attribute. Do not be surprised when a number has zeroes to the left of it, e.g. 001. These are called *leading zeroes* and have no effect on the value of the number; they can be ignored.

The facts for each Descriptor were arranged horizontally across a line. To enter them we must now turn them into a vertical format such as

item-id: NAME

LINE	CONTENTS
001	A
002	1
003	.
004	.
005	.
006	.
007	.
008	.
009	L
010	10

We are working on the Descriptor for NAME; type in the information for each line as it appears:

001+A <return>

The response is the next line which is 002+. Line 2 (002) requires the position of the attribute here being described (the AMC). NAME is attribute number 1. Enter

002+1 <return>

The response is 003+. Lines 3 through 8 may be needed in the future and must be reserved now. This is done by typing in a period

003+. <return>

The next line is 004+. Again, enter

004+. <return>

Now line 005+ comes up. Again type in a period and complete the line i.e.

    005+. <return>

For each line as it appears in sequence, one line at a time, repeat the step until line 8 is completed. This segment is displayed on the screen as

    003+.
    004+.
    005+.
    006+.
    007+.
    008+.
    009+

The data values for NAME are left justified, on line 9 enter

    009+L <return>

The response is 010+. Enter

    010+10 <return>

With line 010 we have completed the Descriptor required for the attribute NAME. For line 011+ press only <return> to indicate that we are ready to leave Input mode.

    011+ <return>

The response is

    TOP
    .

This means that we are at the beginning of the item and see the EDITOR prompt the period. Here is how the screen looks so far:

    >ED DICT GADGETS NAME QTY COLOR
    NAME
    NEW ITEM
    TOP
    .I

```
001+A
002+1
003+.
004+.
005+.
006+.
007+.
008+.
009+L
010+10
011+
TOP
.
```

There are just a few more steps before we go on to the next Descriptor. As you recall, for lines 3 through 8 we used a period to reserve the lines for the future. The period is the value on each of those lines. Now we need to remove the period but keep the line. No value at all is described as a *null value*. This is not the same as <return> or the space bar for a blank. The procedure for changing text that has already been entered is as follows: first you must be in the EDITOR to make a change. You know that you are in the EDITOR by recognizing its prompt, the period, and so can give the command. The general command format to replace is

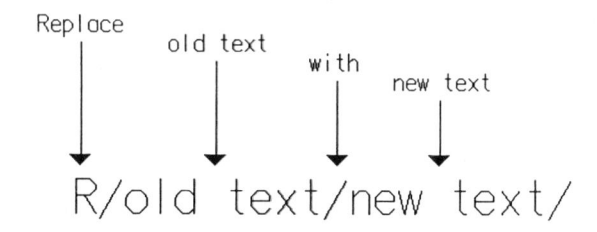

```
Replace   old text       with    new text
   |         |            |         |
   ↓         ↓            ↓         ↓
   R /   old text   /   new text /
```

FIGURE 3.5: THE REPLACE FORMAT

At this time we use slashes to *delimit* or indicate the boundaries between old and new text. The slashes here are called *delimiters*.

To replace the period with nothing (which leaves the line with a null value), the general command format is

Getting Started: Hands On

```
      Replace
      |  period
      |  |  with
      |  |  |  nothing
      ▼  ▼  ▼  ▼
      R / . / /
```

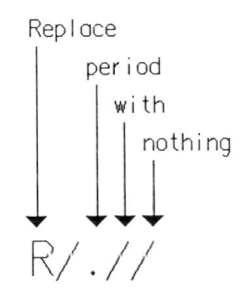

FIGURE 3.6: REPLACE OLD WITH NULL

Here you want to replace old text that appears in several places (the periods on lines 3 through 8) and it is much easier to make all the changes at one time instead of giving a separate instruction for each line. This is done by altering the command. When you place 99 between R and the first slash, the system replaces the first occurrence of the old text wherever it appears on the next specified number of lines from here down. 99 is usually more than adequate. Therefore type in

R99/.// <return>

which means

```
      Replace the first occurrence on the next 99 lines of
      |    period
      |    |  with
      |    |  |  nothing
      ▼    ▼  ▼  ▼
      R99 / . / /
```

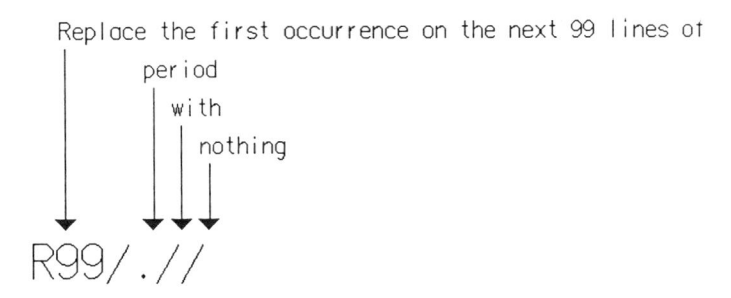

FIGURE 3.7: REPLACE ON MULTIPLE LINES

The response is the lines on which the changes were made - lines 3 through 8 with nothing on them which is exactly what we want.

        003
        004
        005
        006
        007
        008
        EOI 010
        .

At the bottom is EOI 010. This means that the End Of Item is on line 10. Line 11 had only <return> to leave Input mode and is discarded. The plus signs + no longer appear next to line numbers because you terminated Input mode. In this way, you left Input mode (where you enter new text), and re-entered Command mode (where you give instructions). Both modes are within the EDITOR processor and display the same prompt, the period.

Enter

    F <return>

Response

    TOP
    .

The command P Prints the item to the screen. Enter

    P <return>

The response to P is a display of the latest version of the complete item. If your system responds

    CMND?

or

    INVALID COMMAND

type in

    P L22 <return>

once at the beginning of each EDIT session to set up Print. Then type P again.

Inspect the item. Later on you will be able to make corrections before filing the item; for now file it as is and plan to alter it if necessary when we cover how to change text in Chapter 4.5.

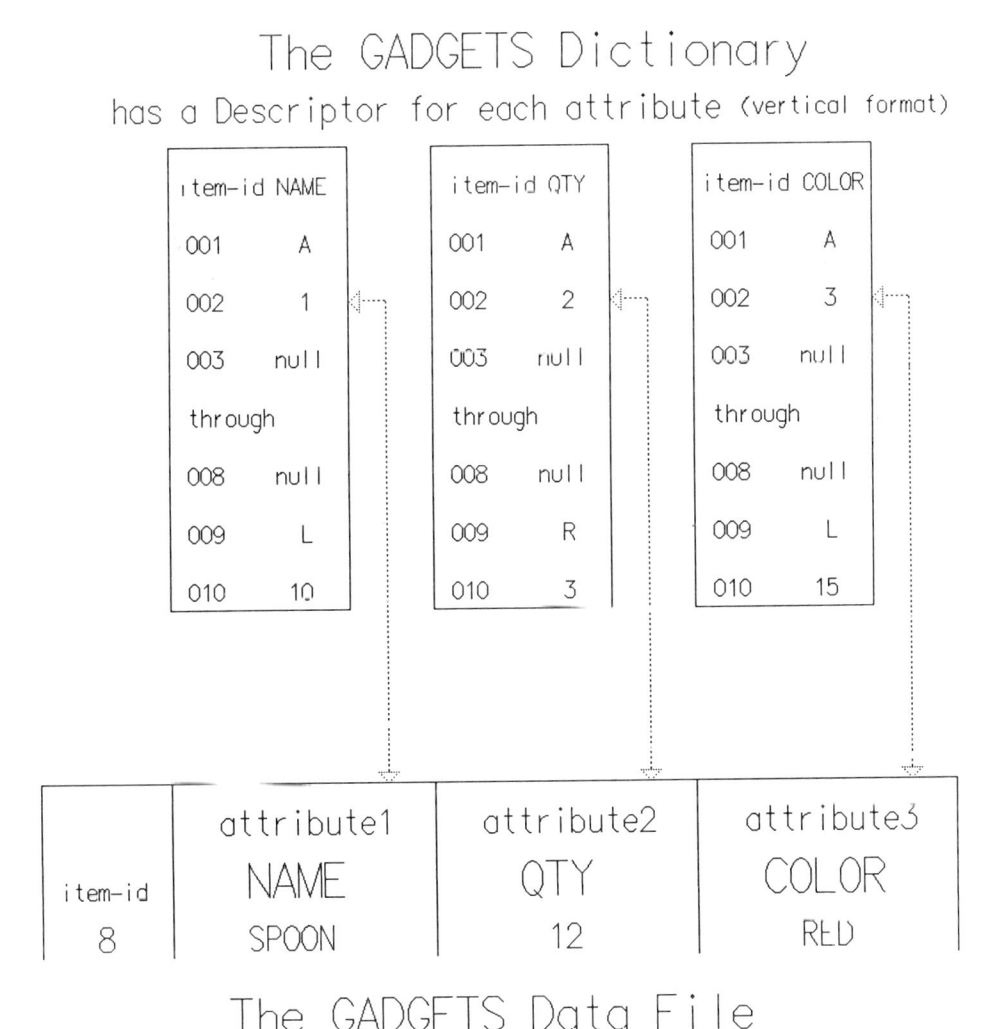

The GADGETS Dictionary
has a Descriptor for each attribute (vertical format)

item-id NAME	item-id QTY	item-id COLOR
001 A	001 A	001 A
002 1	002 2	002 3
003 null	003 null	003 null
through	through	through
008 null	008 null	008 null
009 L	009 R	009 L
010 10	010 3	010 15

item-id	attribute1 NAME	attribute2 QTY	attribute3 COLOR
8	SPOON	12	RED

The GADGETS Data File
has the data values for each item   (horizontal format)

FIGURE 3.8: THE GADGETS DICTIONARY AND DATA FILE

Enter

    FI <return>

This FIles or saves the entire item (lines 1 through 10 in our sample). The response is

    'NAME' FILED.
    QTY
    NEW ITEM
    TOP
    .

NAME appears in quotes, since it is user-supplied, to distinguish it from system terms. The Descriptors are presented in the same sequence as in the ED DICT command. After NAME is FIled, QTY comes up automatically.

Follow the same steps to type in the facts for QTY. Enter

    I <return>

When line 001+ is displayed, just as in the preceding routine enter

    001+A <return>

For line 002+ the AMC is

    002+2 <return>

Lines 003+ through 008+ are handled exactly as before: for each line, type in a period and press <return>.

    003+. <return>
    through
    008+. <return>

Line 009+ is R

    009+R <return>

For line 010+ type in 3

Getting Started: Hands On 49

010+<u>3</u> <return>

After line 010+ we are ready to leave Input mode. Press <return>

011+ <return>

The complete screen display for QTY thus far is

```
QTY
NEW ITEM
TOP
.I
001+A
002+2
003+.
004+.
005+.
006+.
007I.
008+.
009+R
010+3
011+
TOP
.
```

Now repeat the same final steps taken with NAME to finish QTY. Enter

R99/.// <return>

The response is the display of lines 3 through 8 ending with EOI 010 exactly as before

```
003
004
005
006
007
008
EOI 010
.
```

Enter

>   F <return>

Response

>   TOP
>   .

Enter

>   P <return>

The response is the updated version of the item.

Enter

>   FI <return>

The response is

>   'QTY' FILED.   (and COLOR comes up next:)
>   COLOR
>   NEW ITEM
>   TOP
>   .

Enter

>   I <return>

and then the following data for each line as it appears:

>   001+A <return>
>   002+3 <return>
>   003+. <return
>   004+. <return
>   005+. <return
>   006+. <return
>   007+. <return
>   008+. <return
>   009+L <return>
>   010+15 <return>

```
011+ <return>
TOP
.
```

Continue with

```
R99/.// <return>
```

The response is the display of lines 3 through 8 ending with EOI 010 exactly as before

```
003
004
005
006
007
008
EOI 010
.
```

Enter

```
F <return>
```

Response

```
TOP
.
```

Enter

```
P <return>
```

The response is the updated version of the item.

Enter

```
FI <return>
```

The response is

```
'COLOR' FILED.          and the TCL prompt
>
```

The Dictionary is now complete because we have provided the information required for each Descriptor that was listed in the command

```
ED DICT GADGETS NAME QTY COLOR
```

Since COLOR was the last item-id in the ED command, after we FIled it we returned to TCL.

Do not be overwhelmed at this point by the seemingly needless precision that each step requires. But it is absolutely essential in order to accomplish what we set out to do. If you are in a strange place you rely on a detailed map to get around. As you gradually become more familiar with the new locale, you no longer need the guide and can find your own way. The same is true of learning to use the computer: follow the instructions to avoid becoming lost and therefore aggravated. At all times be aware of where you want to go - what you are trying to do and how to go about doing it. TCL was compared to a traffic director for the system but you, the user, are really in charge. As you learn to travel from one specialized function to another, you control the route to be taken to your destination.

The following summarizes the steps that you have already taken. The column marked FORMAT is a framework to which you must add the details for the data on which you are working. The column labeled EXAMPLE shows what was done with the test data for the Descriptors in the GADGETS Dictionary.

SUMMARY: CREATE the DICTIONARY DESCRIPTOR

COMMENTS	FORMAT	EXAMPLE
Invoke the EDITOR to handle text	>ED DICT filename item-id1 item-id2... \<return\>	>ED DICT GADGETS NAME QTY COLOR \<return\>
The attribute name is the Descriptor's item-id	Response attribute NEW ITEM TOP .	NAME NEW ITEM TOP .
Call for Input mode to take text	Enter I \<return\>	see format

Getting Started: Hands On

+ indicates Input mode Attribute Definition Item; enter A	Response 001+<u>A</u> <return>	see format
Attribute Mark Count enter attribute number	Response 002+_ <return>	002+<u>1</u> <return>
Enter a period	Response 003+<u>.</u> <return>	see format

Repeat the above step, one line at a time, through line 008+

Justification? L for letters or R for numbers	Response 009+_ <return>	009+<u>L</u> <return>
Enter maximum output length	Response 010+_ <return>	010+<u>10</u> <return>
Leave Input mode by <return>	Response 011+<return>	see format
You are at the beginning of the item	Response TOP .	see format
Replace the periods with null values	Enter <u>R99/.//</u><return>	see format
Display of lines changed + no longer appears; you left Input mode	Response 003 004 005 006 007 008	see format
EOI is the last line in the item	EOI 010 .	
	Enter <u>F</u> <return>	see format

	Response TOP .	see format
Print the item to the screen	Enter P <return>	see format
Display of the updated version of the complete item	Response 001 through 010 hold the appropriate values for your data 010 EOI 010 .	001 A 002 1 003 004 005 006 007 008 009 L 010 10 EOI 010 .
Inspect the item and FIle it	Enter FI <return> Response 'item-id' FILED. next attribute NEW ITEM TOP .	see format 'NAME' FILED. QTY NEW ITEM TOP .

Follow the above steps starting with I for each attribute as it appears. After the last attribute is completed the response is

        'item-id' FILED.   'COLOR' FILED.
        >   >

You have returned to TCL as shown by the > prompt.

3.6 CREATE THE DATA FILE

The system has been informed of the structure of the data by the Dictionary and is now ready to accept the data itself. Take a moment to look at the facts in the GADGETS Data File in Section 3.5: each row across the table holds the values for one item. For example, item-id 8 has the following values

    attribute1 NAME = SPOON
    attribute2 QTY = 12
    attribute3 COLOR = RED

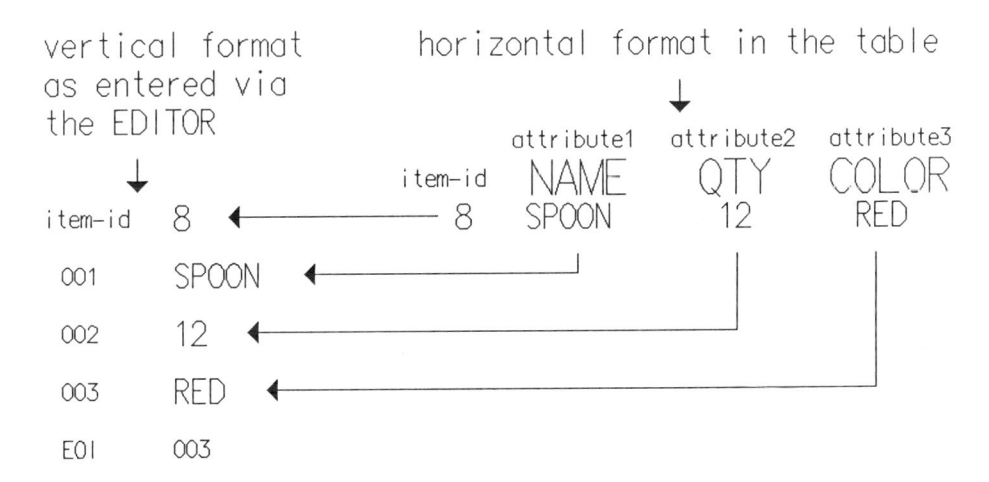

```
vertical format              horizontal format in the table
as entered via                              ↓
the EDITOR
                             attribute1  attribute2  attribute3
    ↓              item-id     NAME        QTY        COLOR
item-id   8   ←───────── 8     SPOON        12         RED
   001   SPOON   ←────────────────┘          │          │
   002    12     ←───────────────────────────┘          │
   003    RED    ←──────────────────────────────────────┘
   E01    003
```

FIGURE 3.9: AN ITEM IN THE GADGETS DATA FILE

As we have already seen, the EDITOR requires us to enter the values in vertical format.

We are going to give the system the facts about every item (in this case each GADGET) in the file, one at a time, as shown above. The general procedure is similar to the one used to build the Dictionary for the first block of reserved space; at this time you type in the Data File for the second block of space. By now you remember that you call on the ED-

ITOR with the command ED. To this you must add the names of what you want to EDit. This time we use the name of the file without DICT before it. The general format is

>ED filename item-id1 item-id2 ....

Specifying the item-id(s) in the command sentence in this manner is the faster way to EDit. However you do not have to show the item-id in the ED command for either the Dictionary or the Data File. If you use only

ED {DICT} filename

most systems respond with a request for the item-id to be EDITed

ITEM ID:

Enter the item-id after the colon and press <return>. This is merely an extra step to give the system the item-id. We use the speedy method and put all of the item-ids in the command sentence. Enter

>ED GADGETS 8 9 20 30 7 21 50 42 49 <return>

The item-ids in the command can be given in any sequence you want. However since they appear on the screen in the same order as in the command, it is most convenient for us to use the same sequence as in the table.

Starting with the first item the system checks and finds it has no item called 8. (Actually it has nothing at all because you are at the beginning of setting up a file. This command is used at other times, therefore the search for the item is done automatically.) Except for the item-id the response is the same as when we EDITed each new Descriptor:

8
NEW ITEM
TOP
.

In order to enter new text, the command is I for Input just as before.

Enter

I <return>

Again the screen displays a familiar sight on the left: the line number followed by the plus sign, which indicates that you are in Input mode as requested. The number 001+ on the screen calls for the first attribute of the item known as 8. Here 001+ corresponds to attribute1, which is column 1 in the original table. Look at the table and you find it is SPOON. Type in

001+SPOON <return>

The response 002+ is for the second attribute, which here is the quantity 12. Type it in

002+12 <return>

The response is 003+. The third attribute is RED; type it in.

003+RED <return>

The response is 004+. There is no more to say about item 8; the values for its three attributes: NAME, QTY, and COLOR have been entered. Indicate the end of the item by

004+ <return>

Thus, just as before, we leave Input mode and enter Command mode but remain within the EDITOR. The response is

TOP
.

The system goes to the TOP (beginning) of the item. Enter

P <return>

This Prints to the screen what has been entered. The response is

001 SPOON
002 12
003 RED
EOI 003
.

The plus signs have disappeared because you are no longer in Input mode. EOI means End Of Item and shows that for this particular item three lines were used. The item-id tags the item but does not appear in this listing. Satisfied that the information is correct, enter

    FI <return>

This is the FIle or save command. The response is

    '8' FILED.
    9
    NEW ITEM
    TOP
    .

The steps we have taken to enter data item 8 are combined together:

```
>ED GADGETS 8 9 20 30 7 21 50 42 49
NEW ITEM
TOP
.I
001+SPOON
002+12
003+RED
004+
TOP
.P
001 SPOON
002 12
003 RED
EOI 003
.FI

'8' FILED.
9
NEW ITEM
TOP
.
```

In the command the second item-id is 9. Find item 9 in the table and the values for its attributes: attribute1 NAME = SPOON, attribute2 QTY = 10, and attribute3 COLOR = YELLOW. Repeat the steps beginning with

I

through

FI

for each item in the table. After the last item, 49, is FIled control returns to TCL and the > prompt is displayed.

Try to be as careful as you can be when typing in data. If you check the screen before completing the line, you can quickly correct errors by using the back space key. Suppose you entered SPOOON instead of SPOON and never noticed the mistake in spelling. As far as the computer knows, this is another kind of GADGET; the machine has no way of knowing that you mean SPOON if you say SPOOON. At some time in the future you may want a total count of all the SPOONs on hand; SPOOON will not be included and your entry is worthless. Stay alert to avoid this kind of mistake.

SUMMARY: CREATE THE DATA FILE

Note that this summary is for what has already been done. The FORMAT column shows the procedure and must be completed with your own data. The column marked EXAMPLE has the steps for the test data in the GADGETS Data File.

COMMENTS	FORMAT	EXAMPLE
Invoke the EDITOR to handle text	>ED filename item-id(s) <return>	>ED GADGETS 8 9 20 etc. <return>
	Response item-id	8
The item is new	NEW ITEM TOP	NEW ITEM TOP
The EDITOR prompt	.	.
Call for Input mode to take text	Enter I <return>	see format
+ indicates Input mode	Response	

Enter the value for attribute1	001+_ <return>	001+<u>SPOON</u> <return>
Enter the value for attribute2	Response 002+_ <return>	002+<u>12</u> <return>
Enter the value for attribute3	Response 003+_ <return>	003+<u>RED</u> <return>

Use one line for each attribute until you have completed the row. The number of the last line depends on how many attributes the item has. After the last attribute for the item has been entered, leave Input mode by pressing <return> only

	line number+ <return>	004+<return>
You are at the beginning of the item	Response TOP .	see format
Print the item to the screen	Enter <u>P</u> <return>	see format
+ no longer appears; you have left Input mode Note that the item-id was displayed earlier	Response display of item	 001 SPOON 002 12 003 RED EOI 003
Inspect the item and FIle it	Enter <u>FI</u> <return>	see format
Item FIled; the next item appears	Response 'item-id' FILED. next item-id NEW ITEM TOP .	'8' FILED. 9 see format

Repeat from I for each item in the table.
After the last item is FIled

	Response 'item-id' FILED.	'49' FILED.
TCL prompt	>	>

3.7 LOGGING OFF

If you must leave the terminal before you have finished entering all the information, log off; do not just walk away. This is wise because first of all, while you are logged on everything in your account is accessible to anyone using the terminal; and second, some accounts track the user's time spent on the system and this time will be included in your accounting time. To log off you must be in TCL with the > prompt. Type in

>OFF <return>

A sample response is

< CONNECT TIME = 110 MINS.;CPU = 18133 UNITS;LPTR PAGES =0 >
< LOGGED OFF AT 12:59:42 ON 09 JAN 1987 >

Each part of this response is explained:

CONNECT TIME:	the total time you were logged on to the system
CPU:	the amount of time using the central processing unit in milliseconds
LPTR PAGES:	the number of pages printed
LOGGED OFF:	the time and date at which you entered OFF. The system is ready for the next user and displays the LOGON message.

You can easily log on again at your convenience. Once you have logged off you can turn the terminal off, such as for overnight but be careful to do this only when there is a logon message on the screen.

3.8 ERROR EXAMPLES

The system has a built-in stock of messages and displays the appropriate one whenever there is a problem. The code number in brackets can be ignored for now; the message itself explains what is wrong. Until the command is retyped in the correct form and entered, you cannot continue working. You may have seen some of the following common errors:

ERROR	COMMENT
LOGON ;GREY	Remove the semicolon, it is not
USER-ID?	part of the account.name

>CREATE FILE GADGETS 3 17 [3] Verb?	Hyphen omitted Correct format is CREATE-FILE
>CREA TE FILE GADGETS 3 17 [3] Verb?	As above; also remove space between the A and T
>CREATE-FILE GADGETS 3 D17 [416] RANGE ERROR IN MODULO OR SEPA- RATION PARAMETER	Remove the letter D
>CREATE-FILE GADGETS 3 17 [413] THE FILE NAME ALREADY EXISTS IN THE MASTER DICTIONARY	The command has already been entered and the file exists whether there is data in it or not
>ED GADGETSS [201] 'GADGETSS' IS NOT A FILE NAME	The filename must be spelled exactly as supplied originally
>ED GAGDETS [201] 'GAGDETS' IS NOT A FILE NAME	Same as above
>ED HARDWARE 43 [201] 'HARDWARE' IS NOT A FILE NAME	The file has not been created
>ED [10] FILE NAME MISSING	Verb must be followed by a filename
>I [3] VERB?	You cannot enter Input Mode from TCL; you must be in the EDITOR with the period . prompt
>FI [3] VERB?	You cannot FIle from TCL; you must be in the EDITOR with the period . prompt

>P   P is a different verb at TCL; it sup-
                       presses output to the screen. Enter
                       P <return> to cancel the first P. Use
                       the ED command to enter the ED-
                       ITOR, then you can P (Print the item
                       to the screen)

3.9 REVIEW QUESTIONS

1. *What does AMC stand for? Where is it used?*
2. *What Processor handles all text? What is its prompt?*
3. *Explain logging on.*
4. *What does EOI mean?*
5. *What is the purpose of a Descriptor? Where is it found?*
6. *When do you log off? Why?*
7. *What is the Replace command and how is it used?*
8. *How are errors corrected before a line is completed?*
9. *When are line numbers followed by plus signs?*
10. *There are two kinds of justification. Explain to what each applies and why.*
11. *What happens when you spell the account name incorrectly at LOGON?*
12. *What is a prompt? Give two examples.*
13. *How is new text entered into the system? How do we indicate that we have finished entering new text?*
14. *What is the cursor?*
15. *In what form must letters be typed into the computer - lower case, upper case, or a combination?*

```
>P
```
P is a different verb at TCL; it suppresses output to the screen. Enter P <return> to cancel the first P. Use the ED command to enter the EDITOR, then you can P (Print the item to the screen)

3.9 REVIEW QUESTIONS

1. *What does AMC stand for? Where is it used?*
2. *What Processor handles all text? What is its prompt?*
3. *Explain logging on.*
4. *What does EOI mean?*
5. *What is the purpose of a Descriptor? Where is it found?*
6. *When do you log off? Why?*
7. *What is the Replace command and how is it used?*
8. *How are errors corrected before a line is completed?*
9. *When are line numbers followed by plus signs?*
10. *There are two kinds of justification. Explain to what each applies and why.*
11. *What happens when you spell the account name incorrectly at LOGON?*
12. *What is a prompt? Give two examples.*
13. *How is new text entered into the system? How do we indicate that we have finished entering new text?*
14. *What is the cursor?*
15. *In what form must letters be typed into the computer - lower case, upper case, or a combination?*

Chapter 4

Keeping the file current: Update

4.1 OVERVIEW

In the previous chapter we created Dictionary Descriptors showing the structure of the Data File and then the Data File itself containing the data values. These were the first steps in preparing the data to produce usable information. This chapter covers two broad ranges of operations on the data. First, we see what has been entered in the system by using various forms of the LIST verb. Second, we alter the data via the ED ITOR processor which handles all text manipulation: Adding, Changing, and Deleting. These three activities are referred to as *updating*.

As with any processing, the most important part is knowing what you want to do and then deciding how to go about doing it. All data is stored in the format of a file. Dictionaries and their associated Data Files are our present concern.

As previously noted, there may be minor variations in the way output is presented. For example, your system may use a different name for a column heading; however the essential factors are the same for all installations.

4.2 WHAT IS IN THE FILE? THE LIST COMMANDS

Thus far all responses have been displayed on the screen. At times it is convenient to have hard copy - output printed on paper - for reference. If your system has a printer, you have the choice of routing the output to the screen or to the printer when using certain commands.

A tremendous assortment of printers are on the market and you must consult the manual for the model you have. Before using the printer, become thoroughly familiar with operations such as loading the paper, flipping switches ON and OFF, and releasing the paper. Output from all forms of the LIST verb can be directed to the printer. At the very end of the command sentence add the printer specification.

```
LPTR        or
(P          or (P)
```

All are abbreviations for *LINE PRINTER* and are interchangeable.

Since it is impossible to remember everything in the computer, there are ways to inspect what has been entered. Different forms of the LIST verb produce different kinds of information: filenames, Descriptors, and all or part of Data Files. The variety of LIST verbs covered in this section may seem unnecessary but it gives the new user an opportunity to choose the verb form that produces the wanted output. You probably will find LISTFILES and LIST-ITEM (discussed below) best suited to your general needs. The words in the command sentence depend on what you want to see. You must know the filename before you can retrieve any facts from it, therefore start with the command that outputs filenames. You may want to see the names of all your files or check the spelling of only one.

LISTFILES

As described in Chapter 2 one part of each account's Master Dictionary is a directory of the account's files. Normally a command has a minimum of two parts: the verb - what to do; and the filename - what to do it to. Note that only one filename can be used at a time. Here the verb and what it is to act upon have been merged into one command word which outputs a LISTing of all the files in the account's Master Dictionary. For output to the screen enter

```
>LISTFILES <return>
```

For output to the printer enter

```
>LISTFILES (P) <return>
```

The portion of the response that concerns us now is

```
F/NAME....CODE...F/BASE...F/MOD...F/SEP

GADGETS...D......21696....3.......1
  .
  .
  .
[405] 31 ITEMS LISTED.
```

Keeping the file current: Update 67

    F/NAME or MD is the filename (this is an instance of variation)

    CODE is the type of file

    F/BASE, F/MOD, and F/SEP are the base frame, modulo, and separation of the file. They vary with the account and are not used by us now. The user created files, identified by a D code, appear together; on some systems other D code files may be included but you can recognize your own filenames. Whenever you refer to one of them spell the name exactly as it is given in the response.

After execution of LIST, the total number of items LISTed is automatically given at the end of the output. This number also varies depending on the contents of the account; in the example there were 31 items. Your particular system may or may not show [405] the message number but it will give the total of the items LISTed.

In the examples in the text the complete command sentences are shown as they should be entered but only the relevant output is included. Information such as page number, date, and summary is omitted.

LIST

After you know the name of the file, you can retrieve all or some of the facts in it. Recall from the previous chapter that the Dictionary and the Data File share the same name. Whenever the Dictionary is the target area for any verb, DICT must be in the command. When DICT is not indicated, processing acts upon, or defaults to, the Data File. Let us next look at all the item-ids in a Data File. For a complete LISTing of the item-ids the format is

    `>LIST filename`

Enter

    `>LIST GADGETS <return>`

Before looking at the sample response remember that each system stores and presents the data in its own internal sequence. Do not be surprised when it is not what you expect. Data is presented in *stored* (physical) order rather than logical order. All the facts are output, however the sequence may vary from one time to another.

Response

    GADGETS

    50
    7
    20
    8
    21
    9
    42
    30
    49
    [405] 9 ITEMS LISTED.

LIST ONLY

The item-ids are the keys to the items and the means to their retrieval. Items in a file usually have attribute values and we can request as few or as many as we want to be displayed. You must know the exact name of each attribute before you can request it. When we created the Descriptors for the Dictionary the names were given in the ED DICT command. By now you may have forgotten the name(s) or possibly the spelling. As long as you know the filename you can get to the facts stored in the Dictionary. To see the names of the attributes the general command format is

    >LIST ONLY DICT filename

Enter

    >LIST ONLY DICT GADGETS <return>

Response

    GADGETS...

    NAME
    GADGETS
    QTY
    COLOR

Keeping the file current: Update 69

GADGETS is the filename; it is the heading and also repeated with the attribute names.

LIST-ITEM

We continue to explore ways of retrieving facts that have been stored. Perhaps the name is not enough and you want to inspect the complete Descriptor. The verb format is

>LIST-ITEM DICT filename

Enter

>LIST-ITEM DICT GADGETS <return>

The response is a vertical display of each Descriptor; part of the output is shown below. Sometimes a response is too long to fit on one screen and the system waits for your signal to continue. The screen seems to be halted and there is no prompt. Press <return> when you are ready to "turn to the next page"; this is called *scrolling*. If you do not want to see any more, you can exit the LISTing by pressing the control key and X together, <control> X, and then let go of both. Do not use the <return> key. You go back to TCL and see the > prompt.

```
NAME
001 A
002 1
003
004
005
006
007
008
009 L
010 10

QTY
001 A
002 2
003
004
```

```
            005
            006
            007
            008
            009 R
            010 3
```

Note that LIST-ITEM does not generate the total number of items LISTed. This verb can also be used with the filename to produce all of the item-ids and their attribute values; these too are in vertical format. Enter

>LIST-ITEM GADGETS <return>

The response in part is

```
             50
        001 FORK
        002 23
        003 TAN

              7
        001 SPOON
        002 1
        003 BROWN
```

LIST WITH ATTRIBUTES

It is not necessary to output the entire contents of a file at all times. We can request attribute(s) by name(s) to be shown with the item-ids. Just add the attribute name(s) after the filename in the command. Start with one attribute and find the COLOR of each item. Enter

>LIST GADGETS COLOR <return>

Response

GADGETS	COLOR
50	TAN
20	TAN
7	BROWN
8	RED
21	RED

```
 9    YELLOW
42    RED
30    BLUE
49    AVOCADO
```

1. The GADGETS file:

```
item-id   NAME    QTY   COLOR
   8      SPOON    12    RED
```

2. The command sentence:

>LIST GADGETS COLOR NAME

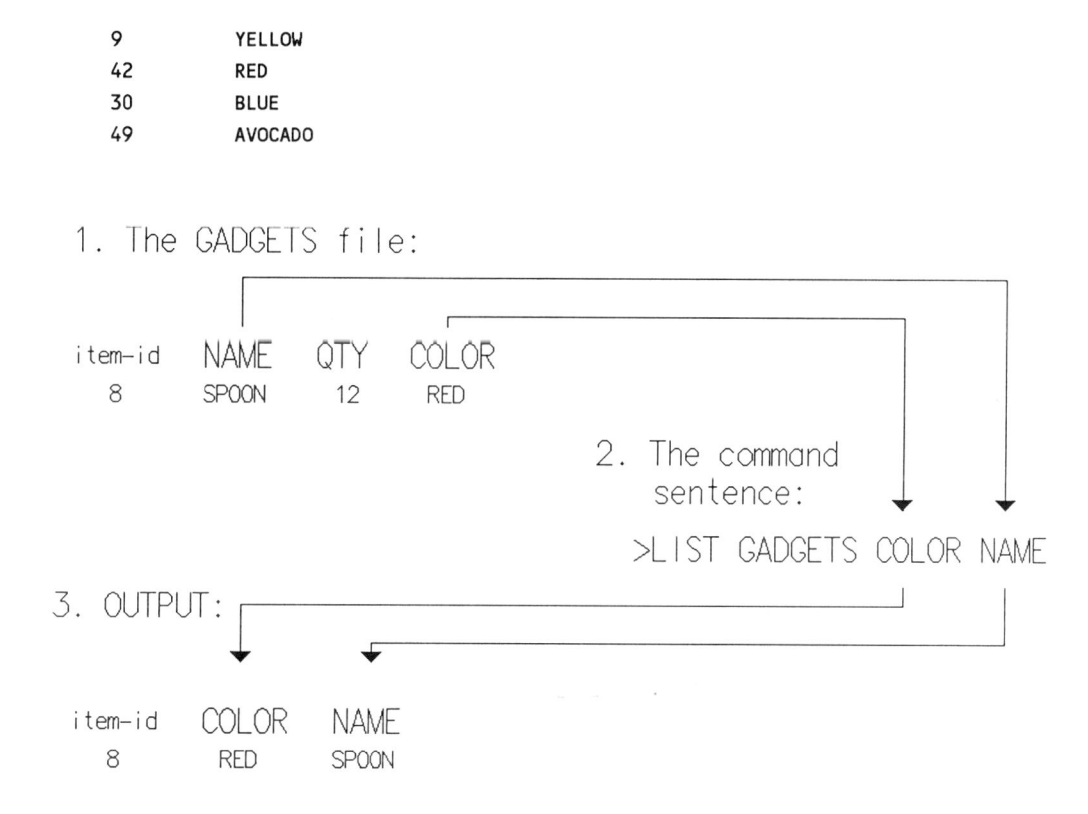

3. OUTPUT:

```
item-id   COLOR   NAME
   8       RED    SPOON
```

FIGURE 4.1: SPECIFYING ATTRIBUTES FOR OUTPUT

You may specify any attributes and in any sequence; they need not be in the same order as the columns in the table. Enter

>**LIST GADGETS NAME COLOR QTY** <return>

Response

GADGETS	NAME	COLOR	QTY
50	FORK	TAN	23
7	SPOON	BROWN	1
20	LADLE	TAN	19
8	SPOON	RED	12
21	LADLE	RED	4
9	SPOON	YELLOW	10
42	SPATULA	RED	17

```
    30        WHISK      BLUE       8
    49        SPATULA    AVOCADO    25
```

At this time there is no shortcut for listing all the attributes; each one to be output must be given in the command. The alternative is to use LIST-ITEM and see all the attributes.

EXPLICIT ITEM LIST

LIST thus far has output all the items in the file. You may want to see only one or several items and outputting the entire file is a waste of time. In this case you can request the item-id(s) that you want to see and the balance of the file will not be output. The item(s) that you want are flagged or delimited for the system; for our present purposes use double quotes around each item-id (some systems require the use of single quotes). One or more such items make up an *explicit item list* which follows the filename in the command. When an explicit item list is given, the system processes only those items in the list; when there is no list, the system defaults to the whole file.

The total command line limit is 148 characters. When you use an explicit item list you must keep in mind that every letter, number, symbol, and blank in the command sentence counts as one character. Therefore it is impossible to say exactly how many items may be given in an explicit item list. The size of the item-ids, and of the file and attribute names all affect the total. Count every character and if you exceed the maximum use more than one command.

Even a sentence within the limit may not fit on one line of the screen. As your typing nears the right side of the screen plan to continue on the next line. This should logically be done when you come to a normal break between words. If you miscalculate and are in the middle of a word and at the end of the line, backspace to a break. First press the space bar. Next press the control and shift keys and the underline all at the same time: <control> <shift> _ then release, and last press <return>. The new prompt is the colon : and it appears at the left end of the new line. Complete the sentence and at the end press <return> as normally done.

Find the quantity for items 7, 8, and 9 instead of for the entire file. To the standard format

```
LIST GADGETS
```

Keeping the file current: Update

add the explicit item list with each item-id in double quotes and a space between it and the next item-id

"7" "8" "9"

Without an attribute at the end of the sentence the command accomplishes nothing; we want to see the QTY so place it in the command. Enter

>LIST GADGETS "7" "8" "9" QTY <return>

Response

GADGETS	QTY
7	1
8	12
9	10

Before continuing, it is essential to determine first what you want to see. Where are these facts stored? Use the command that goes to the target area and fetches what you want to inspect. The Dictionary contains file-names, and attribute names and their structure; the Data File contains the item-ids and the data values.

LIST Verb Summary

TO DISPLAY	USE THE COMMAND	OUTPUT
filenames	>LISTFILES	all files in user's Master Dictionary (account)
all item-ids in one file	>LIST filename	item-ids of all the items in the file
only attribute names in one file	>LIST ONLY DICT filename	the names of all the attributes
the complete Descriptor for each attribute in one file	>LIST-ITEM DICT filename	the complete Descriptor for each attribute

complete items in one file	>LIST-ITEM filename	all items:item-ids and all attribute values
all item-ids and attribute value(s) in one file	>LIST filename attributename(s) (the attributes can be in any sequence)	all items: item-ids and values for attribute(s) named
particular item(s) and attribute value(s)	>LIST filename explicit item list attribute name(s) (each item-id must be in double quotes)	requested item(s) and attribute value(s)

4.3 INTRODUCTION TO UPDATING

The purpose of this book is to acquaint the beginner with the Pick Operating System via hands-on experience. Normally businesses use application programs designed to maintain data integrity. This means that as the data is entered it is checked for correct format, falling within a reasonable range, and so on. There are also security safeguards to protect the data from unauthorized access. The EDITOR processor makes it possible for the person with no programming knowledge to manipulate text. Although this method suits the learner's needs it is not the most practical way of working and circumvents all controls. We therefore warn the new operator to be extremely careful: always create test data and use only test data for practicing the procedures. Never use the EDITOR for "live" data.

Data must be modified constantly to reflect changes in current conditions or to correct data entry errors. This *updating* comprises three types of activity: Add new data to the file, Change items already in the file, and Delete data from the file. While all three operations literally do change the data in the file, in the update context *change* means alter existing data. Some examples of update are: a new employee must be added to the personnel file, the stock inventory for hammers must be changed when a new shipment arrives, the carpet manufacturer changes the color name from cerise to raspberry, and the 24 ounce size of marmalade is discontinued and must be deleted from the file. Take a moment to analyze what you want to do. We shall cover the variety of procedures; be patient and give yourself time to absorb all the details.

You are already familiar with the EDITOR and some of the instructions from the preceding chapter. Do not be confused when you see items dis-

Keeping the file current: Update 75

played horizontally as with LIST (unless the item is too wide) and vertically as with LIST-ITEM and the EDITOR. Another point to keep in mind is that the internal storage order of items may change when they are updated and they may be presented later in a different sequence.

All updating calls for a number of steps, some of which vary according to what has to be done. As we go through the operations to Add, Change, and Delete, we build up a procedure that covers the range of activities. The complete operation can be broken down into three sections; two of which are common to Add, Change, and Delete. Whatever the task, the first command must invoke the EDITOR and get things started. These initial steps are Part 1 of the Update Procedure; always start from here. The next segment of the job differs with the type of update. Obviously you cannot give the same instructions to add a new item as to alter an existing item. Part 2 contains the particular steps required by each activity. The last part of the procedure, like the first, is used for all updating. All three parts must be followed.

As we explore the update possibilities we always refer to Part 1 to begin, then develop the specifics for Part 2, and finally complete the operation with Part 3. This method highlights the shared steps making them easier to remember and avoids repetition. Each of the three parts is summarized after we go through the steps for it.

Earlier in the chapter you added an explicit item list to the LIST verb; an explicit item list can also be used with ED. Note that the EDITOR does not require delimiters with the item-id(s) as LIST does; with ED double quotes are optional.

Part 1 for all updates is the command to summon the EDITOR. Note that commands with the ED or EDIT verb are output to the screen and cannot be directed to the printer. The commands are the same as in the preceding chapter and repeated in the summary below.

SUMMARY: PART 1 of the UPDATE PROCEDURE

The initial steps for all updates are the same and the first command is to summon the EDITOR. Just as in the preceding chapter the command format for working in the Dictionary is

```
>ED DICT filename attribute1 attribute2 etc.
```

and for the Data File

```
>ED filename item-id1 item-id2 etc.
```

As mentioned in Chapter 3, you may inadvertently send the line before typing in the explicit item(s). For example,

```
ED DICT filename
```

or

```
ED filename
```

The response is a request for the

```
ITEM ID:
```

Enter the item-id after the colon.

In both cases the system now has the item-id and tries to retrieve it. When the item is a new one, it does not exist in the file and therefore cannot be found. The response is either

```
NEW ITEM
TOP
.
```

or the item is in the file, the system fetches it, and displays

```
TOP
.
```

We are at the beginning of the item, new or not new, and see the EDITOR prompt, the period. This marks the end of Part 1; next we branch out to cover the unique instructions to Add, Change, and Delete in turn.

4.4 INPUT NEW DATA: ADD

A NEW ITEM

Suppose a new GADGET must be added to the file: the item-id is 63, a BLUE STRAINER, and the quantity is 12. Start with Part 1. This update is in the Data File and we do not have to specify the Data File. Enter

>ED GADGETS 63 <return>

The response is

    NEW ITEM
    TOP
    .

The system has searched the GADGETS file for item 63 and has not found it; therefore the response states that 63 is new. To enter text we must be in Input mode, therefore type in

I <return>

Consecutively numbered lines appear, one at a time, starting with 001+. The + after each line number indicates Input mode and you enter the facts right after the + just as you did in the preceding chapter. Before starting to enter the data make sure that the attributes are in the same sequence as in the table. The order should be

    Item-id   63
    NAME   STRAINER
    QTY   12
    COLOR   BLUE

Type in the appropriate data for each line. Attribute1 NAME STRAINER goes on line 1, attribute2 QTY 12 on line 2, and attribute3 COLOR BLUE on line 3. It is essential to enter the data in the right place. If you type in BLUE on line 1 as the NAME, and 12 on line 3 for the COLOR, the system accepts this new gadget named BLUE, with the color of 12. Remember GIGO. Enter the underlined data for each line as it comes up

    001+STRAINER <return>
    002+12 <return>
    003+BLUE <return>
    004+

All the attributes have been typed in; leave Input mode by

<return>

Response

    TOP
    .

Just as you did in Chapter 3, enter

    F <return>

Response

    TOP
    .

Enter

    P <return>

The response is a display of the complete item

    001 STRAINER
    002 12
    003 BLUE
    EOI 003
    .

Enter

    FI <return>

Response

    '63' FILED.
    >

The last three steps - F, P, and FI - are also familiar and will be used in other update activities.

Beginners are easily overwhelmed by all these new terms and what happens when they go astray. You are going to learn how to handle all sorts of problems. In the exercises you may see that you have made an error; make a note of it and continue working. By the end of the chapter you will be able to correct mistakes.

A NEW ATTRIBUTE

In the above example the structure of the file as described in the Dictionary Descriptors was not altered in any way. The present Descriptors apply to the new data item as well as all the items that already were in the file. Now let us give the data a new attribute for each item: the code identifying the supplier, which we call VENDOR. The revised Data File in table form is shown below:

FILE NAME: GADGETS

GADGETS

item-id	NAME	QTY	COLOR	VENDOR
8	SPOON	12	RED	ACE.88
9	SPOON	10	YELLOW	PEAK.77
20	LADLE	19	TAN	TOPS.55
30	WHISK	8	BLUE	PEAK.77
7	SPOON	1	BROWN	ACME.66
21	LADLE	4	RED	TOPS.55
50	FORK	23	TAN	ZENITH.22
42	SPATULA	17	RED	ACE.88
49	SPATULA	35	AVOCADO	TOPS.55
63	STRAINER	12	BLUE	HIGH.33

Adding a new attribute to an existing file requires two stages: first, a Descriptor for this attribute is added to the Dictionary; and second, the value for the new attribute is added to each item in the Data File. Since we already have attribute1 NAME, attribute2 QTY, and attribute3 COLOR, VENDOR will be attribute4. The Descriptor for VENDOR contains the following facts:

line 001	A	the Code or Attribute Definition Item
line 002	4	Attribute Mark Count
line 003 through		
line 008	null	
line 009	L	justification
line 010	15	output length

The steps to add a new Descriptor are exactly the same as for creating a Descriptor in Chapter 3; they are repeated here. As Part 1 indicates, the initial command to enter is

>ED DICT GADGETS VENDOR <return>

Response

    NEW ITEM
    TOP
    .

As in the previous example, we are adding new text and must be in Input mode, press

I <return>

One at a time, the numbered lines each with a plus sign appear. Enter the data shown above for lines 1,2,9, and 10; for lines 3 through 8 enter a period. For line 11 press only <return> to leave Input mode. This is what we have done so far

    001+A <return>
    002+4 <return>
    003+. <return>
    004+. <return>
    005+. <return>
    006+. <return>
    007+. <return>
    008+. <return>
    009+L <return>
    010+15 <return>
    011+<return>

Response

    TOP
    .

The next step is to replace all the periods on lines 3 through 8 with null

Keeping the file current: Update 81

values. Enter

>   R99/.// <return>

The response is a display of the changed lines i.e. 003 through 008 each with a null value. Follow the instructions in the preceding example to

>   F
>   P
>   FI

Make a note of any errors so that you can correct them after reading the section on making changes.

The Descriptor is now complete; the next step is to go to the Data File and enter the values for VENDOR of each item in the file. Return to Part 1. First consider that we must go through the entire file to add the new values. The command starts with

>   >ED GADGETS item-id1 item-id2 etc.

Wait a moment, this is the slowest way to get the job done. Even with a small test file this would be a tedious job. The most efficient way to EDIT all the items in the file is to use an asterisk * in the command sentence. Each item is automatically presented in internal stored order and we stay in the EDITOR until all the items have been completed. There must be a space between the filename and the asterisk. Enter

>   >ED GADGETS * <return>

The response depends on the stored or internal order of the file which differs from time to time. Eventually every item will appear.

>   item-id
>   TOP
>   .

We are at the beginning of the item whose item id is over the word TOP and ready for the second part of the update. First see what is already in the item. Enter

82 Database and Word Processing for the New User

    P <return>

The response is a display of this item

    001 data
    002 data
    003 data
    EOI 003
    .

To add new text call on Input mode and enter

    I <return>

When adding at the end of the item the response is the number of the last line and + for Input mode. In the example the last line is 003 therefore the display is

    003+

Find the item-id in the table and read carefully across to VENDOR because the sequence in which the items are presented is probably not the same as in the table. Enter the value for VENDOR

    ___ <return>

The response repeats

    003+

Press <return> to show that Input is complete. The response is the old EOI

    EOI 003
    .

Do not be alarmed, the line number will be corrected later. Enter

    F <return>

Response

Keeping the file current: Update

TOP
.

Enter

    P <return>

Response is a display of the new version of the item with the lines resequenced to include the line just added.

    001 data
    002 data
    003 data
    004 the new data
    EOI 004
    .

The End Of Item is now line 4. Enter

    FI <return>

When an asterisk is used you remain in the EDITOR and another item appears automatically. The next item on the screen is probably not the next item in the table because the items come up in stored order. The response is

    'item-id' FILED.
    next.item-id
    TOP
    .

Follow the same procedure starting with the first P. For line 003+ enter the appropriate value for VENDOR for the item you are currently working on. After the last item in the file has been FIled you leave the EDITOR and see the > prompt of TCL.

    'item-id' FILED.
    >

As mentioned, an explicit item list could have been used instead of the asterisk. The GADGETS file is so small that the item-ids easily fit within the maximum limits of the command sentence. However this is not as easy as using *. The only difference between the two methods is that you control the sequence with the explicit item list.

Above, only one line was added to the end of the item; more than one line can be added in the same way. After I, the last line number of the item appears with +. That same line number + comes up for each line as you enter data. The line numbers are adjusted later however many lines are added. You can keep track of the actual line numbers as you work if necessary. Follow the normal procedure and press <return> to end Input mode. The response is the old EOI line number before the Adds. This will also be corrected.

Let us make up a test data item for trying out some of the update operations and purposely put in errors. This is a handy way to experiment without disturbing the other data items in the file. The following new item is full of blunders to be corrected; add it to the GADGETS file. The item-id must be unique and so call it 999 because there is no item with that item-id in the file. Enter

>ED GADGETS 999 <return>

Response

NEW ITEM
TOP
.

Enter

I <return>

Enter the following data. (The item is deliberately a disaster.)

001+ LADLE <return>
002+ TAN <return>
003+ CROWN.11 <return>
004+ CROWN.11 <return>
005+ F <return>
006+ P <return>
007+ <return>

Response

Keeping the file current: Update

```
   TOP
   .
```

Enter

```
   F <return>
```

Response

```
   TOP
   .
```

Enter

```
   P <return>
```

Response

```
   001 LADLE
   002 TAN
   003 CROWN.11
   004 CROWN.11
   005 F
   006 P
   EOI 006
   .
```

Read through each line of the item and see what should be corrected.

> Line 1 (NAME) is LADLE and is OK
> Line 2 (QTY) should be 7
> Line 3 (COLOR) should be TAN
> Line 4 (VENDOR) is CROWN.11 and is OK
> Line 5 should be deleted
> Line 6 should be deleted

When working on a large item or making many changes in a small one, we can save the corrections as we go. The command

```
   FS
```

files the latest update and permits us to remain in the item and in the EDITOR. We want to save this item and continue to work on it instead of having to leave the EDITOR and then return. Enter

    FS <return>

The item is saved and also retained as the current item, we remain in the EDITOR. The response is

    TOP
    .

INSERT TEXT

We are now at the TOP of the same item - 999 - and ready to make the first correction. Normally we would press P to inspect the item before making changes, but we already have it on display. Think back a moment to when we added the VENDOR values to the end of each item. The same procedure will not work here if we want to insert the new data after line 1 for the quantity 7 to fall on line 2. Enter the number of the line for the insert to follow.

    1 <return>

If the response is the line requested which is

    001 LADLE
    .

then skip to I below.

    However if the response is

        CMND?

your system requires a

        G with the line number

G means GO TO. Whenever you call for a particular line number you must use

        Gn

with no space between the G and the line. Here enter

    G1

to display

    001 LADLE
    .

To enter new text call for Input mode. Enter

    I <return>

The response is the line just given above I with a plus sign. Here we see

    001+

Type in whatever is to be inserted on the next line, i.e.

    7 <return>

At this time we are inserting only one line and so are ready to leave Input mode. Press

    <return>

Response

    .

Continue with the following steps to see the current version of the item:

    F <return>

Response

    TOP
    .

Enter

    P <return>

This response is how the item looks now

```
001 LADLE
002 7
003 TAN
004 CROWN.11
005 CROWN.11
006 F
007 P
EOI 007
.
```

Note that the line numbers have been resequenced to include the insert after line 1; the 7 is on line 2 where it belongs, and TAN has been pushed down to line 3 where it should be. Because we added one line, the EOI is now on line 7, one more than it was before the insert. The item still has problems that we shall correct later, meanwhile save it by typing in

    <u>FI</u> <return>

Response

    '999' FILED.
    >

The system cannot go backwards. For example, suppose you enter 7 and then I to insert text after line 7. Suddenly you realize that you should have entered 6. Send <return> to exit Input mode, press F <return> to get to the TOP of the item, and then 6 <return> to position text after line 6.

Just as multiple lines can be added to the end of an item they can be inserted within an item. When this is done the original line number to follow appears with + after each new line is entered, always the same number. The line numbers are corrected later to include the inserted lines.

4.5 REPLACE DATA: CHANGE

The most frequent type of update is probably changes to existing items in the Data File. At this time only an attribute can be modified; the item-id is the key to the item and must not be altered in any way.

Suppose you are told that the new strainer, item 63, should be BROWN and not BLUE. Think through the steps to take: the change is in the Data File and the item-id is 63. Refer to Part 1, then use the ED command with the filename GADGETS and the explicit item 63. Enter

```
>ED GADGETS 63 <return>
```

Response

```
TOP
.
```

First Print the item to the screen to see exactly where the change is to be made. Enter

```
P <return>
```

Response

```
001 STRAINER
002 12
003 BLUE
004 HIGH.33
EOI 004
.
```

BLUE is on line 3. Enter the number of the line to be changed

```
3 <return>
```

Response

```
003 BLUE
.
```

As you recall we used one form of the Replace command R99/.// to replace the periods with null values in the Descriptors. The 99 instructed the system to replace the first period with null wherever one appeared on the next 99 lines. The change we are making now applies to only one line and we do not use 99. The standard format for Replace is

```
R/old text/new text/
```

Here we are replacing the old text BLUE with the new text BROWN, enter

    R/BLUE/BROWN/ <return>

The response is the changed version of the line above the Replace command

    003 BROWN
    .

This display does not mean that the change is permanent. You must complete the final steps that we have been using to make the update on disk. If you omit the last part of the update, you still have a BLUE strainer in the file. By now you are experienced and can

    F   Flip the changes
    P   Print the item to the screen and inspect it
    FI   FIle the item

As an aside, there is a way of doing less work. You may be able to use some of the old text instead of replacing it completely. Here we could keep the B and replace LUE with ROWN.

    R/LUE/ROWN/

Or perhaps you have extra characters which must be removed from the old text: BROWNN should be BROWN. A short cut correction is to replace the extra character N with nothing

    R/N//

and you are left with BROWN.

R followed by a number, as in R99, replaces the old text wherever it appears on the next specified number of lines but only the first occurrence on a line.

Sometimes the old text to be changed appears more than once on a line. To make all the changes on one line at one time use Replace Universal with the form

    RU/old text/new text/

Suppose you typed in SPIIN instead of SPOON. The correction can be made with R and the complete old and new texts; with a short word it does not matter very much. If the text is long, it is quicker to replace all of the I's with O's.

```
RU/I/O/
```

The response would be

```
SPOON
```

Every I on the line is replaced with O. You realize that R and RU must come directly after the line being corrected.

U and a number can be combined to replace *all* occurrences on the next indicated number of lines. The format is

```
RU99/old text/new text/
```

Remember that all forms of R work from the current line (the line immediately before the R) down; if you want to change text for the whole item start at the TOP.

As with any changes make sure that the results will be what you want. Perhaps you intended to type in ROOFING and by mistake made it RIIFING. If you use RU and replace all the I's with O's, you end up with ROOFONG because every I on the line was replaced. The most efficient way of working is to think first. Reminder – the fastest corrections can be made before the line is completed; inspect the text and use the back space before pressing <return>.

4.6 REMOVE DATA: DELETE

The sample files are extremely simple but be aware of the inter-relationships of data and the effects of careless deletions. For example, a file of hardware supplier information has name, code, address etc.. The supplier ships parts that are in several files. When one part is discontinued and removed from its file do not erase the supplier information from its file until you are sure that he no longer delivers any parts in any file. Otherwise you lose data that you need for parts that are still being sent.

In some cases it may be wise to flag non-current items or to store facts in an inactive file rather than discard them. Think through the effects of deleting and be guided by your particular needs; consult with a colleague.

Generally speaking it is wise to follow the sequence we have used in updating: first Add, then Change, and last Delete. Be particularly careful when removing data from the files. Whether a line, a whole item, or an entire file once deleted it is gone forever; there is no trash basket where you can recover what has been thrown away.

Let us return to special item 999 to practice deleting. Enter

>ED GADGETS 999 <return>

Response

TOP
.

Enter

P <return>

Response

```
001 LADLE
002 7
003 TAN
004 CROWN.11
005 CROWN.11
006 F
007 P
EOI 007
```
.

DELETE A LINE

As we read down the item we find the first problem on line 5 - the line should come out. When we used the Replace command we gave the line number to work on; to delete, enter the line number to be removed

5 <return>

Response

```
    005 CROWN.11
    .
```

We are now positioned at line 5 with the data value CROWN.11. The command DE (DElete) removes the *current* line - the one at which we are positioned - and also whatever is on the line. Enter

```
    DE <return>
```

The response is the EDITOR prompt

```
    .
```

Always inspect the latest version of the item. Enter

```
    F <return>
```

Response

```
    TOP
    .
```

Enter

```
    P <return>
```

Response

```
    001 LADLE
    002 7
    003 TAN
    004 CROWN.11
    005 F
    006 P
    EOI 006
    .
```

The old line 5 was deleted, consequently line 6 moved up into its place and became the new line 5. The old line 7 also moved up one and is now line 6. Whenever one line is deleted everything that follows goes up by one line. Check the item carefully. If it is correct FIle it, but item 999 is not yet ready to save. As you see lines 5 and 6 must be DEleted. Can you guess what usually has happened when you see lines with F and P?

It is common to forget to press <return> after Input mode is complete. Then F and P become part of the item. In this example only the <return> was used after P was entered for line 6.

DELETE MULTIPLE LINES

Note that there are now two consecutive lines to be DEleted: 5 and 6. Enter the first of them

>   5 <return>

Response

>   005 F
>   .

When used alone DE defaults to the current line. When there is more than one line to be DEleted we do not have to repeat the command for each line. DEn removes *n* or *this many consecutive lines* starting with the current line. In the example, *n* is 2 because two lines are to be deleted; there is no space between DE and the number. Beginning with line 5 DE2 will DElete lines 5 and 6. Enter

>   DE2 <return>

The response is the EDITOR prompt

>   .

Enter

>   F <return>

Response

>   TOP
>   .

Enter

>   P <return>

Response

    001 LADLE
    002 7
    003 TAN
    004 CROWN.11
    EOI 004
    .

Enter

    FS <return>

As you see DEn (here DE2) goes straight down and wipes out n lines in sequence. Lines 5 and 6 are gone forever. It is essential to remember the difference between calling for the line number to work on and using a number with DE.

Suppose you intend to erase line 3: you <u>should</u> type in 3 to get to the line, inspect it, and then use DE to DElete line 3. What happens when you put the number 3 in the DElete command? Enter

    F <return>

to get to the TOP of the item, then

    DE3 <return>

Response

    .

Enter

    F <return>

Response

    TOP
    .

Enter

P <return>

Response

    001 CROWN.11
    EOI 001
    .

What a shock. We were at the TOP or first line of the item. DE3 erased three lines beginning with line 1; what was formerly line 4 is now line 1 and it is all that is left of the item.

It is time to take a conceptualized look at what has been happening in the procedures thus far. The EDITOR workspace is divided into two *buffers* which are like scratch pads. An existing item being EDITed is copied from disk into the primary buffer. Alterations to the item and also new text are held in the secondary buffer. The command F Flips, or copies, the contents of the secondary buffer onto the primary buffer. The P command Prints the latest version of the item to the screen for our inspection.

At this stage we can decide what to do with the item because the system is using two buffers.

1. If we want to keep the last version of the item, we use FI or FS which FIles the updated contents of the primary buffer to disk: an old item is replaced by its new form or a new item is added.

2. If we do not want to file the last version of the item, we can discard the contents of the secondary buffer with the command EX (EXit). Now the existing item remains on disk unchanged; any alterations to it or new text are thrown away. Note that EX can also be used to leave an item after a routine display to the screen.

FI and EX leave the buffers ready for the next item.

EX is handy for throwing away recent changes such as the mistake just made. Do not FIle the above version of the item with the unexpected change from the DE3 example. Enter

    EX <return>

The response is

    [220] '999' EXITED
    >

Note that the EDITOR has also been EXited and we see the TCL prompt. What does the item look like without the most recent alteration? Enter

    >ED GADGETS 999 <return>

Response

    TOP
    .

Enter

    P <return>

Response

    001 LADLE
    002 7
    003 TAN
    004 CROWN.11
    EOI 004
    .

This item is in the same state as it was when brought from disk. The changes in the secondary buffer after the DE3 command (when the item was reduced to one line) were discarded after the EX command. EX is extremely useful but must be handled with care. The version of an item immediately before the last FS or FI is saved. The form of an item after changes is not kept because it is EXited before FS or FI. Now that we have checked 999 we are satisfied to let it remain as it is on disk and enter

    EX <return>

Response

    [220] '999' EXITED
    >

Note that when there is an asterisk or explicit item list with more than one item in the command, the next item is presented. Here there are no more items and so you return to TCL.

Sometimes when working in the EDITOR with either * or an explicit item list you may want to "get out" for one reason or another. The suffix K (Kill the remaining item-ids) stops the presentation and returns to TCL; K can be used with EX and FI.

```
.EXK
```

EXits the current item and ignores whatever is left.

Response

```
'item-id' EXITED
>
```

In contrast,

```
.FIK
```

FIles the current item and, as above, ignores whatever is left.

Response

```
'item-id' FILED.
>
```

DELETE AN ITEM

Special item 999 has served its purpose and there is no reason to keep it any longer. Now we shall remove the entire item: the item-id and all the attribute values. Start with Part 1; enter

```
>ED GADGETS 999 <return>
```

Response

```
TOP
.
```

Keeping the file current: Update

Print the item to the screen and look it over before continuing. Enter

    P <return>

The response is the complete item as we saw it before, and the EDITOR prompt. After you are positive that this is the item to remove use the FD command. Note that in the command below, the letter F does not refer to the file but only to the item. Enter

    FD <return>

After FD, some systems delete the item immediately, others ask you to verify with a query such as

    Are you sure (Y/<N>)?

If you decide not to delete the item, enter

    N <return>

The response is the EDITOR prompt and you can continue in the item or EX. To complete the delete enter

    Y <return>

The response is

    '999' DELETED.
    >

TCL displays its prompt; we have left the EDITOR. FD is the exception to the normal Update Procedure and the final steps of Part 3 are not used. For a quick check try to EDit the item that was just deleted with FD. Enter

    >ED GADGETS 999 <return>

The response is

    NEW ITEM
    TOP
    .

This proves that item 999 is no longer in the file. Enter

    EX <return>

to EXit the item and the EDITOR and go on to the next job.

The new item 63 which we added to the file a short time ago is not being shipped and must be removed from the file. Such is the way of data update. Follow the same steps used in deleting item 999 with FD.

DELETE MULTIPLE ITEMS

If we had known about this earlier we could have deleted both 999 and 63 in one operation by using an explicit item list in the ED command. Since both items have now been removed do not enter the following commands; they are shown to illustrate DEleting multiple items.

    >ED GADGETS 999 63

Each item is displayed in turn as it is given in the command. First is

    999
    TOP
    .

The command is

    FD

Response

    '999' DELETED.
    63
    TOP
    .

The system has fetched 63 the next item in the list and remains in the EDITOR. Enter

    FD

Response

'63' DELETED.
>

After the last item in the list is completed we return to TCL.

SUMMARY: PART 2 of the UPDATE PROCEDURE

ADD

    A New Item

        .I <return>
        001+ enter data for this line <return>
        002+ enter data for this line <return>
        etc. Consecutively numbered lines appear one at a time. When all the data has been entered go to the end of ADD.

    At the End

        .P <return>
        .I <return>
        Response is the last line number + enter data <return>
        Response is the same line number + enter data <return>
        The same line number is repeated for each line. Enter data on appropriate line(s). When all the data has been entered go to the end of ADD.

    Insert

        .P <return>
        Response is a display of the entire item
        Enter line number the insert is to follow <return>
        Response is the requested line number and data on it.
        .I <return>
        Response is the requested line +
        Enter data to be inserted on the next line <return>
        Response is the same line number + repeated for each line. Enter data on proper line(s). When all the data has been entered go to the end of ADD.

    End of Add

        <return> to leave Input mode
        Response is
        TOP
        .

Complete Part 3 of the Update Procedure at the end of Section 4.7

CHANGE

For all Changes
.P <return>
Response is a display of the entire item
Enter line number to change <return>
Response is the requested line number and data.

Replace format
.R/old text/new text/ <return>
Use
R   to Replace old text with new text on this line
R99 to Replace the first occurrence on the next 99 lines
RU   to Replace all occurrences on this line
RU99 to Replace all occurrences on the next 99 lines

Complete Part 3 of the Update Procedure at the end of Section 4.7

DELETE

For all Deletes
.P <return>
Response is a display of the entire item

One Line
Enter line number to be deleted <return>
Response is the requested line number and data.
.DE <return>
. Response is the EDITOR prompt.
Complete Part 3 of the Update Procedure

Multiple Lines
Enter line number of first line to be deleted <return>
Response is the requested line number and data.
.DEn <return> DEletes n consecutive lines starting with the line directly above the DElete command.
. Response is the EDITOR prompt.
Complete Part 3 of the Update Procedure

Keeping the file current: Update

Entire Item
.FD <return>
'item id' DELETED
>
Omit Part 3; control automatically returns to TCL

4.7 FINAL STEPS OF UPDATE

Actually you have already been using these commands after you completed Part 2 for Add, Change, and Delete. The last steps are combined here because they are common to all updates. Whatever the type of update activity get into the habit of

F Flip or merge the contents of the two buffers and
P Print the current version of the item to the screen. Inspect the item.

There are now three options depending on what you want to do:

1. If you want to save the item as it appears but also continue to work on it, the command

    .FS <return>

    makes it easy. It copies the current version of the item to disk and you remain in the item and in the EDITOR. The response is

    TOP
    .

    You are at the beginning of the same item as before FS. Perform whatever operations are necessary starting with Part 2 or Part 3 of the Update Procedure. Part 1 is not required because you are already in the EDITOR and at the TOP of the item. To leave this item you must use FI or EX as explained below.

2. If you want to FIle and then leave the item use

    .FI <return>

It FIles the final form of the item to disk; if the item was on file before, the old form is discarded and only the new is retained.

What follows depends on whether or not there was an asterisk or explicit item list or neither in the initial ED command.

With * or a list the EDITOR presents the next item

```
item-id
TOP
.
```

You are at the beginning of the item shown and remain in the EDITOR as indicated by the period prompt. Perform the update for the item through Part 3. Continue to work on each item as it appears. When you reach the last item it is the same as if there were no asterisk or list. The response is

```
'item-id' FILED.
>
```

The EDit process is complete. Control returns to TCL which displays its > prompt.

3. An item can be EXited at any time; EX is included in Part 3 only because it is one way to leave the EDITOR. If the item was previously on disk, it is retained in its old form; all updating since the last FS or FI is not filed. WARNING: this means that a new item as well as recent alterations to an existing item are discarded. The command is

```
.EX <return>
```

The response is

```
[220] 'item-id' EXITED
```

As above, when there is an asterisk or explicit item list the next item is presented. When there are no more items to be EDited, control returns to TCL and its prompt > is displayed.

Here is a summary of these last steps:

SUMMARY: PART 3 of the UPDATE PROCEDURE

The next two steps are always used

    .F <return>

Response

    TOP
    .
    P <return>

Response

    001 The updated version of the item is Printed to the screen.
    002
    etc.
    EOI
    .

Use one of the following:

    FS <return>

to save the updated version and remain in the item and in the EDITOR.

Response

    TOP
    .

Leave by FI or EX

    FI <return>   FIle the item to disk

Response

    'item-id' FILED.
    item-id   of the next item if there is one
    TOP
    .

or

>

after the last item, or

    .EX <return>

which means EXit the item; do not save the last version

Response

```
[220] 'item-id' EXITED
item-id                    of the next item if there is one
TOP
.
```

or

>

after the last item.

The K suffix with FI or EX Kills (ignores) the remaining item-ids and returns to TCL.

In summary, all update starts from TCL when we summon the EDITOR. Text is added, changed or deleted; and the updates can be kept or discarded. When the task is complete, control returns to TCL. Many of the steps are the same or similar for all updating. In time you will become familiar with them; meanwhile give yourself a chance to absorb all these new procedures.

The importance of using test data cannot be overemphasized. After a test Dictionary and Data File have been created for experimenting and are no longer needed they should be deleted to free the disk space. A word of caution: be positive that you will not need the file anymore. Once deleted it is gone forever. Do not delete the GADGETS file, we shall be using it again. The following is included here because it can be considered an update activity.

The command to delete a file works at TCL level and is not a function of the EDITOR. The format is

```
>DELETE-FILE filename
```

The response is the TCL prompt

```
>
```

Just as we tested the item deletion we can check that the above file is erased by trying to see it

```
>LIST filename
```

The response should be

```
[10] FILE NAME MISSING
```

which proves it is gone.

After all the manipulation on the GADGETS file, it is wise to LIST it and verify the contents. Make whatever revisions are necessary to insure the accuracy of the data.

SUMMARY: EDITOR TERMS

DE	DElete the line above
DEn	DElete n many lines starting with the line above
to invoke the EDITOR use	
ED DICT filename	optional: explicit item list (quotes unnecessary) or *
ED filename	optional: explicit item list (quotes unnecessary) or *
EX	EXit the item and discard latest changes
F	Flip the contents of the secondary buffer onto the primary
FD	Delete the item from disk
FI	FIle the item to disk, if no more items leave the EDITOR
FS	File the item to disk and remain in the item and the EDITOR
I	call for Input Mode to enter new text
K	suffix with EX or FI, Kill the remaining item-ids
P	Print the item to the screen

prompt	the period . in the EDITOR
R/old text/with new text/	Replace the first occurence on this line
R99/old/with new/	Replace the first occurence on the next 99 lines
RU/old/with new/	Replace all occurences on this line
RU99/old/with new/	Replace all occurences on the next 99 lines
<return>	in Command Mode: continue display in Input Mode: use alone to terminate Input Mode
TOP	beginning of the item

4.8 ERROR EXAMPLES

ERROR	COMMENT
>LIST GADGETS 9 [24] THE WORD "9" CANNOT BE IDENTIFIED	Quotes are missing around 9
>LIST GADGETS "7 [2] Uneven number of delimeters (' " \).	Closing quote after 7 is omitted
>LIST GADGETS * [24] THE WORD "*" CANNOT BE IDENTIFIED	LIST automatically gives the whole file; * is not used with LIST
.ED GADGETS 63 CMND?	You are already in the EDITOR as shown by the period prompt
>ED GADGETS* [201] 'GADGETS*' IS NOT A FILE NAME	There must be a space between the filename and *
>ED GADGETS ITEM ID:EX NEW ITEM TOP	EXit an item only at the EDITOR prompt Here the system waits for the item-id

.EX	Wherever the period appears alone
[220] 'EX' EXITED	you may EXit the item
>R/SPOON/LADLE/	You must be in the EDITOR to use
[3] Verb?	the Replace command

When creating a Descriptor for the Dictionary

.	
.	
EOI 010	
.R99/.//	Here R99 is at the end of the item
EOI 010	
.Γ	
.P	
001 A	As you see it has no effect
002 9	
003 .	
004 .	
005 .	
006 .	
007 .	
008 .	
009 R	
010 6	
EOI 010	
.F	
TOP	Get to the TOP of the item
.R99/.//	
003	
004	
005	The periods on the lines below
006	the Replace command have been
007	replaced with null values
008	
001 SPOON	
002 12	DE must follow the request for the
003 RED	line to be DEleted
EOI 003	
.DE	here it follows the display of the item
SEQN?	

4.9 REVIEW QUESTIONS

1. What are three ways to leave the EDITOR?
2. How can you EDIT the whole file most efficiently?
3. What is the difference between FI and FS?
4. Is it essential to use test data? Why?
5. What does the K suffix do? With which commands is it used?
6. How many and in what order are attributes requested for output?
7. What is the advantage of having two EDITOR buffers?
8. How do you get to a particular line in an item? If, for example, you are at line 7 how do you call for line 4?
9. What does update mean?
10. How do we delete one line in an item? Multiple lines? An entire item?
11. What do you do if a response is too long to fit on one screen?
12. What two steps are required when a new attribute is added to an existing file?
13. How can you find a filename? How can you see the item-ids in a file? The complete items?
14. Give three variations of the Replace command and explain when they are used.
15. What is an explicit item list? What is the difference between using one with LIST and with EDIT?

Chapter 5

Producing Information from the Data

5.1 WHAT IS ACCESS?

Up to this point the verb LIST has output the entire contents of a file unless an explicit item list was given. A great deal more can be produced from the data such as: Which GADGETS are RED? What is the average quantity? How does the file look when sorted alphabetically by NAME? What is the total quantity of SPOONs? You, as the user, decide what you want to know. How to get information from the raw data is the subject of this chapter.

The built-in capabilities of the Pick System provide a variety of functions. The test data files used in the examples have deliberately been kept small. In this way processing can easily be done mentally and the results compared to the computer output. If you know that the response is correct, you know that you have worded the command properly. Adapt the examples to suit your own needs and do not be afraid to experiment.

As you have seen from the start, the computer can follow only those instructions it can understand, those that have been built into it. When a command is given properly, the process is performed quickly and accurately. To produce the types of information described above we use certain normal English words that make up a *data retrieval* or *query* language. ACCESS (*ENGLISH* on the Microdata system, *INFO/ACCESS* on the ADDS MENTOR, and *RECALL* on Ultimate) is the name of the language and also of the specialized processor that performs this function in the Pick Operating System. While these terms may seem strange, the actual procedure is simple and easy to understand. First think what you want done and how you express it in everyday language. As we cover different ways of outputting information you will be able to translate the idea, often with few or no changes, into an acceptable instruction.

The output of the verbs in this chapter - LIST, COUNT, SUM, STAT, and SORT - can be routed either to the screen or to the printer.

5.2 EXTRACT DATA: LIST WITH SELECTION CRITERIA

The sentence can be long and contain many optional elements, but usually only two parts are required: the verb which describes what to do such as LIST, COUNT, or SORT; and the filename which says what to do it to. As we go through each variation of a command try it on your system and see if the results are what they should be. This is the best way to learn the procedures. You may be surprised at some of the weird answers you see from incorrect formats. Sometimes you will get a message that explains the error; other times you will get a response but not the correct one. It is highly recommended when starting that you pretend to be the computer and process the sample data. Compare your output with that of the computer. Remember GIGO; earlier it referred to data entry, now it can also be applied to errors in the wording of the command sentence.

Many system messages are already familiar; you will continue to see them plus some new ones. There are two types: the error message, which flags a problem and contains an explanation so that the error may be corrected; and the summary message, which appears with output. Both types are self-explanatory and helpful. As previously noted, only the relevant parts of sample command output are shown; page numbers, headings, system messages, and so forth are frequently omitted. Remember that data is output in internal sequence and the order in yours may not be the same as shown in the sample responses.

In this chapter it will be possible to set up requirements that the data must pass before it is selected for processing. Data that does not meet the specifications is ignored. This is an important capability because it provides a great range to database manipulation. Without a test, LIST GADGETS QTY outputs the QTY for each item in the file. But we may want the QTY only for the SPOONs. The command should find the quantity for all the SPOONs in the GADGET file.

Before QTY can be listed each item must be tested on its NAME. If the NAME is SPOON the item meets the requirement and is chosen; if the NAME is not SPOON the item fails the test and is ignored. In short, the computer selects from the file only those items that meet the requirement.

Whether a simple phrase such as

   NAME equals SPOON

or complex phrases such as

COLOR equals RED and also quantity greater than 12

the test is called *selection criteria.* In order to be selected, the item must pass the test. Each phrase contains an object to be tested, such as the QTY and the test itself, such as equals 12.

The verb is LIST and it must be first in the sentence. The filename follows the verb. So far we have

    LIST GADGETS

which as you know lists the entire file. To select only those items with the quantity of 12 we must add the word WITH and the selection criteria. The object to be tested is the value for the attribute QTY

    WITH QTY

All tests consist of a comparison or relationship between two things. To start, consider some of the relations that one value can have to another: it can be equal to, greater than, or less than the second value. These terms indicate the relationship between two elements and therefore are known as *relational operators.* Either the short form of letters or symbols is permitted.

RELATIONSHIP	RELATIONAL OPERATORS
Equal to	EQ or =
Greater than	GT or >
Less than	LT or <

Note that there must be a space on each side of the operator. The value for QTY is tested to see if it is equal to 12 and so EQ or = is the relational operator for this comparison. Equal to what? The last part of the test is a fixed value, here 12.

The computer reads through the file. It compares the QTY for the item to 12. If the value for the QTY is equal to 12, the item is selected by its item-id; if the QTY is any other number the computer moves on to the next item. The values for quantity can be different for every item in the file but the 12 does not change, it remains the same throughout the reading of the file. A fixed value of this kind is called a *literal value* and must be enclosed in double quotes which we consistently use to delimit values.

Enter

>LIST GADGETS WITH QTY = "12" <return>

The system now reads through the GADGETS file, tests each QTY value against 12, and lists only the item-ids for those items with quantity equal to 12.

Response

8

If more than the item-id is to be displayed add the name(s) of the attribute(s) at the end of the sentence. You have already done this with LIST in Chapter 4 and recall that any number of attributes can be requested in any sequence. Enter

>LIST GADGETS WITH QTY = "12" QTY COLOR NAME <return>

Response

GADGETS	QTY	COLOR	NAME
8	12	RED	SPOON

Now that you know how the equal sign is used, note that it can be omitted. When no relational operator appears the system assumes, or defaults to, equal. All other operators must be specified.

Output of the LIST verb varies in its sequence; your LISTings will probably not be in the same order as the samples in the text but all the items will appear in the output.

Note that OR is implied between literal values in a test. If you want to know what RED and BROWN GADGETS are in the file it means that you will accept a color equal to RED or to BROWN. The phrase starts

WITH COLOR

equal is understood after the attribute named COLOR. "RED" and "BROWN" are literal values and must be in quotes; OR is implied between them. Enter

Producing Information from the Data 115

```
>LIST GADGETS WITH COLOR "RED" "BROWN" COLOR NAME <return>
```

Response

GADGETS	COLOR	NAME
7	BROWN	SPOON
8	RED	SPOON
21	RED	LADLE
42	RED	SPATULA

Find the GADGETS that have a quantity greater than 12. Use either the letters GT or symbol > as the relational operator. Enter

```
>LIST GADGETS WITH QTY > "12" QTY <return>
```

Response

GADGETS	QTY
50	23
20	19
42	17
49	25

"Greater than 12" means precisely what it says: the number 12 is equal to 12 but is not greater than 12 and therefore it is not included.

Selection criteria can contain further requirements. What GADGETS have a quantity greater than 12 and also the COLOR TAN? Here both tests must be passed before the item can be selected. If it passes only one test – quantity greater than 12 but COLOR not TAN; or COLOR TAN but quantity not greater than 12 – the item is ignored. Here we call for tests on two different attributes: QTY and COLOR. Each attribute must have its own selection criterion phrase

```
WITH QTY > "12"

WITH COLOR "TAN"
```

You must use the word AND to connect the above phrases. Enter

>LIST GADGETS WITH QTY > "12" AND WITH COLOR "TAN" QTY NAME COLOR <return>

Response

GADGETS	QTY	NAME	COLOR
50	23	FORK	TAN
20	19	LADLE	TAN

The system permits a maximum of nine AND clauses but it is hard to imagine such an awkward sentence.

Find what RED GADGETS are supplied by vendor PEAK.77. Again there are two tests to be passed: the item must have COLOR equal to RED and also VENDOR equal to PEAK.77. Note that the following command fits on one line on the screen although it is continued on a second line in the text. Enter

>LIST GADGETS WITH COLOR "RED" AND WITH VENDOR "PEAK.77"
COLOR VENDOR NAME <return>

Response

[401] NO ITEMS PRESENT.

Check the sample Data File. There are RED GADGETS and there are GADGETS from VENDOR PEAK.77 but no item passes both tests and the response is correct.

FORMAT FOR LIST:

REQUIRED	OPTIONAL	OUTPUT ATTRIBUTE(S)
LIST filename	explicit item list and/or selection criteria WITH one attribute AND WITH each extra attribute	optional default to item-ids

If you had any problems with the bare bones of the ACCESS sentence format you may be more comfortable inserting *Throwaway words*. These are special words that are allowed by the system and their sole function is to provide greater clarity for the user. For example

Producing Information from the Data

```
LIST GADGETS WITH QTY > "12" AND WITH COLOR "TAN"
```

can also be written

```
LIST ANY ITEMS IN THE GADGETS DATA FILE WITH A QTY > "12" AND WITH THE COLOR
OF "TAN"
```

Both produce the same response and the choice is up to the user.

THROWAWAY WORDS

A
AN
ANY
ARE
DATA
FILE
FOR
IN
ITEMS
OF
OR
THE

The command line limit of 148 characters also applies to sentences containing Throwaway words.

5.3 THE VERBS COUNT, SUM, STAT

COUNT

Now try a new verb: COUNT. It produces a count of the total number of items. When used with selection criteria the count is for those items that pass the test(s); without selection criteria the count is the total number of all the items in the file. The sentence takes the standard ACCESS format: verb, filename, and optional extras. To start, use the verb and filename to produce the count of the items in the file. Enter

```
>COUNT GADGETS <return>
```

Response

```
[407] 9 ITEMS COUNTED
```

Add selection criteria to the above to find how many items in the file are TAN. This is like saying how many items have TAN as the value in the attribute named COLOR. The selection criteria phrase is

```
WITH COLOR "TAN"
```

Enter

```
>COUNT GADGETS WITH COLOR "TAN" <return>
```

Response

```
[407] 2 ITEMS COUNTED
```

This particular system message number 407 is generated by the COUNT verb and gives the number of items that were counted. This is the only information that is given. By checking the sample data we find that gadgets 20 and 50 have the COLOR TAN; 2 items is correct. When you think through this command and its response, you understand why an attribute name at the end of the sentence is meaningless because it has no effect on the counting.

The command

```
COUNT GADGETS WITH COLOR "TAN" NAME
```

produces exactly the same response as the sentence in the previous example. Omit output specifications when using COUNT.

FORMAT FOR COUNT:

REQUIRED	OPTIONAL	OUTPUT ATTRIBUTE(S)
COUNT filename	explicit item list and/or selection criteria WITH one attribute AND WITH each extra attribute	omit output attribute

SUM

Another specialized verb is SUM; it generates the total of the values for one designated attribute. Find the total for quantity of every item in the file. In addition to the verb and the filename the system must know what attribute is to be used for the SUM; the name of the attribute is placed at the end of the sentence. Enter

>SUM GADGETS QTY <return>

Response

TOTAL OF QTY = 119

As you can see from the test data, 119 is the total of all the QTY values. When using SUM remember there are now three required parts in the sentence: SUM, the filename, and the attribute to be SUMmed. As with COUNT any additional attribute(s) have no effect on the process. Selection criteria can be inserted to obtain a SUM for GADGETS that meet specified requirements.

Find the SUM of all the quantity values that are less than 12. Enter

>SUM GADGETS WITH QTY < "12" QTY <return>

Response

TOTAL OF QTY = 23

Check the response by looking at the sample data to find which GADGETS have QTY < 12. GADGETS 9, 7, 21, and 30 have quantity values of 10, 1, 4, and 8 respectively. The sum is 23 as shown. By checking in this way, you can be sure that you are using the correct format for the sentence. SUM generates only a total and not the individual elements that comprise it.

If you enter

>SUM GADGETS WITH QTY < "12" <return>

and omit the attribute to be SUMmed, the response follows.

```
TOTAL OF GADGETS = 97
```

Who knows what the 97 comes from? The computer could not give the right answer because it was not given the correct instruction. The system can only follow your commands and do what you say, not what you mean.

FORMAT FOR SUM:

REQUIRED	OPTIONAL	OUTPUT ATTRIBUTE
SUM filename	explicit item list and/or selection criteria WITH one attribute AND WITH each extra attribute	required attribute to be SUMmed

Find the total of quantity for all the SPOONs. The selection criterion is WITH NAME "SPOON". The computer will test the name of each GADGET as it reads through the file; if the NAME is SPOON, the value for quantity is added, if the NAME is not SPOON, the value for quantity is ignored. Enter

```
>SUM GADGETS WITH NAME "SPOON" QTY <return>
```

Response

```
TOTAL OF QTY = 23
```

Note that the attribute QTY must be given at the end of the sentence to indicate what is to be SUMmed. Again look at the test data to verify the response.

STAT

STAT is a short form of STATISTICS and produces three calculations on the specified attribute:

TOTAL - the sum of all the values
AVERAGE - the average (TOTAL divided by COUNT)
COUNT - the number of items processed

Like SUM, STAT requires at the end of the sentence the name of the attribute to be processed. If this is omitted the output is absolutely worthless as you have seen with SUM. STAT generates a great deal of information for us. The format is the STAT verb, filename, and attribute to be STATted. Enter

>STAT GADGETS QTY <return>

Response

```
STATISTICS OF QTY:
TOTAL = 119 AVERAGE = 13.22 COUNT = 9
```

If the statistics are needed for several items rather than for the whole file use an explicit item list. For STAT on items 7, 8, and 9 enter

>STAT GADGETS "7" "8" "9" QTY <return>

Response

```
STATISTICS OF QTY:
TOTAL = 23 AVERAGE = 7.66 COUNT = 3
```

The result is for the three items given in the item list. Does the response look familiar? The total of 23 was also given for the SUM of the GADGETS named SPOON. Check the table: 7, 8, and 9 are the item-ids of all the SPOONs. There is a lot of flexibility in the way the sentence can be constructed. WITH NAME "SPOON" and the explicit item list "7" "8" "9" select the same data for processing. Always think through what is to be done and then translate the most sensible version of your idea into the ACCESS sentence.

FORMAT FOR STAT:

REQUIRED	OPTIONAL	OUTPUT ATTRIBUTE
STAT filename	explicit item list and/or selection criteria WITH one attribute AND WITH each extra attribute	required attribute to be STATted

Compare the output of the four verbs covered so far by using the same file and selection criteria:

COMMAND	OUTPUT
LIST GADGETS WITH QTY < "12" QTY	LISTing and summary of total number of items LISTed

```
    GADGETS      QTY

      7           1
     21           4
      9          10
     30           8
[405] 4 ITEMS LISTED
```

COMMAND	OUTPUT
COUNT GADGETS WITH QTY < "12" 4 ITEMS COUNTED	Total number of items COUNTed
SUM GADGETS WITH QTY < "12" QTY TOTAL OF QTY = 23	Total of attribute SUMmed
STAT GADGETS WITH QTY < "12" QTY TOTAL = 23 AV = 5.75 COUNT = 4	Total of attribute STATted Number of items counted Total divided by count gives average

SUMMARY

VERB	OUTPUT
LIST	list of item-ids (attributes optional) and the count of items LISTed
COUNT	number of items COUNTed
SUM	sum of the values for the attribute SUMmed
STAT	total, average (total divided by count), and count for the attribute STATted

The above summary in chart form follows.

VERB	OUTPUT			
	LIST	COUNT	TOTAL	AVERAGE
LIST	X	X		
COUNT		X		
SUM			X	
STAT		X	X	X

Choose the verb that produces the required information.

Using the computer on such small data files may seem ridiculous but it serves two purposes. The various functions that have been discussed work in the same way regardless of file size. Once you understand the concept you can apply it to a large database. Equally important is to use simple test data for the beginner to process mentally and compare the results to the computer output. By checking the computer response against the brain-calculated answer the user can tell if the sentence was entered correctly.

Some verbs and what they generate have been covered. Now consider taking two steps to produce more information. For example find what GADGETS items have a quantity that is less than the average quantity. First it is necessary to know the average for QTY for the entire file. This was done already: the average is 13.22 and we round it to the nearest whole number which is 13. The second step is to check all the quantity values and list those with a value below the average. Enter

>LIST GADGETS WITH QTY < "13" QTY NAME VENDOR <return>

Response

GADGETS	QTY	NAME	VENDOR
7	1	SPOON	ACME.66
8	12	SPOON	ACE.88
21	4	LADLE	TOPS.55
9	10	SPOON	PEAK.77
30	8	WHISK	PEAK.77

To give the examples greater variety create another small test Data File, this time with the item-id made up of alphabetic characters. Normally, this is not practical because two vendors may have the same name and then the item-id would no longer be unique. We eliminate this problem by adding a period and two numbers after the name. As an example ACE.88 and ACE.99; the numbers are different and therefore both the item-ids are unique. If any more vendors named ACE are added to the file each can have a different number and there will be no duplication. The file contains vendor data; the name of the Dictionary and the Data File is VENDOR. The item-id is the same as attribute4 VENDOR in the GADGETS file and each item has three attributes:

attribute1 (SHIPS.VIA): the method of shipment (alphabetic)
attribute2 (STATE): part of the vendor's address
attribute3 (ZIP): the zip code of the address (the address is not complete but provides enough sample data for us now).

Create a Descriptor for each attribute; the facts for the Dictionary Descriptors of the new file are as follows:

The VENDOR Dictionary

	attribute1 SHIPS.VIA	attribute2 STATE	attribute3 ZIP
001 Attribute Definition Item	A	A	A
002 Attribute Mark Count	1	2	3
003 through 008 for all attributes have null values (dot replaced by null)			
009 Justification	L	L	R
010 Output Length	10	2	5

Create the VENDOR Data File with these values:

item-id	attribute1 SHIPS.VIA	attribute2 STATE	attribute3 ZIP
ACME.66	AIR	IL	12345
TOPS.55	TRUCK	MA	67890
ACE.88	TRUCK	NY	23456
PEAK.77	PP	IL	12345
SUMMIT.33	TRUCK	SC	45678
ZENITH.22	RAIL	AR	56789

Review the steps in Chapter 3 to create the Dictionary and the Data File.

When two files have some fact(s) in common it is possible to travel from one file to another via the common data. There is an attribute in the GADGETS file called VENDOR which contains the vendor's name. There is also a file named VENDOR which has the same vendor data as the item-ids. Because the vendor name appears in both files it can be used to go from one file to another. Do not be confused because the same word - here VENDOR - is the name of a file and also the name of an attribute in another file. This is because we have chosen the names; as far as the system is concerned, the one has nothing to do with the other. To illustrate using common data find the quantity for SPOONs from suppliers in IL. When you look at the GADGETS and VENDOR files you see that the first step is to find which VENDORs are in IL. Enter

>LIST VENDOR WITH STATE "IL" STATE <return>

Response

VENDOR	STATE
ACME.66	IL
PEAK.77	IL

The second step is to find which of the above vendors supplies SPOONs. This command requires the continuation of the line by holding control and shift together and the underline

<control> <shift> _

Enter

>LIST GADGETS WITH VENDOR "ACME.66" "PEAK.77" <control> <shift> _ <return>
AND WITH NAME "SPOON" QTY NAME VENDOR <return>

Response

GADGETS	QTY	NAME	VENDOR
7	1	SPOON	ACME.66
9	10	SPOON	PEAK.77

This is only one possibility for using the ACCESS language to extract information from files. Adapt and expand the examples to suit your own data.

5.4 MORE SELECTION CRITERIA

THE REST OF THE RELATIONAL OPERATORS

You have probably noticed that the relational operators used thus far do not cover all possible relationships. Perhaps you want values that are equal to and also greater than another value for example, 10. For everything that is 10 or higher one combination operator is used: GE or >= (both mean greater or equal). When the test is >= "10" values of 10 or more pass.

A combination is also available for less than or equal: LE or <= (less or equal). Note that there is no blank between the letters or symbols here or above; the union is handled as one operator. For example, LE "7" or <= "7" takes values of 7 and less than 7.

In the LIST examples we saw output for GADGETS with a quantity greater than 12. Item 8 is not included because its QTY is 12. To find the GADGETS with quantity of 12 or more enter

```
>LIST GADGETS WITH QTY >= "12" QTY <return>
```

Response

```
GADGETS  QTY

50       23
20       19
8        12
42       17
49       25

[405] 5 ITEMS LISTED
```

So far we have specified requirements such as COLOR RED, quantity less than 12 etc.. Data that met the criteria were accepted, the balance ignored. Sometimes it is easier to specify what is not acceptable than what is. To list all the GADGETS except the FORKs entails giving every literal value that is not a FORK:

```
LIST GADGETS WITH NAME "SPOON" "LADLE" "WHISK" "SPATULA"
```

Each item is tested against each name and it passes if it has any one of the names specified. The result is a list of all but the FORKs. In ordinary

Producing Information from the Data 127

language you would say: LIST all the GADGETS whose NAME is not FORK. The relationship here is *not equal*; a much simpler way to express what we want. There are three relational operators for this purpose and all mean the same #, NE, and NOT. Enter

```
>LIST GADGETS WITH NAME NOT "FORK" <return>
```

Response

```
    7
   20
    8
   21
    9
   42
   30
   49
[405] 8 ITEMS LISTED
```

With only five different names in the file, using *not equal* may not seem like much of an achievement, but if you want all but a few states from a large listing, the advantage is obvious.

Find all the vendors' STATEs except MA and NY. Here are two literal values for the same attribute which is STATE: MA and NY. If the test were to find the STATEs equal to MA and NY, OR would be implied between them. But here the test is for *not equal* and the implied OR does not work. You must use AND NE before the second literal value (and as many as follow)

```
NE "MA" AND NE "NY"
```

Enter

```
>LIST VENDOR WITH STATE NE "MA" AND NE "NY" STATE <return>
```

Response

```
VENDOR      STATE

SUMMIT.33   SC
PEAK.77     IL
ZENITH.22   AR
ACME.66     IL
```

List all the GADGETS that are not FORKs and also not TAN. The normal format is used: WITH NAME NOT "FORK" is the first selection criterion phrase on the attribute NAME; AND connects the second selection criterion phrase on the different attribute COLOR: WITH COLOR NOT "TAN". As in the preceding example the relational operator, here NOT, must be repeated. Enter

>LIST GADGETS WITH NAME NOT "FORK" AND WITH COLOR NOT "TAN" NAME COLOR <return>

Response

GADGETS	NAME	COLOR
7	SPOON	BROWN
8	SPOON	RED
21	LADLE	RED
9	SPOON	YELLOW
42	SPATULA	RED
30	WHISK	BLUE
49	SPATULA	AVOCADO

It is often desirable to check data before processing. You may have an employee personnel file and each record must show either M or F; any other character is an error. The values can easily be checked by listing those that are neither M nor F, e.g.

LIST ... WITH GENDER NOT "M" AND NOT "F" ...

The output shows where the errors are, the corrections are made, and the data is accurate. This is a common application of extracting incorrect data by testing for non-equality.

The last tests were on alphabetic characters; when the values were equal they were selected for processing. Letters can also be tested on the basis of their position in the alphabet. Thus R is greater than F, and S is less than Y. When multiple characters are involved the test is performed on one letter at a time starting from the left. *Seersucker* is less than *seesaw*, and *mouth* is greater than *moustache*. *Greater than* (GT or >) can be expressed as AFTER and *less than* (LT or <) is the same as BEFORE. Find the vendors with STATE greater, or later in the alphabet, than IL. Enter

>LIST VENDOR WITH STATE AFTER "IL" STATE <return>

Response

VENDOR	STATE
SUMMIT.33	SC
TOPS.55	MA
ACE.88	NY

THE RELATIONAL OPERATORS in the ACCESS SENTENCE

RELATIONSHIP	ABBREVIATION	SYMBOL
equal	EQ (both can be omitted)	=
greater than	GT or AFTER	>
less than	LT or BEFORE	<
greater or equal	GE	>=
less or equal	LE	<=
not equal	NE or NOT	#

5.5 JUSTIFICATION

In Chapter 3 when the Dictionary for the Data File was created, a Descriptor was made up for each attribute of the data. Attributes containing alphabetic characters are left justified; attributes containing numeric values are right justified. Therefore, R or L, as appropriate, was entered on line 9. The attribute QTY in the GADGETS file contains numeric data, and so line 9 in its Descriptor shows R. Thus the value in QTY is processed from right to left, the standard direction for numbers. When an attribute such as NAME contains letters, it is left justified and comparisons proceed from left to right as already discussed.

Up to this point numeric comparisons such as QTY < "12" were made on attributes described as right justified and so there have been no problems. If you recall from Chapter 3 it was not necessary to describe the item-id, only the attributes. Now when we want to use the item-ids of the GADGETS Data File in comparisons we make a startling discovery: all item-ids are automatically given left justification by the system whether alphabetic or numeric. An item-id made up of letters is normally left justified and presents no difficulty. However a numeric item-id must be described as right justified before it can be used in arithmetic comparisons or the results are not at all as expected. If numbers are processed starting from the left, 123 is less than 58 because the leftmost digit 1 is less than the leftmost 5. You can readily see how useless left justification is for numbers.

The solution is simple: create a new Dictionary Descriptor for the item-id. Remember that this has no effect on the item-id in the file which continues to show the same value: item-id 8 remains item-id 8. The new Descriptor needs a name and R for right justified on line 9. When the system sees the new Descriptor name it goes to the Dictionary and finds that the Descriptor is a synonym referring to the item-id and also that the item-id is to be processed as right justified. In this way the new Descriptor can substitute for a numeric item-id whenever comparisons or calculations are made. Choose a meaningful name for the Descriptor, e.g. RJID is easy to remember for Right Justified Item-iD. Follow the procedure in Chapter 3 to create a Descriptor in the Dictionary for GADGETS with the following data:

```
RJID
line 001    S         Attribute Definition Item
line 002    0         Attribute Mark Count
line 003 through 008 have null values (period replaced by null)
line 009    R         Justification
line 010    3         Output length
```

The S on line 1 indicates that this is a Synonym Descriptor. The zero on line 2 shows that the item is a synonym for attribute 0 which is the item-id. From now on, whenever you want a comparison on an item-id in the GADGETS file simply specify RJID as you would with an attribute. The system will use the original item-id but will handle it according to the structure described in the synonym Descriptor we have just created. Some systems omit S type Descriptors from the output of LISTDICT. However this type will be displayed by the command

```
>ED DICT filename *
```

Then when you are at the TOP of the item you can press P to display the complete item on the screen.

To illustrate what happens in a comparison on left justified numbers enter

```
>LIST GADGETS < "30" <return>
```

Response

    20
    21

Check the output. What happened to 7, 8, and 9? Remember that the item-id is left justified and evaluation proceeds from left to right. Accordingly 7, 8, 9 are greater than 30 because 7, 8, 9 are greater than 3. Try the new synonym; enter

    `>LIST GADGETS WITH RJID < "30"` <return>

Response

    7
    20
    8
    21
    9

Processing has been performed with right justification and the response is correct. As you know, when no attribute name is given at the end of the sentence for output the system defaults to displaying the item-ids and therefore the numbers appear as left justified. Add RJID to the command, enter

    `>LIST GADGETS WITH RJID < "30" RJID` <return>

Response

GADGETS	RJID
7	7
20	20
8	8
21	21
9	9

The GADGETS column shows the automatic left justified display of item-ids; the RJID column has the same numbers shown as right justified, starting from the right as we normally write numbers. The form of the ouput is optional and you need not specify the right justified attribute at the end of the sentence unless you wish.

Two selection criteria phrases can be used to produce items that fall within a range. Find what items in the file have item-ids between 8 and 25. As we have just proved, the right justified attribute must be used for testing item-ids. We want a list of all GADGETS greater than or equal to 8 and also less than or equal to 25. Since both phrases apply to the same attribute RJID, use AND between the two tests (omit WITH). Enter

>LIST GADGETS WITH RJID >= "8" AND <= "25" RJID <return>

Response

GADGETS	RJID
20	20
8	8
21	21
9	9

5.6 REARRANGE OUTPUT: THE SORT VERB

SORT, a powerful verb in the ACCESS processor, can present all or a selected part of a file in a specified sequence. The original file remains in its stored order; a copy is sorted according to the user's instructions and then output like a list. The sort is performed on a designated *Sort Key* which determines the sequence of the new arrangement. Let us return to the telephone directory. Every subscriber has a different telephone number which is the unique identifier for the account. The telephone number is the item-id by which the subscriber information is retrieved. But the file sorted by telephone numbers is worthless unless the number is known. Therefore the data is extracted from the file into a new sequence using the last name as the Sort Key. The result is the listing of subscribers in alphabetical order that we use. As you know *name* is not a unique Sort Key because several people can have the same last name. We refer to last name as the Primary Sort Key because it is the major, or first, Sort Key that was used. All the items with the same last name are sorted again with the first name as the Secondary Sort Key. If there are persons with the same last and first names, a third sort is made using the middle name or initial as the Tertiary Sort Key. An example is

Brand   Charles
Brown   Anna

    Brown   George
    Brown   George Spiro
    Brown   Matt
    Brown   Peter
    Brown   Peter I.G.
    Brunch   Jan

When the sort is on a non-unique Sort Key additional sorts can be made. If the sort is on a unique Sort Key, obviously no further sorting can be done. The differences in users' needs dictate the arrangement of the file: what is to be used as Sort Key(s) and what attributes are to be shown for each item.

Start with a LISTing of the VENDOR file to see how the items are stored. Enter

>LIST VENDOR <return>

Response

    ACME.66
    ZENITH.22
    PEAK.77
    SUMMIT.33
    TOPS.55
    ACE.88

The items are given in their internal stored order. These positions do not change; when the file is sorted it is copied, arranged, and output in the new order. Unlike the output from LIST, SORTed data will be presented in the same sequence by all systems at all times.

>SORT VENDOR <return>

Response

    ACE.88
    ACME.66
    PEAK.77
    SUMMIT.33
    TOPS.55
    ZENITH.22

Compare the output of LIST and SORT. All the sorted names are arranged alphabetically in ascending order which is from low to high (A to Z). Numeric ascending order is from 0 to 9.

As you can see from the previous example when the sentence consists of only the verb SORT and the file name, the system defaults in two ways: first to using the item-id as the Sort Key and then to sorting in ascending order. The output is the item-ids. However the name(s) of the attribute(s) to be displayed can be added at the end of the sentence just as with LIST. Enter

>SORT VENDOR STATE <return>

Response

VENDOR	STATE
ACE.88	NY
ACME.66	IL
PEAK.77	IL
SUMMIT.33	SC
TOPS.55	MA
ZENITH.22	AR

Selection criteria can also be added to extract only those items for sorting that pass the test. Find which VENDORS use TRUCKs and sort the items in ascending order. Enter

>SORT VENDOR WITH SHIPS.VIA "TRUCK" SHIPS.VIA <return>

Response

VENDOR	SHIPS.VIA
ACE.88	TRUCK
SUMMIT.33	TRUCK
TOPS.55	TRUCK

By adding another selection criterion phrase we see which VENDORs use TRUCKs and have a STATE less than or equal to NY. Whatever data meets both requirements is then sorted. Enter

Producing Information from the Data 135

```
>SORT VENDOR WITH SHIPS.VIA "TRUCK" AND WITH STATE <= "NY" SHIPS.VIA STATE <return>
```

Response

VENDOR	SHIPS.VIA	STATE
ACE.88	TRUCK	NY
TOPS.55	TRUCK	MA

This time SUMMIT was omitted because its STATE is SC and therefore did not meet the second test.

The file can also be sorted on an attribute; add BY and the name of the attribute to be used as the Sort Key. There are different kinds of transport in the SHIPS.VIA attribute - air, truck etc.. How does the file look when arranged by SHIPS.VIA? BY SHIPS.VIA gives the instruction; SHIPS.VIA at the end of the sentence calls for the attribute to be output. Remember that when no attribute is requested for output only the item-ids are shown. Enter

```
>SORT VENDOR BY SHIPS.VIA SHIPS.VIA <return>
```

Response

VENDOR	SHIPS.VIA
ACME.66	AIR
PEAK.77	PP
ZENITH.22	RAIL
ACE.88	TRUCK
SUMMIT.33	TRUCK
TOPS.55	TRUCK

This tiny sample data file can produce other variations of SORT. First find the VENDORs that use TRUCK and then sort them by STATE. The selection criterion is SHIPS.VIA "TRUCK", the Sort Key is STATE. Enter

```
>SORT VENDOR WITH SHIPS.VIA "TRUCK" BY STATE SHIPS.VIA STATE <return>
```

The response follows.

VENDOR	SHIPS.VIA	STATE
TOPS.55	TRUCK	MA
ACE.88	TRUCK	NY
SUMMIT.33	TRUCK	SC

To extract from the above those vendors that come after the letter G add another selection criterion phrase: AFTER "G" which applies to the item-id and must follow the file name. The rest of the sentence stays the same. Enter

>SORT VENDOR AFTER "G" WITH SHIPS.VIA "TRUCK" BY STATE SHIPS.VIA STATE <return>

Response

VENDOR	SHIPS.VIA	STATE
TOPS.55	TRUCK	MA
SUMMIT.33	TRUCK	SC

ACE.88 is omitted because it comes before G.

When the sort is on a non-unique key - an attribute where more than one item has the same value such as TRUCK - additional sorts can be made. The second sort is made on a secondary key; a third sort is on a tertiary key and so on. Note that this often will not show when there is only a small amount of test data. The values in the table for the attributes SHIPS.VIA and STATE are not unique because, for example more than one item has TRUCK and more than one has IL. When the file was sorted with SHIPS.VIA as the Sort Key you saw how all the items with the same SHIPS.VIA were grouped together in the output e.g. ACE.88, SUMMIT.33, and TOPS.55 have TRUCK as their SHIPS.VIA. The system has defaulted to displaying them in ascending order. Actually it has automatically performed a secondary sort using the item-id as the key. However we can specify an attribute as key for the secondary sort by adding another BY and the attribute name. How does the file look sorted first by SHIPS.VIA and then by STATE? The instructions in the sentence are followed by the computer in the same way that the sentence is read: first sort by SHIPS.VIA and then sort by STATE. Enter

>SORT VENDOR BY SHIPS.VIA BY STATE SHIPS.VIA STATE <return>

Response

VENDOR	SHIPS.VIA	STATE
ACME.66	AIR	IL
PEAK.77	PP	IL
ZENITH.22	RAIL	AR
TOPS.55	TRUCK	MA
ACE.88	TRUCK	NY
SUMMIT.33	TRUCK	SC

Three items have the value TRUCK for SHIPS.VIA. They have been sorted again on STATE in ascending order with TRUCK MA coming before TRUCK NY which comes before TRUCK SC. Note the difference in the results when the order of the BY phrases is reversed: now the primary sort is on STATE and the secondary sort is on SHIPS.VIA. Enter

>SORT VENDOR BY STATE BY SHIPS.VIA STATE SHIPS.VIA <return>

Response

VENDOR	STATE	SHIPS.VIA
ZENITH.22	AR	RAIL
ACME.66	IL	AIR
PEAK.77	IL	PP
TOPS.55	MA	TRUCK
ACE.88	NY	TRUCK
SUMMIT.33	SC	TRUCK

The test data file is small and there is only one example of data sharing the same value for STATE i.e. IL. The secondary sort on SHIPS.VIA puts AIR before PP.

The GADGETS file provides similar possibilities for SORT but you must always be alert to the justification of numeric data. Because the item-id in this file is numeric we created a synonym attribute described as right justified. This new attribute must be used for SORTing when the item-id is the Sort Key; if the left justified item-id is used the output is worthless. Let us see how the GADGETS file looks when arranged in ascending numeric order on the right justified version of the item-id as Sort Key. Enter

>SORT GADGETS BY RJID <return>

138 Database and Word Processing for the New User

Response

```
7
8
9
20
21
30
42
49
50
```

The item-ids have been sorted on the right justified synonym and are in correct sequence. However the system defaults to displaying the item-id which is left justified and therefore the numbers are printed from left to right. This was also shown in a LIST example. With SORT you have the same option of adding the right justified attribute (or any other) to the output. Enter

>__SORT GADGETS BY RJID RJID__ <return>

Response

GADGETS	RJID
7	7
8	8
9	9
20	20
21	21
30	30
42	42
49	49
50	50

If you had any doubts about the problems with using a left justified numeric item-id as the Sort Key, take a good look at the following example. Enter

>__SORT GADGETS__ <return>

Response

Producing Information from the Data   139

```
20
21
30
42
49
50
7
8
9
```

The output has been sorted from the left-most digit and is hardly in acceptable numeric order. Now you should be convinced why a right justified Sort Key must be used.

Find the GADGETS named either SPOON or LADLE and then sort them by item-id. The right justified item-id must be used here. Enter

```
>SORT GADGETS WITH NAME "SPOON" "LADLE" BY RJID NAME QTY <return>
```

Response

GADGETS	NAME	QTY
7	SPOON	1
8	SPOON	12
9	SPOON	10
20	LADLE	19
21	LADLE	4

Early in this chapter OR was implied between "RED" and "BROWN" to output GADGETS with either COLOR. Here OR is implied between "SPOON" and "LADLE". OR is a Throwaway word; it may make the sentence clearer to the user but is not required.

Thus far the system has defaulted to sorting in ascending order (from low to high). The file can also be arranged in descending order (from high to low). The instruction is BY-DSND followed by the name of the attribute to be used as the Sort Key. Note that an attribute name must be used with BY-DSND and there is no default here to item-ids. The right justified synonym for the GADGETS file item-id, RJID, was used for an ascending sort. Use the same synonym, RJID, again to produce a descending sort on item-ids. Enter the following command.

>SORT GADGETS BY-DSND RJID RJID <return>

Response

GADGETS	RJID
50	50
49	49
42	42
30	30
21	21
20	20
9	9
8	8
7	7

No matter what type of characters make up the item-id, a synonym attribute must be used for a descending sort. Therefore we must create a synonym Descriptor in the VENDOR Dictionary for the item-id. A logical name is IDSYN and it contains

```
001  S
002  0
003 through 008 have null values (period replaced by null)
009  L
010  15
```

Use this new synonym for sorting in descending order on the alphabetic item-id. Enter

>SORT VENDOR BY-DSND IDSYN <return>

Response

```
ZENITH.22
TOPS.55
SUMMIT.33
PEAK.77
ACME.66
ACE.88
```

How does the GADGETS file look after it has been sorted first on NAME as Primary Sort Key and then by COLOR as Secondary Sort Key?

Both sorts are to be in ascending order. Enter

>SORT GADGETS BY NAME BY COLOR NAME COLOR <return>

In the response below the results of the Primary Sort on NAME are shown separately so that the Secondary Sort on COLOR can be seen more easily.

GADGETS	NAME	COLOR
50	FORK	TAN
21	LADLE	RED
20	LADLE	TAN
49	SPATULA	AVOCADO
42	SPATULA	RED
7	SPOON	BROWN
8	SPOON	RED
9	SPOON	YELLOW
30	WHISK	BLUE

As you see LADLE RED comes before LADLE TAN; the SPOONs are sequenced BROWN, RED, YELLOW. Make a slight change in the sentence and have the secondary sort on COLOR in descending instead of ascending order. Enter

>SORT GADGETS BY NAME BY-DSND COLOR NAME COLOR <return>

Response

GADGETS	NAME	COLOR
50	FORK	TAN
20	LADLE	TAN
21	LADLE	RED
42	SPATULA	RED
49	SPATULA	AVOCADO
9	SPOON	YELLOW
8	SPOON	RED
7	SPOON	BROWN
30	WHISK	BLUE

Now LADLE TAN comes before LADLE RED; the SPATULAs and the SPOONs are also in the opposite sequence from the previous example. The item-ids appear automatically with each item but have no effect on the sorted order.

Find the GADGETS with QTY values within two ranges: between 0 and 12, or between 20 and 30 and arrange them in ascending order. The Throwaway word OR is not required between the two tests but can be included to make the sentence clearer:

```
WITH QTY >= "0" AND <= "12" OR >= "20" AND <= "30"
```

Enter

```
>SORT GADGETS WITH QTY >= "0" AND <= "12" >= "20" AND <= "30" BY QTY QTY <return>
```

Response

GADGETS	QTY
7	1
21	4
30	8
9	10
8	12
50	23
49	25

Item 7 through item 8 in the output have quantities that fall between 0 and 12; items 50 and 49 have quantities between 20 and 30. All the items meet the selection criteria and are sorted in ascending order on the Sort Key QTY.

Although there is a degree of flexibility in constructing the sentence, the logical order should always be a consideration. Understandability for the human user is as important as for the computer. Also remember that every special character and the blank have a numeric value. When combined with letters or numbers they affect the comparison and distort the results. It is wise to avoid sorting values made of mixtures like A104, 6 9, or F...BL.

5.7 STRING SEARCHES

When the selection criterion such as NAME "SPOON" was used, the test applied to the entire value for NAME. If the name equalled "SPOON" the item was selected; if the name was "SPATULA" it was not. Selection criteria can also be applied to only a part of a value. In a test for values starting with the letter S both SPOON and SPATULA are selected.

SPOON, SPATULA or any group of characters are called *strings*. Every data value is viewed as a string e.g. TOPS.55 (a VENDOR in the GADGETS file) and TRUCK (a SHIPS.VIA in the VENDOR file). This section covers how selection criteria can work on part of a string: for example, does it end with L? Contain an E ? Start with 6? Have seven characters?

Find the vendors with STATE beginning with M; it does not matter what letters follow the M. M and the right square bracket M] instruct the system to select those strings starting with M. Note that M] acts as a literal value and must be enclosed in double quotes. Enter

>LIST VENDOR WITH STATE "M]" STATE <return>

Response

```
VENDOR    STATE

TOPS.55   MA
```

To find data ending with a particular character use the left square bracket [. "[Y" indicates any string ending with Y; whatever comes before Y can be ignored. Enter

>LIST VENDOR WITH STATE "[Y" STATE <return>

Response

```
VENDOR    STATE

ACE.88    NY
```

Part of a file within an alphabetic range can be listed. Find the STATEs in the VENDOR file starting with the letters A through K. The selection criteria are STATE >= "A]" AND <= "K]". Enter

>LIST VENDOR WITH STATE >= "A]" AND <= "K]" STATE <return>

Response

VENDOR	STATE
ACME.66	IL
ZENITH.22	AR
PEAK.77	IL

The new capability for searching strings can be combined with what has already been covered. The format remains the same. Find the VENDORs between N and W that use TRUCKs and are in MA or NY. Between N and W applies to the item-id and follows the filename. Enter

>LIST VENDOR >= "N]" AND <= "W]" WITH SHIPS.VIA "TRUCK"
 AND WITH STATE "MA" "NY" SHIPS.VIA STATE <return>

Response

VENDOR	SHIPS.VIA	STATE
TOPS.55	TRUCK	MA

Use a character with both brackets to find values with that particular character anywhere within the string. For example, use [E] to find the VENDORs that have E at the start, at the end, or inside the item-id. Note that here there is an exception to the norm: for a string search on the item-id the system does not default to equal. Either EQ or = must be used as the relational operator. Enter

>LIST VENDOR = "[E]" <return>

Response

ACME.66
ZENITH.22

```
PEAK.77
ACE.88
```

The caret ^ is used in string searches as a placeholder for any character. It requires only that some character be in that position. One application is to check the number of characters in a value. ZIP in the VENDOR file must have five characters, any other amount is not acceptable. Use five carets ^^^^^ one to represent each digit. The computer searches the file and lists the items that have more or less than five characters for the ZIP. Keep in mind that the test is only for something in the position; the validity of the data is not checked. Enter

```
>LIST VENDOR WITH ZIP NOT "^^^^^" <return>
```

Response

```
[401] NO ITEMS PRESENT.
```

We now know that all the items have five characters for ZIP.

The output from this kind of test is a list of errors to be corrected before the data in the file is processed.

The caret can be combined with literal values. For example, find the ZIP codes that contain the series: 6, any number, then 8. Beginning with 6 is shown as [6; any one character is shown as ^; ending with 8 is shown as 8]. All are combined into one literal value with double quotes outside all of the parts "[6^8]". Enter

```
>LIST VENDOR WITH ZIP "[6^8]" ZIP <return>
```

Response

VENDOR	ZIP
SUMMIT.33	45678
TOPS.55	67890
ZENITH.22	56789

The string 6^8 occupies different positions in the ZIPs that are output but all pass the test because they contain 6^8 at the beginning, end or inside.

SUMMARY: STRING SEARCH

Imagine that the bracket opening indicates the balance of the string:

X]
begins with X and anything follows

[X
begins with anything and ends with X

[X]
contains X

^
placeholder for any character

Earlier in the chapter there is a list of Throwaway words, which are ignored by the computer. The opposite is *Reserved words*, which have special meanings; they work in only one context and have particular significance to the system. This includes all ACCESS verbs, all relational operators, WITH, AND, and BY. As you look back over the many forms of the sentences you can understand the role of Reserved words in processing and why they cannot be used in any other way.

SUMMARY: THE ACCESS SENTENCE FORMAT

REQUIRED	REQUIRED	OPTIONAL	SPECIFY FOR OUTPUT
What to do	What to do it to		
VERB	filename	Explicit Item List	
	default: item-ids	Selection Criterion Phrase(s) see next SUMMARY	
LIST	as above	"	default: item-ids optional: attribute(s)
COUNT	as above	"	(none)
SUM	as above	"	attribute to be SUMmed

STAT	as above	"	attribute to be STATted
SORT	as above	"	default: item-ids
			optional: attribute(s)

Sort Key(s)
default: ascending Sort
default: item-ids
or use BY attribute

descending Sort:
BY-DSND attribute
Note: use a synonym for the item-id

SUMMARY: SELECTION CRITERION FORMATS

Each selection criterion phrase is a test consisting of:

the object to test	a relational operator	a literal value in quotes	example
default: item-ids	default: EQ =		LIST VENDOR "ACE.88" STATE
	Exception: use EQ or = for a string search on the item-id		LIST VENDOR = "[E]"
or WITH attribute	or GE AFTER >		LIST GADGETS WITH NAME "SPOON"
	LT BEFORE <		LIST GADGETS WITH QTY < "12"
	GE >=		
	LE <=		
	NOT NE #		

start each additional test either with
AND
to output data that passes all tests   LIST VENDOR WITH STATE >= "A]"
                                         AND <- "K]" STATE

	LIST GADGETS WITH QTY > "12"
	AND WITH COLOR "TAN"
or imply (use is optional)	
OR	
to output data that passes any test	LIST VENDOR WITH STATE "IL"
	{OR} "MA" STATE
	LIST GADGETS WITH COLOR "RED"
	{OR} WITH NAME "LADLE"
Exception: when testing for not equal	
NOT NE ≠	
use AND instead of OR, implied or	LIST VENDOR WITH STATE NE "MA"
stated	AND NE "NY" STATE

5.8 ERROR EXAMPLES

Whether or not you have seen system error messages, the following are common mistakes and help point out what <u>not</u> to do. Generally, errors result either from carelessness or unfamiliarity with new procedures. Do not be discouraged when you see error messages; use them as guides to make corrections. These examples cover a variety of slip-ups. Test yourself to see if you can spot the error and then correct it.

ERROR	COMMENT
>LIST VENDOR WITH STATE = "NY" AND [18] THE LAST WORD MAY NOT BE A CONNECTIVE.	Sentence should not end with AND
>LIST VENDOR WITH ZIP NOT 12345 [24] THE WORD 12345 CANNOT BE IDENTIFIED	Put double quotes around 12345
>SORT GADGET BY QTY [10] FILE NAME MISSING	Filename misspelled
>STAT GADGETS WITH QTY> "24" [24] THE WORD "QTY>" CANNOT BE IDENTIFIED	There must be a space on each side of the relational operator; attribute is omitted

Producing Information from the Data 149

```
>LIST GADGETS WIH QTY < "13"
[24] THE WORD "WIH QTY" CANNOT BE IDENTIFIED
```
Spell WITH correctly

```
>SUM VENDOR
TOTAL OF VENDOR = 165
```
How can you SUM alphabetic item-ids?

```
>LIST GADGETS WITH COLOR "RED"
AND VENDOR "PEAK.77"
[71] AN ILLEGAL CONNECTIVE MODIFIES THE WORD 'VENDOR'
```
The word WITH must follow AND

```
>LIST GADGETS WITH QTY > "5" AND < 10"
[2] Uneven number of delimiters ( ' " \)
```
Quotes needed before 10

```
>COUNT VENDOR WITH STATE 'ND'
[401] NO ITEMS PRESENT.
'ND' NOT ON FILE.
```
Use double quotes

```
>COUNT VENDOR WITH STATE "ND"
[401] NO ITEMS PRESENT.
```
Note the same message as above. The response is correct since there is no ND in the file

```
>LIST VENDOR "ACE" "TOPS" ADDRESS
[24] THE WORD "ADDRESS" CANNOT BE IDENTIFIED
```
There is no attribute ADDRESS in the VENDOR file

```
>STAT GADGETS QTY NAME
STATISTICS OF QTY;
TOTAL = 119 AVERAGE = 13.22 COUNT = 9
```
QTY is the attribute to be STATted; NAME is ignored

```
>SUM GADGETS WITH QTY < "12"
TOTAL OF GADGETS = 97
```
The attribute to be SUMmed must be at the end of the sentence; 97 is meaningless

```
>COUNT GADGETS QTY "1"
[407] 9 ITEMS COUNTED
```
WITH is omitted; response is a COUNT of all items in the file

>SORT GADGETS BY VENDOR VENDOR GADGETS [5] THE WORD "GADGETS" IS ILLEGAL.	GADGETS is not an attribute
>LIST GADGETS WITH NAME NOT "FORK" AND COLOR NOT "TAN" [71] AN ILLEGAL CONNECTIVE MODIFIES THE WORD 'COLOR'	The word WITH must appear after AND
>SORT VENDOR BY-DSND VENDOR [5] THE WORD "VENDOR" IS ILLEGAL.	For a Sort in descending order on the item-id use a Synonym Descriptor attribute
>LIST VENDOR WITH STATE >= "A]" AND <= "M" STATE ACME.66...IL ZENITH.22.AR PEAK.77...IL	There is no STATE M; if you want STATES beginning with M use "M]"
>SORT GADGETS BY RJID [705] ILLEGAL CONVERSION CODE: '.'	Periods were not replaced by null on lines 3 through 8 when the RJID Descriptor was created; correct it
>LIST VENDOR "[E]" [401] NO ITEMS PRESENT. [202] '[E]' NOT ON FILE.	Equal must be specified in a string search on the item-id, use EQ or =
>LIST VENDOR WITH STATE NE "IL" "NY" STATE ZENITH.22...AR SUMMIT.33...SC TOPS.55.....MA ACE.88......NY	Implied OR does not work with NE; use AND NE between "IL" and "NY" if NY is not to be output

5.9 REVIEW QUESTIONS

1. What is a Reserved Word?
2. Give four examples of relational operators.
3. What is the difference between ascending and descending sorts? Can they be combined in one command sentence?
4. What are the two types of system messages?
5. What justification is necessary for comparisons to be made on numeric data? Why?
6. Is it practical to use all alphabetic characters for the item-id? Why?
7. What are selection criteria and why are they used?
8. Are output attributes used with the SUM verb? With COUNT?
9. What is the default Sort Key?
10. What two parts of an ACCESS sentence are required?
11. What is a literal value? How is it shown?
12. What is a string?
13. Define a unique Sort Key, a non-unique Sort Key.
14. What are Throwaway Words?
15. What happens when a file is sorted?

Chapter 6

Outputting Familiar Data in New Ways

6.1 OVERVIEW

We are accustomed to seeing the output of the verbs LIST and SORT in a standard default format: at the top of the response there is a heading with page number, time and date; the next line has the column headings; and the individual data items are below. At the bottom is a system message with the total number of items output. This chapter covers other ways to display the familiar data. Although the data itself continues to be the same, it can look very different with new formatting.

For example, we can replace or suppress the default headings and/or the column headings along with the summary line. Item-ids can also be suppressed. It is possible to display all the values for an attribute such as quantity, and show the grand total at the end. Another practical procedure is to SORT data and generate subtotals. The last exercise will output attribute(s) automatically without naming them in the command sentence.

You have seen many responses from LIST and SORT. For the new operations we use these verbs with *modifiers* which are Reserved words that alter the normal action of the verbs. Each modifier performs a particular task. The procedures are considered part of ACCESS which was introduced in the preceding chapter. As before when we use the new terms properly, the system does all the work for us.

6.2 HEADINGS AND FOOTINGS

SUPPRESSION

Without realizing it you have already used some modifiers. When you added BY and BY-DSND to the SORT sentence you modified or affected the action of the verb. When you used WITH or WITH....NOT in a selection criterion phrase you modified the action of LIST and SORT.

Start with a look at the default heading. As shown below the first heading line consists of the page number, and time and date in the same format as seen at LOGON. Column headings consist of the filename over the item-ids, and the attributename(s) over the attribute values. The bottom line is the system message [405] with the total number of items.

```
    PAGE   1                              11:13:50  16 JAN 1987
    VENDOR      STATE

      .           .
      .           .
      .           .

    [405] 6 ITEMS LISTED.
```

Note that only the output relevant to the topic rather than the entire file is shown in the sample responses.

First let us suppress the default heading by using the modifier

```
    HDR-SUPP
```

Enter

```
    >LIST VENDOR HDR-SUPP <return>
```

Response

```
    VENDOR

    ACE.88
    TOPS.55
    ACME.66
    SUMMIT.33
    PEAK.77
    ZENITH.22
```

HDR-SUPP suppresses both the default heading and the summary line; the column heading(s) are displayed as usual.

Another modifier eliminates the heading, column heading(s), and the summary line:

COL-HDR-SUPP

Enter

>LIST VENDOR STATE COL-HDR-SUPP <return>

Response

ACME.66
ACE.88
TOPS.55
.
.
.

Sometimes you may want to output one or more attributes, but not the item-ids. For example, to output only the STATE (in ascending alphabetical order for the VENDOR file), the modifier to suppress item-ids is

ID-SUPP

Remember to call for at least one output attribute when suppressing the item-ids. If there are no item-ids and no attribute(s) you end up with nothing but a summary of the number of invisible items. The command sentence is exactly what you expect. Enter

>SORT VENDOR BY STATE STATE ID-SUPP <return>

Response

STATE

AR
IL
IL
MA
NY
SC

[405] 6 ITEMS LISTED.

ID-SUPP when used alone does not affect the summary line. It can be combined in a command sentence with HDR-SUPP or COL-HDR-SUPP.

The same suppressions can be made by *options*. Here the options act on the verb exactly as the modifiers do; they are interchangeable. The option - either preceded by an opening parenthesis or enclosed in both parentheses - is placed at the end of the sentence. Modifiers and corresponding options are as follows:

To Suppress	Use Modifier	Or Option
Heading and Summary Line	HDR-SUPP	(H
Heading, Column Headings and Summary Line	COL-HDR-SUPP	(C
Item-ids	ID-SUPP	(I

Options can be combined; the single parenthesis serves both e.g. (but some systems require a comma between options)

    (CI

Enter

    >SORT VENDOR BY STATE STATE (CI <return>

Response

    AR
    IL
    IL
    MA
    NY
    SC

C, like COL-HDR-SUPP, suppresses the heading, the column headings, and the summary line. I, like ID-SUPP, suppresses the item-ids.

HEADINGS

Now that we have eliminated various default output, let us substitute our own text for the default heading. The modifier is

```
HEADING
```

and it instructs the system to print the text that follows instead of the usual heading. The user supplied text string is enclosed in double quotes which delimit it like a literal value. A sample heading is

```
"VENDOR FILE"
```

Combine the modifier and the text string:

```
HEADING "VENDOR FILE"
```

Enter

```
>LIST VENDOR HEADING "VENDOR FILE" <return>
```

Response

```
VENDOR FILE
VENDOR

ACME.66
ACE.88
TOPS.55
 .
 .
 .
[405] 6 ITEMS LISTED.
```

Although our heading has replaced the normal one, the column heading and summary line appear as usual.

Next we come to a different group of options that are used with modifiers. Just as modifiers affect the action of the verb, modifier options affect their modifiers. For example, one of the modifier options permitted with the modifier HEADING is Date. All modifier options consist of one or two letters enclosed in single quotes within double quotes. To display the date in the heading text string use

```
'D'
```

Since processing is from left to right the position for the date is indicated by the position of 'D' in the string. If we write

```
"VENDOR FILE 'D'"
```

the date comes after the text VENDOR FILE. If we use

```
"'D' VENDOR FILE"
```

the date is displayed before the string as in the following example. Enter

```
>LIST VENDOR HEADING "'D' VENDOR FILE" <return>
```

Response in part

```
16 JAN 1987 VENDOR FILE
```

'D' may also have text on both sides of it.

Text is not required with HEADING. The date can be shown alone if that is all you want. In that case use double quotes outside 'D'

```
"'D'"
```

Note that HEADING can appear anywhere after the filename in the sentence. Enter

```
>LIST VENDOR HEADING "'D'" WITH STATE "IL" STATE <return>
```

Response

```
16 JAN 1987
VENDOR    STATE

ACME.66   IL
PEAK.77   IL
```

The modifier option

```
'T'
```

gives the time and date in the same format as in the default heading. Change the text string to

"VENDOR FILE AT 'T'"

and enter

>LIST VENDOR HEADING "VENDOR FILE AT 'T'" <return>

Response in part

VENDOR FILE AT 14:31:18 29 DEC 1987

Thus far the headings have started at the left side of the page. If you want the heading centered, place the modifier option

'C'

inside the string. T and C can be combined within the single quotes as 'TC'. Enter

>LIST VENDOR HEADING "VENDOR FILE AT 'TC'" <return>

Response with heading

VENDOR FILE AT 14:31:56 03 JAN 1987

FOOTINGS

Footings are exactly like headings only they appear at the bottom of each page. The summary line is below the last footing. The modifier is

FOOTING

The same modifier options are used with HEADING and FOOTING.

Two slightly different modifier options can be used for page number.

'PN'

displays the page number as left justified which means there is no gap between text and number, e.g.

PAGE 1

The other choice is

>'P'

which prints the page number as right justified in a space for four characters. This leaves a gap if there are only one or two digits:

>PAGE   1

Both alternatives can be used with or without text. The convention is usually PAGE or PAGE NO.

Display a footing with text, date, and page number. Enter

>LIST VENDOR FOOTING "VENDOR FILE AT 'D' PAGE NO. 'P'" <return>

Response

>PAGE   1   14:40:16 03 OCT 1986

.
.
.

>VENDOR FILE AT 03 OCT 1986 PAGE NO.   1

>[405] 6 ITEMS LISTED.

Note that the default heading appears at the top regardless of the footing. To avoid the duplication consider using HDR-SUPP or (H.

We can output the footing text on two lines with the modifier option

>'L'

What follows the L is printed on a new line. To move the page number to the next line, put 'L' before the text such as PAGE and 'PN' or 'P'. Enter

>LIST VENDOR FOOTING "VENDORS ON 'D' 'L' PAGE 'PN'" <return>

The default heading is at the top of the response followed by the item-ids. The two lines of the footing are at the bottom of the response.

.
.
.

VENDORS ON 14 MAR 1987
PAGE 1

[405] 6 ITEMS LISTED.

Combine modifiers and options in the next example. Use both a heading and a footing, and suppress the default column headings and the summary line. Enter

>LIST VENDOR HEADING "'D'" FOOTING "VENDORS 'L' PAGE NO. 'PN'" (C <return>

Response

16 JAN 1987

.
.
.

VENDORS
PAGE NO. 1

SUMMARY: HEADINGS and FOOTINGS

To Output	Use the MODIFIER	For	Add HEADING/FOOTING Modifier Option
A heading to replace the default heading	HEADING	centered text a new line date time and date page number 4 characters wide page number with no gap	"with text 'C'" "'L' with text" "with/without text 'D'" "with/without text 'T'" "with/without text 'P'" "with/without text 'PN'"
A footing	FOOTING	options as above	

6.3 TOTALS

The section on headings and footings covered how to "dress up" the output. The next two sections introduce modifiers that produce new information from the data.

In Chapter 5 we used the verb SUM to generate a total of the values for an attribute.

```
>SUM GADGETS QTY
TOTAL OF QTY = 119
```

Only the total for the attribute QTY is shown; the individual data values that add up to 119 are not displayed.

The modifier

```
TOTAL
```

outputs two kinds of information: the value for each item of the attribute named, and also the grand total of all the separate attribute values. Follow TOTAL with the name of the attribute to be TOTALed

```
TOTAL attributename
```

such as

```
TOTAL QTY
```

Use LIST and SORT as you have been doing, with or without selection criteria, and your choice of output attribute(s). The attribute named with TOTAL is output automatically and therefore is not specified again. Enter

```
>LIST GADGETS TOTAL QTY <return>
```

Response

```
GADGETS  QTY

50       23
20       19
```

```
    7         1
    8        12
   21         4
    9        10
   42        17
   30         8
   49        25

  ***       119
```

[405] 9 ITEMS LISTED.

The output for TOTAL shows the individual values for QTY in the sample, and the grand total for QTY at the end. The system defaults to three asterisks *** with the grand total amount, here 119. The usual summary line is at the bottom.

An optional modifier can be used with TOTAL to replace the asterisks on the grand total line with user supplied text. Add the modifier

   GRAND-TOTAL

followed by a text string enclosed in double quotes. The format is

   GRAND-TOTAL "text string"

For now keep the text to a limit of ten characters. (In Chapter 7 we will discuss changing length constraints.) Replace *** with the text

   TOTAL IS

The modifier and text string together are

   GRAND-TOTAL "TOTAL IS"

add them to the command sentence. Enter

   >LIST GADGETS TOTAL QTY GRAND-TOTAL "TOTAL IS" <return>

The response follows.

```
GADGETS   QTY

   .        .
   .        .
   .        .
  42       17
  30        8
  49        5

TOTAL IS 119
```

GRAND-TOTAL has a modifier option that underlines the last value in the column and thus highlights the grand total amount.

```
'U'
```

is enclosed with or without text in double quotes. Insert 'U' in the GRAND-TOTAL text string which we just used:

```
GRAND-TOTAL "TOTAL IS 'U'"
```

and enter

```
>LIST GADGETS TOTAL QTY GRAND-TOTAL "TOTAL IS 'U'" <return>
```

Response

```
   .        .
   .        .
   .        .
  30        8
  49       25
          ===
TOTAL IS 119
```

'U' can also be used without a text string but remember to add the double quotes. Enter

```
>LIST GADGETS TOTAL QTY GRAND-TOTAL "'U'" <return>
```

Response

```
    .     .
    .     .
    .     .
   30     8
   49    25
         ===
  ***   119
```

The GRAND-TOTAL can be any text string (space permitting) to replace ***. For example

```
GRAND-TOTAL ">>>"
```

outputs

```
>>>  119
```

SUMMARY: TOTAL and GRAND-TOTAL

To Output	Use the Modifier
Individual attribute values and their grand total	TOTAL attributename
A customized grand total line with underline modifier option	GRAND-TOTAL "text string" "with/without text 'U'"

6.4 SUBTOTALS VIA CONTROL BREAKS

Our goal is always to produce as much information as possible from the raw data. Control Breaks, as you will see, output the data in a more meaningful format than we have seen so far. To review briefly, the LIST verb outputs the file in internal order which means it is not organized in any way. We must use the SORT verb to see the file arranged in a particular order. SORT the GADGETS file with NAME as the sort key, and output the values for NAME and QTY. The item-ids appear automatically. Enter

```
>SORT GADGETS BY NAME NAME QTY <return>
```

The response follows.

GADGETS	NAME	QTY
50	FORK	23
20	LADLE	19
21	LADLE	4
42	SPATULA	17
49	SPATULA	25
7	SPOON	1
8	SPOON	12
9	SPOON	10
30	WHISK	8

First notice that all the names are in ascending alphabetical order. Therefore all the GADGETS with the same NAME are together. The file is output in one continuous column and we must look for the NAME changes. Even with a small test data file it would be easier to see where the changes occur if there were a break or separation between, for example, FORK and LADLE. We can instruct the system to do just that with another break between LADLE and SPATULA, and so on.

These *Control Breaks* occur each time the value of the Sort Key changes. Note that the break is always on the same attribute used as the Sort Key. The groupings are essential before there can be breaks. The modifier is

    BREAK-ON

followed by the name of the attribute on which to break.

    BREAK-ON attribute

This attribute is output automatically, and so (as with TOTAL) there is no need to repeat it at the end of the sentence. For a control break wherever the NAME changes, add to the command

    BREAK-ON NAME

Enter

    >SORT GADGETS BY NAME BREAK-ON NAME QTY <return>

Response

```
GADGETS    NAME      QTY

50         FORK      23

           ***

20         LADLE     19
21         LADLE     4

           ***

42         SPATULA   17
49         SPATULA   25

           ***

7          SPOON     1
8          SPOON     12
9          SPOON     10

           ***

30         WHISK     8

           ***

***
[405] 9 ITEMS LISTED.
```

In the response each NAME group is separated and stands out clearly. However the actual data is the same as in the preceding example.

What happens when BREAK-ON is used with LIST? Because LIST outputs the items in internal order, they are not organized in any way and there are no groupings. Breaks occur each time the BREAK-ON attribute value changes which could be every one or two items. In the sample output below it is only a coincidence that two SPOONs - 9 and 8 - happen to be stored next to each other at this moment. The output has no meaning.

```
>LIST GADGETS BREAK-ON NAME <return>
```

Response

GADGETS	NAME
50	FORK
***	
7	SPOON
***	
20	LADLE
***	
9	SPOON
8	SPOON
***	
21	LADLE
***	
42	SPATULA
***	
30	WHISK
***	
49	SPATULA
***	
***	

SORT and BREAK-ON go together. As you see, the output of

SORT GADGETS BY NAME BREAK-ON NAME ...

makes it possible to compute sub-totals. We can find the sub-total for QTY within each NAME group - a sub-total QTY for the FORKs, the LADLEs, the SPATULAs, the SPOONs, and the WHISKs - and then a grand total for the QTY of the entire file.

When combined with BREAK-ON, the modifier TOTAL calculates the sub-totals as well as the grand total. Both modifiers are used in their normal formats. The instructions are placed in the sentence in the order in which they are performed:

first, SORT GADGETS BY NAME
second, BREAK-ON NAME
third, TOTAL QTY

Outputting Familiar Data in New Ways

Since both modifiers automatically output their attributes' values, it is not necessary to add NAME or QTY at the end of the command. Enter

>SORT GADGETS BY NAME BREAK-ON NAME TOTAL QTY <return>

Response

GADGETS	NAME	QTY
50	FORK	23
	***	23
20	LADLE	19
21	LADLE	4
	***	23
42	SPATULA	17
49	SPATULA	25
	***	42
7	SPOON	1
8	SPOON	12
9	SPOON	10
	***	23
30	WHISK	8
	***	8
***		119

This version of the command outputs:

1. The individual values for QTY
2. A sub-total of QTY flagged by *** for each NAME
3. The grand total for QTY - the total of the individual values which is the same as adding the sub-totals for each break.

The grand total of 119 is what we see with SUM and TOTAL, but the new format of the output gives a clearer picture of what it consists of.

BREAK-ON has a modifier option to replace the asterisks with the value where the break occurs.

"V"

enclosed in double quotes, with or without text, after BREAK-ON displays the value at the break.

In the following example, the TOTAL modifier is not used. Enter

```
>SORT GADGETS BY NAME BREAK-ON NAME "'V'" <return>
```

Response

GADGETS	NAME
50	FORK
	FORK
20	LADLE
21	LADLE
	LADLE
42	SPATULA
49	SPATULA
	SPATULA
7	SPOON
8	SPOON
9	SPOON
	SPOON
30	WHISK
	WHISK

The value at the break is displayed instead of ***. FORK is at the end of the FORK group and so on.

When

```
BREAK-ON attributename "'V'"
```

and

```
TOTAL attributename
```

are used together they output the break value and the subtotal for the value on the same line, as in this example. Enter

```
>SORT GADGETS BY NAME BREAK-ON NAME "'V'" TOTAL QTY <return>
```

Response

GADGETS	NAME	QTY
50	FORK	23
	FORK	23
20	LADLE	19
21	LADLE	4
	LADLE	23
42	SPATULA	17
49	SPATULA	25
	SPATULA	42
7	SPOON	1
8	SPOON	12
9	SPOON	10
	SPOON	23
30	WHISK	8
	WHISK	8
***		119

'V' can be combined with user-supplied text and all enclosed in double quotes. The text string could be

```
"SUBTOTAL FOR 'V'"
```

or

```
"THE 'V' TOTAL"
```

You can use whatever is appropriate.

Before entering the command we must change line 10 in the Descriptor for NAME. The output length of ten characters has been long enough for all the NAMEs. Now, however, we are adding text to the NAME which is printed in the NAME column because the break occurs there. (Output length is covered further in Chapter 7.) So we must change the number on line 10 to 25 in order to output up to 25 characters under NAME.

The parts of the following command are shown here on separate lines for clarity.

```
>SORT GADGETS BY NAME
BREAK-ON NAME
"SUBTOTAL FOR 'V'"
TOTAL QTY <return>
```

Enter them on one line as follows:

>SORT GADGETS BY NAME BREAK-ON NAME "SUBTOTAL FOR 'V'" TOTAL QTY <return>

Response

GADGETS	NAME	QTY
50	FORK	23
	SUBTOTAL FOR FORK	23
20	LADLE	19
21	LADLE	4
	SUBTOTAL FOR LADLE	23
42	SPATULA	17
49	SPATULA	25
	SUBTOTAL FOR SPATULA	42
7	SPOON	1
8	SPOON	12
9	SPOON	10
	SUBTOTAL FOR SPOON	23

30	WHISK	8
	SUBTOTAL FOR WHISK	8
***		119

As you have seen, each step adds a new way to present the data. Combine the procedures to create formats suitable for your reports. Take the time to experiment.

Temporarily add seven new items to provide more test data in the GADGETS file:

item-id	NAME	QTY	COLOR
11	SPOON	4	RED
12	SPOON	3	YELLOW
23	LADLE	11	TAN
52	FORK	1	TAN
41	SPATULA	8	RED
5	SPOON	2	BROWN
6	SPOON	9	BROWN

Line 10 in the NAME Descriptor was recently changed to allow room for additional text. Change line 10 in the COLOR Descriptor to 30 for the same reason.

The preceding examples of SORT and control breaks sorted the file on one Sort Key which was NAME. The newly expanded GADGETS file provides enough test data to show the results of a secondary Sort on COLOR. The Primary Sort is on NAME as in the preceding example. Enter

>SORT GADGETS BY NAME BY COLOR NAME COLOR QTY <return>

Response

GADGETS	NAME	COLOR	QTY
50	FORK	TAN	23
52	FORK	TAN	1
21	LADLE	RED	4
20	LADLE	TAN	19

23	LADLE	TAN	11
49	SPATULA	AVOCADO	25
41	SPATULA	RED	8
42	SPATULA	RED	17
5	SPOON	BROWN	2
6	SPOON	BROWN	9
7	SPOON	BROWN	1
11	SPOON	RED	4
8	SPOON	RED	12
12	SPOON	YELLOW	3
9	SPOON	YELLOW	10
30	WHISK	BLUE	8

The output is the file SORTed first in ascending order on NAME. Each group of NAMEs has then been given a Secondary Sort on COLOR, also in ascending sequence. Here is part of the above output separated by dashes to show where the breaks occur:

```
  ----------------------------------------------- NAME break
  21   LADLE     RED      4
           ------------------------------------- COLOR break
  20   LADLE     TAN     19
  23   LADLE     TAN     11
  ----------------------------------------------- NAME break
  49   SPATULA   AVOCADO 25
           ------------------------------------- COLOR break
  41   SPATULA   RED      8
  42   SPATULA   RED     17
  ----------------------------------------------- NAME break
```

The result of the Primary Sort is groupings of the same NAME. The break where the NAME changes is called a *major control break*, such as between LADLE and SPATULA. The Secondary Sort produces subdivisions within the major groups by COLOR such as between LADLE RED and LADLE TAN. These breaks are called *minor control breaks*.

BREAK-ON can be used more than once in a command. Each time it is followed by the name of the attribute on which to break. Thus for the example above we use

```
BREAK-ON NAME
BREAK-ON COLOR
```

If there were a Tertiary Sort there could be another break on the attribute used as the third Sort Key. In such a case the Primary Sort provides for the major control break, the Secondary Sort for an intermediate control break, and the Tertiary Sort for the minor control break. Up to 15 control breaks are allowed.

Return to the Secondary Sort on COLOR within the Primary Sort on NAME. How many LADLEs are RED? How many LADLEs are TAN? How many LADLEs are there altogether? The modifier TOTAL works at all BREAK-ON points. When there was only one break

    BREAK-ON NAME

TOTAL output the QTY subtotal for each NAME. When there are two breaks

    BREAK-ON NAME
    BREAK-ON COLOR

TOTAL outputs the QTY subtotal first for each COLOR within the same NAME and then the subtotal for all the COLORs with that NAME.

Inspect the separate parts of the command in the order they are performed:

    first, SORT GADGETS BY NAME
    second, BY COLOR
    third, BREAK-ON NAME
    fourth, BREAK-ON COLOR
    fifth, TOTAL QTY.

Enter

    >SORT GADGETS BY NAME BY COLOR BREAK-ON NAME BREAK-ON COLOR TOTAL QTY <return>

Response

GADGETS	NAME	COLOR	QTY
50	FORK	TAN	23
52	FORK	TAN	1
		***	24
	***		24

```
     21        LADLE      RED          4
                          ***          4
     20        LADLE      TAN         19
     23        LADLE      TAN         11
                          ***         30
               ***                    34

     49        SPATULA    AVOCADO     25
                          ***         25
     41        SPATULA    RED          8
     42        SPATULA    RED         17
                          ***         25
               ***                    50

      5        SPOON      BROWN        2
      6        SPOON      BROWN        9
      7        SPOON      BROWN        1
                          ***         12
     11        SPOON      RED          4
      8        SPOON      RED         12
                          ***         16
     12        SPOON      YELLOW       3
      9        SPOON      YELLOW      10
                          ***         13
               ***                    41

     30        WHISK      BLUE         8
                          ***          8
               ***                     8

     ***                             157
```

At each break - first where the value for COLOR changes, and next where the value for NAME changes - the system defaults to *** on the lines. If you wish replace the asterisks with the value at the break by using the modifier option 'V' after each BREAK-ON.

The following command falls within the limit of 148 characters; for clarity we show it broken up into separate pieces. Enter the command as two parts:

```
>SORT GADGETS BY NAME
BY COLOR
BREAK-ON NAME
"SUBTOTAL FOR 'V'"
BREAK-ON COLOR
<control> <shift> _ <return>
```

and the prompt on the screen is

:

continue with

```
"SUBTOTAL FOR 'V'"
TOTAL QTY
GRAND-TOTAL "TOTAL 'U'"
<return>
```

Response

GADGETS	NAME	COLOR	QTY
50	FORK	TAN	23
52	FORK	TAN	1
		SUBTOTAL FOR TAN	24
	SUBTOTAL FOR FORK		24
21	LADLE	RED	4
		SUBTOTAL FOR RED	4
20	LADLE	TAN	19
23	LADLE	TAN	11
		SUBTOTAL FOR TAN	30
	SUBTOTAL FOR LADLE		34
49	SPATULA	AVOCADO	25
		SUBTOTAL FOR AVOCADO	25
41	SPATULA	RED	8
42	SPATULA	RED	17
		SUBTOTAL FOR RED	25
	SUBTOTAL FOR SPATULA		50

5	SPOON	BROWN	2
6	SPOON	BROWN	9
7	SPOON	BROWN	1
		SUBTOTAL FOR BROWN	12
11	SPOON	RED	4
8	SPOON	RED	12
		SUBTOTAL FOR RED	16
12	SPOON	YELLOW	3
9	SPOON	YELLOW	10
		SUBTOTAL FOR YELLOW	13
		SUBTOTAL FOR SPOON	41
30	WHISK	BLUE	8
		SUBTOTAL FOR BLUE	8
		SUBTOTAL FOR WHISK	8
			===
	TOTAL		157

The above groupings, subtotals, and explanatory labels present the data in a format with more meaning for the user than the default output.

The seven items that were added to the GADGETS file have served their purpose to illustrate control breaks. The following items can be deleted: 5, 6, 11, 12, 23, 41, and 52.

SUMMARY: BREAK-ON

To output control breaks
use the   SORT verb

with the modifier   BREAK-ON attributename
                    the same attribute as the Sort Key

To replace *** on the subtotal lines
add the modifier option   "with or without text 'V'"

Note: 1. The BREAK-ON attribute is automatically output.
       2. Up to 15 control breaks are allowed.
       3. Other modifiers commonly used with BREAK-ON are

                    TOTAL attributename
                    with or without
                        GRAND-TOTAL "text string"
                        and/or the underline modifier option "'U'"

6.5 IMPLICIT ATTRIBUTE LISTS

This topic is a unique procedure that, like other material covered in this chapter, provides a new way to output familiar data.

First let us define some terms which may be confusing and go back to the explicit item list we have often used. As you know, the explicit item list consists of particular item-id(s) in the command sentence. The verb acts on them instead of on the entire file. The word "explicit" means the same in English as in computer terms: distinctly stated or expressed. We specify the items in the explicit item list.

Next consider attributes. The verbs LIST and SORT default to outputting the item-ids. In order to output one or more attributes we must name them in the command such as

    LIST VENDOR CITY STATE

The attribute(s) specified for output are also distinctly stated and therefore are called an *Explicit Attribute List*. Without applying the definition this is what we have been using whenever we gave the output attribute name(s). When the same one or more attributes are almost always wanted, this method is unnecessarily time consuming.

There is a way of automatically outputting one or more attributes without specifying them in the command: use an *Implicit Attribute List*. The word "implicit" has the same meaning in English and computer reference: understood though not expressed. Thus an Implicit Attribute List is implied (not distinctly stated). You and the system know it exists but there is no mention of it in the LIST or SORT command. After an Implicit Attribute List is created the system always defaults to it unless you use an Explicit Attribute List which we shall cover shortly.

The first step is to decide what attribute(s) you want to output most of the time. They can be in any order. Let us select three attributes from the Vendor file to output with LIST or SORT unless we give other instructions:

1. CO.NAME
2. CITY
3. STATE

The next step is to create a Synonym Descriptor for each attribute. For an Implicit Attribute List we use a number as the Descriptor name, starting with 1 and continuing in sequence as planned above. There is no limit to the numbers but they must be consecutive. The system references 1 and continues. If you happen to use numbers 1, 2, 3, omit 4, and then use 5 the system goes from 1 to 3 and stops; it cannot get to 5 because there is no 4. Do not skip numbers when making Descriptors for an Implicit Attribute List.

Create the Descriptors just as you have done for a Synonym:

line	contents
001	S
002	the number of the original attribute for which this is a synonym
003 through 008	null values
009	the justification of the original attribute
010	the maximum output length of the original attribute

The command is

>ED DICT VENDOR 1 2 3 <return>

Enter the following for each Descriptor:

	1	2	3
line			
001	S	S	S
002	8	5	2
003 through 008	null values		
009	L	L	L
010	35	10	2

These three Descriptors are the Implicit Attribute List. To see the results enter

>LIST VENDOR <return>

Response

```
VENDOR      1                              2              3

ACE.88      ACE BROS.                      PETERBURG      NY
ZENITH.22   ZENITH                         KENN CITY      AR
    .
    .
    .
```

The default output above is now the item-ids (as normal) plus attributes 1, 2, and 3.

The SORT verb defaults to the same attributes. Try it with a selection criterion phrase. Enter

>SORT VENDOR WITH STATE > "MA" <return>

Response

```
VENDOR      1                              2              3

ACE.88      ACE BROS.                      PETERBURG      NY
SUMMIT.33   THE SUMMIT FOR KITCHENWARE     WARRENTON      SC
```

The Implicit Attribute List works only at output time; all other operations are as usual.

When you want to override the Implicit Attribute List output, use an Explicit Attribute List such as in the command

>LIST VENDOR STATE <return>

Response

```
VENDOR     STATE

ACE.88     NY
TOPS.55    MA
PEAK.77    IL
   .
   .
   .
```

As you see, the attribute STATE overrides the Implicit Attribute List. The same applies to the SORT verb. Enter

>SORT VENDOR WITH STATE > "MA" STATE <return>

Response

```
VENDOR      STATE

ACE.88      NY
SUMMIT.33   SC
```

In Chapter 4 we used

LIST ONLY DICT filename

to output the names of the attributes in the file. We did not use this verb with the Data filename as

LIST ONLY filename

because it outputs the item-ids the same as

LIST filename

We had already used LIST and defaulted to the item-ids and there was no reason to mention another verb to perform the same operation.

The situation is different now because the VENDOR file has an Implicit Attribute List. Every time you

LIST VENDOR

the attributes on the Implicit Attribute List are output with the item-ids. This does not apply to

LIST ONLY filename

which outputs only the item-ids whether there is an Implicit Attribute List or not. LIST ONLY overrides the Implicit Attribute List. To illustrate this enter the following.

```
>LIST ONLY VENDOR <return>
```

Response

```
VENDOR

ACE.88
TOPS.55
ACME.66
SUMMIT.33
PEAK.77
ZENITH.22
```

As you see in the response the Implicit Attribute List has no effect on LIST ONLY.

6.6 ERROR EXAMPLES

Note: to allow space for wider commands and responses the comments have been placed below the error examples.

```
>LIST VENDOR (C) STATE
[24] THE WORD "(C) STATE" CANNOT BE IDENTIFIED
```

COMMENT: (C) must be at the end of the sentence.

```
>LIST VENDOR STATE (C (I
[24] THE WORD "I" CANNOT BE IDENTIFIED
```

COMMENT: (C and (I must be combined as (CI

```
>SORT VENDOR BY STATE ID-SUPP
```

Response

```
Page 1
```

(seven blank lines)

```
7 ITEMS LISTED.
```

COMMENT: No output attribute is specified and ID-SUPP suppresses the default item-ids. Therefore, there is no visible output. Name at least one attribute for output when suppressing item-ids.

```
>LIST VENDOR HEADING "VENDOR FILE AT 'T' PAGE 'PL'"
```

Response

```
VENDOR FILE AT 14:33:18 01 FEB 1987 PAGE 1
    .
    .
    .
```

COMMENT: 'L' must be followed by whatever goes on a new line. If you want PAGE and number on a new line, place 'L' before PAGE

```
>LIST GADGETS TOTAL QTY GRAND TOTAL "THE TOTAL QUANTITY IS"
```

Response

```
[24] THE WORD "GRAND" CANNOT BE IDENTIFIED
```

COMMENT: There must be a hyphen in GRAND-TOTAL

```
>SORT GADGETS BY NAME BREAK-ON NAME TOTAL QTY "'U'"
```

Response

GADGETS	NAME	QTY
50	FORK	
	***	0
20	LADLE	
21	LADLE	
	***	0
42	SPATULA	
49	SPATULA	
	***	U
7	SPOON	
8	SPOON	
9	SPOON	
	***	0
30	WHISK	
	***	0
***		0

COMMENT: 'U' must be used with the modifier GRAND-TOTAL

```
>SORT GADGETS BY NAME BREAK-ON NAME TOTAL QTY NAME QTY
```

Response

GADGETS	NAME	QTY	NAME	QTY
50	FORK	23	FORK	23
	***	23		
20	LADLE	19	LADLE	19
21	LADLE	4	LADLE	4
	***	23		
42	SPATULA	17	SPATULA	17
49	SPATULA	25	SPATULA	25
	***	42		

7	SPOON	1	SPOON	1
8	SPOON	12	SPOON	12
9	SPOON	10	SPOON	10
	***	23		
30	WHISK	8	WHISK	8
	***	8		
***		119		

COMMENT: The BREAK-ON attribute and also the TOTAL attribute are automatically output. Do not name them again to avoid duplication.

```
>SORT GADGETS BREAK-ON COLOR
```

Response

GADGETS	COLOR
20	TAN
	***
21	RED
	***
30	BLUE
	***
42	RED
	***
49	AVOCADO
	***
50	TAN
	***
7	BROWN
	***

```
    8           RED
                ***

    9           YELLOW
                ***
```

COMMENT: There is no Sort Key - BY COLOR - in the command which causes two problems:

1. The system defaults to a Sort on the item-ids which are numeric but left justified and the Sort is therefore useless.
2. The items are in internal stored order and not grouped by COLOR which is necessary to have the breaks on COLOR in the proper places.

```
>SORT GADGETS BY NAME BREAK-ON NAME TOTAL QTY "SUBTOTAL FOR 'V'"
```

Response

```
    GADGETS     NAME        QTY

    50          FORK
                ***          0

    20          LADLE
    21          LADLE
                ***          0

    42          SPATULA
    49          SPATULA
                ***          0

    7           SPOON
    8           SPOON
    9           SPOON
                ***          0

    30          WHISK
                ***          0

    ***                      0
```

COMMENT: "SUBTOTAL FOR 'V'" must follow immediately after the name of the BREAK-ON attribute.

6.7 REVIEW QUESTIONS

1. What happens when the S Descriptors in an Implicit Attribute List are not numbered consecutively?
2. What is the relationship between the Sort Key and the control break attribute?
3. Describe five modifier options available with Headings and Footings and how they are used.
4. What is an Explicit Attribute List? Where is it placed?
5. TOTAL can be used with what modifier? How?
6. How can the value at a control break be displayed?
7. What is a default Heading and what does it contain?
8. What are control breaks? What modifier causes them?
9. Explain the purpose of an Implicit Attribute List. How can you override it?
10. How is a Heading with user supplied text displayed?
11. What is a modifier?
12. Name the two ways to supress the default Heading. What else is suppressed?
13. Compare the output of SUM and TOTAL.
14. What is an Explicit Item List? Why is it used?
15. What does (C do?

Chapter 7

Changing the Output via the Descriptor

7.1 DESCRIPTOR REVIEW AND LINE 10: LENGTH

Up to now we have not given much thought to the Descriptors after they were created. It has been enough to know that the structure of each attribute as defined by its Descriptor determines how the data is output. In this chapter we explore various ways in which Descriptors can be modified to alter output. The operations that we cover here gradually grow more complex than those we have been performing and require more practice to become familiar. Be patient as you move from one section to another and take the time to go back and review the procedures. When you have mastered them you will realize how much data manipulation is possible on the Pick Operating System for a person with no programming knowledge.

Suppose we start with a line-by-line review of the information in a Descriptor:

- 001 defines the type. A is the original Descriptor (Attribute Definition Item); S is a Synonym for an A type Descriptor as used in Chapter 5.
- 002 the AMC (Attribute Mark Count) is the position of that attribute, e.g. NAME is AMC 1 or the first attribute in the GADGETS file.
- 003 through 008 have been reserved with null values.
- 009 justification is the direction of processing: L (Left) for letters or a combination of letters and numbers such as in street address; R (Right) for all numbers. You saw the consequences of justification with a Sort on Left justified numeric data in the GADGETS file. It was necessary to create a new Descriptor with Right justification to produce valid output.
- 010 maximum output length allocates space for the specified number of characters.

Line 10 is not the only factor controlling output length. The number of characters in the Descriptor's name is automatically compared to the number on line 10, whichever is greater is the actual maximum output length. Whether the Descriptor is type A or S does not matter, only its name is considered.

What happens when line 10 in the Descriptor for NAME is changed to 3? NAME is now

    001 A
    002 1
    003 to 008 null
    009 L
    010 3

Enter

>LIST GADGETS NAME <return>

Response

    GADGETS   NAME

    50   FORK
    7   SPOO
              N
    42   SPAT
              ULA
    20   LADL
              E
    .
    .
    .

Note that only part of the response is shown to illustrate the output. This will be done whenever partial output serves the purpose.

Line 10 has 3, NAME has 4 characters and so 4 becomes the output length. Since NAME is Left justified, the first 4 characters beginning at the left are output while the 5th to last characters are *wrapped* or *folded* to the next line.

In Chapter 6.4 on control breaks we added text

"SUBTOTAL FOR 'V'"

to be output in the NAME column. Before entering the command we changed line 10 in NAME from 10 to 25. The reason for increasing the output length was to allow space for

```
SUBTOTAL FOR
```

There are 11 characters in the words plus 2 spaces - one between SUBTOTAL and FOR, and one between FOR and the NAME value which follows - making a total of 13 so far. To this add 'V' representing the value for the NAME originally covered under the NAME output length of 10. We then used 25 for the new total length only because it gives a small extra allowance. If we had not changed line 10 to make room for the added text the output would have been limited to whichever was greater: NAME with 4 characters or length 10. This is how the output would have looked

```
GADGETS    NAME......
   .
   .
   .
           SUBTOTAL F
           OR SPOON
   .
   .
   .
           SUBTOTAL F
           OR SPATULA
```

Note that T can be used for justification of alphabetic text instead of L. With T the wrap occurs on the nearest break between words rather than dividing the word as occurs above. Suppose that the Descriptor for NAME has T for justification on line 9 and continues with 10 as output length on line 10. The output above now looks like

```
GADGETS    NAME......
   .
   .
   .
           SUBTOTAL
           FOR SPOON
   .
   .
```

SUBTOTAL
FOR
SPATULA

The periods in the column headings show the balance of the space allowed for the output. NAME has 4 characters, line 10 has a length of 10, therefore 6 periods fill out the column. This is true for the item-id and all attribute column headings; they are shown in the sample output only when relevant. In the response above with SUBTOTAL F, the first 10 characters of the subtotal text are output to the end of the column; the balance of the text wraps around and continues on the next line. By increasing the maximum length when we did, we eliminated this problem. Whenever you change output format be sure that there will be enough room for the new version.

7.2 LINE 9: JUSTIFICATION

Let us refer to data values that do not fit in their assigned space as "oversized." The two preceding examples were for Left justified attributes. Where does an oversized item-id that is Left justified go? Again start from the Descriptor. When displaying the Descriptors in a Dictionary you have seen one with the same name as the file. This Descriptor is created by the system for the item-id and contains vital information such as how the item can be found. <u>NEVER</u> alter the following in any way:

001 D the code type
002 the beginning frame of the file
003 the file modulo
004 the file separation.

These first four lines must not be changed. However lines 005 through 010 (for our purposes) are comparable to those lines in Attribute Definition Items which we have been referring to as Descriptors.

Line 009 in the item-id Descriptor has a default value of L as mentioned. Earlier, to avoid possible disasters we created Synonym Descriptors with the appropriate justification instead of altering the Descriptor for the item-id. Now that you are experienced you may prefer to make changes directly on line 9 when required.

Changing the Output via the Descriptor 193

Line 010 in the Descriptor for the item-id has a default value of 10 as output length.

To see what happens to an oversized Left justified item-id we added a new (incomplete) test item to the VENDOR Data File. VENDOR has 6 characters, line 10 has 10; the new item has an item-id of 15 characters: MOUNTEVEREST.11. The value for SHIPS.VIA is AIR.

Output looks normal when no attributes are output. Enter

>LIST VENDOR <return>

Response

    VENDOR....

    ACE.88
    TOPS.55
    MOUNTEVEREST.11
    .
    .
    .

The item-id is Left justified. Output starts with the left-most character at the left end of the column and proceeds toward the right. The 15 characters in the oversized item-id continue into the adjacent space.

The problem shows up when an attribute is added to the output and space is no longer available. Enter

>LIST VENDOR SHIPS.VIA <return>

Response

    VENDOR.... SHIPS.VIA

    ACE.88   TRUCK
    TOPS.55   TRUCK
    MOUNTEVERESAIR
    .
    .
    .

Normally one blank shows between columns. Here the oversized item-id uses all of its own 10 spaces plus the space between columns. SHIPS.VIA is Left justified and must start at the left end of its column whether its neighbor is there or not. As a result, the last part of MOUNT-EVEREST.11 does not show. AIR over-writes the last part of the item-id T.11.

If we intended to keep the new item we would have to allow space for it by changing line 10 in the VENDOR Descriptor of the VENDOR Dictionary from 10 to 20. But the item was only for testing.

The results of oversized Right justified data are not the same as for Left justified. However item-ids and attributes with Right justification both behave in the same way: output starts with the right-most character at the right end of the column and proceeds toward the left. After the value fills its own column it continues to output and over-writes anything in its way. When there is no more space, whatever remains of the value is *truncated* or cut off and not output.

First observe what happens to a test GADGETS data item: the item-id is defined as Right justified and has 15 characters: 123456789012345; the value for NAME is FORK. The command

        LIST GADGETS NAME

Outputs

        GADGETS...   NAME

        12   SPOON
        30   WHISK
        6789012345   FORK
        .
        .
        .

The output for the oversized item-id is the first 10 characters starting from the right end of the value. They fill the space and there is no room for the left end - 12345 - which is truncated.

In Chapter 6 when we added text for the grand total line to appear in the item-id column we stayed within the 10 character limit and so the text fit. If the text had been longer and line 10 of the GADGETS Descriptor had the default value of 10, the text would not have fit. The results would have been the same as with an oversized Right justified item-id. For example, the command

    LIST GADGETS TOTAL QTY GRAND-TOTAL "THE GRAND TOTAL IS"

outputs

    GADGETS... QTY

    50   23
    8   12
    .
    .
    .
    D TOTAL IS 160

As you see part of the text for

    THE GRAND TOTAL IS

does not appear because output starts at the right, continues to the left for 10 characters to the boundary of the column, and the left end of the string does not fit.

    THE GRAN

is truncated. When text exceeds the space limit, change line 10 in the item-id Descriptor to allow space for the required number of characters.

An oversized Right justified attribute also proceeds from right to left as far as possible. It uses the space between columns and then over-writes anything in its path. For example, if the item-id for VENDOR is left justified, and the oversized value for ZIP is right justified, the output is

    VENDOR.... ZIP..

    ZENITH0987654321

The value for ZIP has over-written the last part of the item-id which is .22.

When we are careless about calculating the length requirement for item-ids and attributes, the results are unsatisfactory. The output may be spread out with wide spaces between values or forced into vertical format. Thus far there has been space enough on one line in the output to display the attributes; they appear horizontally as they do in the table. When there is not enough space for the attributes to fit on one line across the screen or the page, they are displayed vertically: each attribute name is on the left with its value next to it.

Use a small amount of representative test data to see how the output will look before working with large files. Remember that Length and Justification cannot be considered separately; Length controls the amount of space and Justification, by direction, determines what goes into the space.

SUMMARY: HOW LENGTH and JUSTIFICATION AFFECT OUTPUT

1. Column space is equal to whichever is greater: the name of the attribute or the length in its Descriptor.
2. All values are output according to their Justification:
   L   puts the left-most character at the left end of the column and proceeds to the right
   R   puts the right-most character at the right end of the column and proceeds to the left.
3. A normal length value fits in its column.
4. An oversized value cannot fit in its column and the results are as follows:

	LEFT JUSTIFIED	RIGHT JUSTIFIED
OVERSIZED ITEM-ID:	Without an attribute it continues to the right into the available space. With an attribute the part of the of the item-id that occupies the attribute's column is over-written.	Both an item-id and an attribute continue to the left and over-write what is in the way. When there is no more space, whatever remains of the value is truncated
OVERSIZED ATTRIBUTE:	Fills its column and then wraps to the next line.	

7.3 LINE 3: TAG

Starting in Chapter 3 when we first created a Descriptor, we reserved lines 3 through 8 by giving them null values. For the rest of this chapter we shall use some of those lines: 3, 7, and 8. As you know, whatever resides in the Descriptor directs the processing of the attribute. Therefore, when changing the output form of the data we must make a decision: alter the original A type Descriptor and always see the modified form of the data; or create an S type Descriptor and use it when that particular data form is wanted for output.

So far we have seen the name of the attribute output as the column heading. User supplied text can be substituted for the attribute name as heading. This is done by replacing the null value on line 3 of the Descriptor with the text, which is called a *Tag*.

To illustrate what happens when a Tag is placed in an A type Descriptor use QTY in the GADGETS file. Suppose we change the normal heading QTY to

```
QUANTITY ON HAND
```

Not only will this be automatically output as the column heading but the length of the Tag is now a third consideration when space is allocated for outputting the attribute values. When there is a Tag, the column width is the largest of:

1. the name of the attribute,
2. the figure on line 10, or
3. the number of characters in the Tag

QTY has 3 characters, line 10 has 3, and the Tag has 16 characters (including the two blanks between the words). Therefore, room for 16 characters is set aside for the QTY output values and there is no need to change line 10 in the Descriptor. The Descriptor for QTY is now

```
001 A
002 2
003 QUANTITY ON HAND
004 through 008 null
009 R
010 3
```

Enter

><u>LIST GADGETS QTY</u> <return>

Response

GADGETS...QUANTITY ON HAND

```
50                      23
7                        1
21                       4
 .
 .
 .
```

Whenever a Descriptor is named for output, if there is a Tag it becomes the column heading.

It is possible to print a Tag on two lines such as

QUANTITY ON HAND
IS AS FOLLOWS

When entering the text on line 3 in the Descriptor, indicate where the new line starts by inserting a special delimiter: press the control key and the right square bracket together

<control>]

Only the bracket] appears on the screen. Line 3 is now going to have

QUANTITY ON HAND]IS AS FOLLOWS

Before changing the line choose the fastest way to replace the old text with the new. Instead of typing out both complete texts as in

R/old text/new text/

look for a shortcut as suggested in Chapter 4.5. We are keeping the old text and adding to it. The last two characters of the old are ND (this is the only place where they appear) and so we can

Changing the Output via the Descriptor 199

```
R/ND/ND]IS AS FOLLOWS/
```

Change line 3 as shown.

A word on the slash / which is normally the delimiter in the Replace command: if the slash is part of either the old or the new text you must use a different delimiter, such as ! or $ or ; or . Whichever symbol you choose use it in the required three places, for example

```
R!8!2!
```

Enter

```
>LIST GADGETS QTY <return>
```

Response

```
GADGETS...QUANTITY ON HAND
             IS AS FOLLOWS

50                      23
20                      19
 .
 .
 .
```

The Tag is output every time QTY is called for unless the column headings are suppressed. If this suits you, leave the Tag in QTY. The alternative is to put the Tag in a Synonym Descriptor for QTY and use the name of the S Descriptor to output that particular column heading. Give the new Descriptor a name associated with what it does, like

QTY.ON.HAND
001 S   this is an S type Descriptor
002 2   the Descriptor refers to attribute 2
003 QUANTITY ON HAND   the column heading
004 through 008 null
009 R   right justified output
010 3   length of 3 positions

In this way QTY.ON.HAND outputs the special heading, and QTY outputs the normal heading QTY. The data values are the same in both cases.

Change line 3 in QTY back to null if you do not want the Tag.

After the Implicit Attribute List was created in Chapter 6 the output columns were headed with the numeric names of the attributes: 1, 2, and 3. The numbers do not describe the data values at all; why not give each attribute a meaningful Tag? You might want to use the same name as the A type Descriptor i.e.

>   for 1 CO.NAME
>   for 2 CITY
>   for 3 STATE

or you may prefer a different version of the original. Do as you wish. But <u>never</u> try to give the item-id Descriptor a Tag; lines 1 through 4 must not be altered.

7.4 LINES 7 AND 8: CONVERSIONS AND CORRELATIVES

In addition to line 3, we use lines 7 and 8 in the Descriptor. An instruction on line 7 is called a *conversion*; on line 8 it is a *correlative*. Conversions and correlatives change only the output form of the data; the stored data is not changed. Some of the possibilities include adding a dollar sign and decimal point, extracting part of a value, fetching an attribute from another file, performing calculations, and joining data values with text. In all cases the output is different from what we are used to seeing. We continue to work with the ACCESS verbs LIST and SORT, starting with simple commands to learn what these new procedures can do. At the end of the section we cover the effects of selection criteria on processing and then can decide whether to use a conversion or a correlative.

The same instruction format is used for both lines. The only difference is that line 8 is executed before line 7 (even though we may have expected the opposite sequence). Each of these special instructions is expressed as a different *code* that consists of one to three letters. Some codes require additional information before they can be executed. Whenever the output is not what you expect, check the code; it must conform exactly to the rules. We shall explore ten different conversions/correlatives, one at a time. Look for the similarities and differences among them and also possible ways of combining them to suit your particular needs.

Changing the Output via the Descriptor

Generally, we create Descriptors for the conversions/correlatives so that their unique processing can be called for when it is required. Each case however, dictates whether an A or S type Descriptor is appropriate. Since there is no limit to the number of Synonym Descriptors and more than one can refer to the same A type, we can create Descriptors as needed. Give them logical names that remind you what they do and remember that the maximum output length on line 10 must allow for the changes.

To provide more test data we are going to expand both the GADGETS and VENDOR files by adding attributes. This involves making a new Descriptor in the Dictionary of both files for each new attribute and then entering the actual data values for each item in the Data Files. In this chapter we shall also be moving into and out of the Dictionaries to inspect and change Descriptors. Therefore, you may want to review creating a Descriptor (Chapter 3), and also updating, particularly making changes (Chapter 4).

Add the following Descriptors to the GADGETS file:

line	(attribute5) DATE	(attribute6) COST	(attribute7) SELL
001	A	A	A
002	5	6	7
003 through 008	null values for all the Descriptors		
009	R	R	R
010	11	8	10

Add the following data values for the items in the GADGETS Data File. Read across the line for the values for each item-id as if this were an extension of the table we used originally. DATE is explained in Section 7.4.10. The COST and SELL values are entered as whole numbers in cents without a decimal point and are covered in Section 7.4.8 Arithmetic.

item-id	DATE	COST	SELL
8	6539	100	200
9	6486	75	150
7	6584	225	450
20	6610	150	325
21	6578	250	500

30	6573	300	650
50	6591	110	225
42	6615	200	375
49	6472	210	400

These are the new Descriptors for the VENDOR Dictionary:

line	(attribute4) STREET	(attribute5) CITY	(attribute6) PHONE	(attribute7) CONTACT	(attribute8) CO.NAME
001	A	A	A	A	A
002	4	5	6	7	8
003 through 008 are null values in all the Descriptors					
009	L	L	R	L	L
010	30	20	13	35	35

The length for PHONE allows for incorrect data to be used later for demonstration.

Note that the data values for each item in the VENDOR Data File are displayed in vertical format because the values are too long to fit across a line.

```
item-id     ACME.66
STREET      7 CHANDLER ST.
CITY        BILLINGS
PHONE       516-123-4567
CONTACT     MR. J. J. KING
CO.NAME     ACME TECH INC.

item-id     PEAK.77
STREET      903 STEVENS AVE.
CITY        JOSEPH HARBOR
PHONE       215-277-0123
CONTACT     MR. R. M. DONALD
CO.NAME     PEAK SUPPLY CO.

item-id     ACE.88
STREET      3 KILGORE RD. SUITE 1202B
CITY        PETERBURG
PHONE       516-123-8911
CONTACT     MS. C. MOORE
CO.NAME     ACE BROS.
```

```
    item-id      SUMMIT.33
    STREET       49 LINDA BLVD.
    CITY         WARRENTON
    PHONE        516-234-5678
    CONTACT      MR. ROY POWELL
    CO.NAME      THE SUMMIT FOR KITCHENWARE

    item-id      TOPS.55
    STREET       JANET LANE
    CITY         CHARLES NECK
    PHONE        703-890-1234
    CONTACT      MS. ELLEN VAN
    CO.NAME      TOPS IN GADGETS

    item-id      ZENITH.22
    STREET       3-17 D ST.
    CITY         KENN CITY
    PHONE        273-721-9012
    CONTACT      DR. SIMON GUTH
    CO.NAME      ZENITH
```

Add item-id ACE.99 to the VENDOR Data File as shown below. Many errors are included to provide additional test data.

```
    item-id      ACE.99
    SHIPS.VIA    AIR
    STATE        C4
    ZIP          34A67
    STREET       5 EXPERIMENT WAY
    CITY         TRYOUT
    PHONE        184-279-80041
    CONTACT      MS. JANFULCRO
    CO NAME      ACE TO TEST
```

7.4.1 MASK CHARACTER: MC

MC (Mask Character) is a family of codes that can change the case of letters or block the output of specified types of characters. All of the instructions start with MC to which we add the particular character(s) for each operation. For the first application output data values in lower case letters with the MCL code. Let us output the values for the COLOR in the GADGETS file in lower case. This is the time to decide if the code should be placed in the A type Descriptor or in an S type. In the future we may want the upper case output therefore we create a Synonym Descriptor for the code. This way we can output either upper or lower case by calling for the appropriate Descriptor. The new Descriptor is COLOR.LC and the name suggests what it does. Create the Descriptor and place the code on line 8 where it is called a correlative.

```
COLOR.LC
001 S                           this is a Synonym Descriptor
002 3                           for attribute3
003 through 006 null values
007 null
008 MCL                         the Mask Character code
009 L                           Left justification
010 15                          output length
```

By giving both COLOR and COLOR.LC in the command we can compare their output. Enter

>**LIST GADGETS COLOR COLOR.LC** <return>

Response

```
GADGETS    COLOR        COLOR.LC

50         TAN          tan
21         RED          red
9          YELLOW       yellow
 .
 .
 .
```

The output is the same values for both attributes only the form has been changed by MCL in COLOR.LC.

Note that any or all of the attributes in an Implicit Attribute List can also be used for conversions/correlatives. But remember that you will always see the data in the changed form when the system defaults to outputting those attributes.

MCT outputs the first letter of each word in upper case (caps) and the rest of the word in lower case. The data for STREET in the VENDOR file is suitable for demonstrating the results of MCT. Create a new Synonym Descriptor:

```
STREET.UL
001 S                       this is an S type
002 4                       it is a Synonym for attribute4
003 through 006 null
007 null
008 MCT                     the Mask Character code
009 L                       Left justified output
010 30                      output length
```

Enter

```
>LIST VENDOR STREET.UL <return>
```

Response

```
VENDOR    STREET.UL

ACE.88    3 Kilgore Rd. Suite 1202B
TOPS.55   Janet Lane
PEAK.77   903 Stevens Ave.
  .
  .
  .
```

The MCU code outputs the data in all upper case letters but it does nothing for us at this time because we have entered it in upper case and this is how the output is normally shown.

The three preceding members of the MC family change the case of the output. The other part of the family extracts specific data types by working like a mask, much as a face mask shows the eyes but covers the nose and the mouth.

  MCA

outputs only the alphabetic characters and holds back the other types: numbers and symbols. Ideal test data for this code are the item-ids in the VENDOR Data File which consist of letters, a period, and numbers. Here it is essential to make a Synonym Descriptor. If we put the code in the item-id Descriptor (the D type) we shall never see the complete item-id, only the results of MCA. Create the Descriptor

```
ID.CHECK
001 S                        this is an S type
002 0                        the item-id is considered attribute zero
003 through 006 null
007 null
008 MCA                      the Mask Character Alphabetic code
009 L                        Left justified output
010 12                       output length
```

Enter

```
>LIST VENDOR ID.CHECK <return>
```

Response

```
VENDOR     ID.CHECK

ACE.88     ACE
TOPS.55    TOPS
PEAK.77    PEAK
  .
  .
  .
```

Compare the item-ids to the output of ID.CHECK. MCA has masked off the non-alphabetic characters and output only the letters. To extract the numeric characters and mask the letters and symbols use

```
MCN
```

As previously suggested special instructions like these should be placed in a Descriptor and set aside until needed. But here we are experimenting with many new procedures and creating a Descriptor for each one would take a great deal of time and disk space. Therefore, for these illustrations we shall make use of existing Descriptors to test new codes although this is contrary to what is recommended for normal operations.

Change line 8 in ID.CHECK to

```
MCN
```

Enter

>LIST VENDOR ID.CHECK <return>

Response

```
VENDOR     ID.CHECK

ACE.88     88
TOPS.55    55
PEAK.77    77
   .
   .
   .
```

The response shows only the numbers in the item-id; the letters and the period have been masked out.

MCA and MCN allow one type of character to pass and ignore the other two types. The next examples of MC allow two types to pass and hold back the third type. As before, there are separate codes depending on what is to be output.

MC/A

takes all the characters that are <u>not</u> alphabetic - numbers and symbols - and ignores the alphabetic characters. Change line 8 in ID.CHECK to

MC/A

Enter

>LIST VENDOR ID.CHECK <return>

Response

```
VENDOR     ID.CHECK

ACE.88     .88
TOPS.55    .55
PEAK.77    .77
   .
```

The output consists of the period and the numbers, which are non-alphabetic characters.

To output all characters that are not numeric use

    MC/N

on line 8 in ID.CHECK. Enter

    >LIST VENDOR ID.CHECK <return>

Response

```
VENDOR     ID.CHECK

ACE.88     ACE.
TOPS.55    TOPS.
PEAK.77    PEAK.
  .
  .
  .
```

The examples illustrate the effects of the codes. You decide how to apply them to your data.

SUMMARY: MC (Mask Character) Code

CODE	OUTPUT CASE
MCL	lower
MCT	Upper And Lower
MCU	UPPER

	OUTPUTS	MASKS
MCA	letters	numbers, symbols
MCN	numbers	letters, symbols
MC/A	numbers, symbols	letters
MC/N	letters, symbols	numbers

7.4.2 PATTERN: P

The MC code tests the character type but not the number of characters in the string. In Chapter 5 we used the caret as placeholder to test for the number of characters but could not check for the type. Now we have a way to examine both the type and the number of characters by using the Pattern code. The format is

```
P(the number of characters followed by the type)
```

For example, values for ZIP in the VENDOR file should consist of 5 numeric characters, therefore the code for the Pattern is

```
P(5N)
```

with no spaces between the parts of the code. To see what happens when Pattern is placed in an A type Descriptor put the code on line 7 of the ZIP Descriptor.

Then enter

```
>LIST VENDOR ZIP <return>
```

Response

```
VENDOR    ZIP

ACE.88    23456
TOPS.55   67890
ACE.99
  .
  .
  .
```

The response shows no ZIP value for ACE.99. Why not? The data exists but does not match the pattern and so was not output. As long as the P code is in the ZIP Descriptor a value that does not match the pattern in the code will never be output. This illustrates the need to think through the results of putting code in an A type Descriptor. Replace the code on line 7 with a null value which it had before. The only way to see the actual non-matching data is to create a Synonym Descriptor for the P code. Call it ZIP.TEST.

```
ZIP.TEST
001 S
002 3                  this is a Synonym for ZIP which is attribute3
003 through 006 null
007 P(5N)              the Pattern code
008 null
009 R                  as in ZIP
010 5                  as in ZIP
```

There are now two attributes we can output: we can see the raw data values as originally entered for ZIP, and also where those values do not match the pattern that is in ZIP.TEST. Enter

>LIST VENDOR ZIP ZIP.TEST <return>

Response

VENDOR	ZIP	ZIP.TEST
ACE.88	23456	23456
TOPS.55	67890	67890
ACE.99	34A67	
.		
.		
.		

The trouble is easy to spot: ACE.99 has an A in the ZIP value. Normally this error would be corrected but we are only showing how P can be used.

The same method could ensure that all the data values for STATE consist of two alphabetic characters. The code for this is

P(2A)

and it should be placed in a Synonym Descriptor for STATE.

A Pattern can also test for multiple parts when all the data is in the same format such as in PHONE in the VENDOR Data File. There are 10 nu-

Changing the Output via the Descriptor 211

meric characters separated into three parts by dashes. The elements in the Pattern code are

3N	3 numeric characters
-	delimited by a dash
3N	3 numeric characters
-	delimited by a dash
4N	4 numeric characters

The complete code is

P(3N-3N-4N)

Always use the same delimiters in the code as there are in the data values.

Create a Synonym Descriptor for PHONE called

```
PHONE.TEST
001 S                       this is a Synonym Descriptor
002 6                       for attribute6
003 through 006 null
007 P(3N-3N-4N)             the Pattern code
008 null
009 R                       Right justification
010 13                      output length
```

Just as we did with the ZIP example, name both attributes for output in order to inspect any non-matching data values. Enter

>LIST VENDOR PHONE PHONE.TEST <return>

Response

VENDOR	PHONE	PHONE.TEST
ACME.66	516-123-4567	516-123-4567
ACE.99	184-279-800041	
TOPS.55	703-890-1234	703-890-1234
.		
.		
.		

The PHONE for ACE.99 has an extra digit in the last part. If this were not test data the error would have to be corrected.

When two formats for the data are acceptable both can be given in the Pattern code. Perhaps you are willing to have the data either as 10 continuous digits without delimiters or as in the Pattern just used above. Specify both formats with a semicolon between them when writing the code:

```
P(10N);(3N-3N-4N)
```

Social security numbers can be checked by Pattern; the code may be

```
P(9N)         or
P(3N-2N-4N)
```

or combined as

```
P(9N);(3N-2N-4N)
```

Here the delimiter is a dash but it may not always be so.

In the examples we have used:

    A   for Alphabetic characters
    N   for Numeric characters

Both types are represented by

    X   for Alphanumeric characters

Note that P code can have a combination of character types such as

```
P(3N-2A-2X)
```

7.4.3 GROUP EXTRACTION: G

The G (Group Extraction) code takes one or more parts from a value when the parts are separated by a non-numeric character, such as the VENDOR file item-ids (a period is between groups) and PHONE (a dash is between groups). The code consists of four parts:

Changing the Output via the Descriptor

1. G
2. the number of groups to skip before starting to extract (when no number is given G defaults to 0, skips no groups, and starts with the first group)
3. the separator character between groups
4. the number of contiguous, or adjoining, groups to take.

For our first application, output the area code from the values for PHONE: take the first group, the separator is a dash, and we want only one group, therefore the code is

```
G0-1
```

Since G defaults to 0 we can omit the 0 and

```
G-1
```

produces the same results. For convenience use the Descriptor PHONE. TEST and change line 7 to either of the G codes. Suppose you want to see the area codes for the VENDOR file sorted in ascending order. Enter

```
>SORT VENDOR BY PHONE.TEST PHONE.TEST <return>
```

Response

VENDOR	PHONE.TEST
ACE.99	184
PEAK.77	215
ZENITH.22	273
ACME.66	516
ACE.88	516
SUMMIT.33	516
TOPS.55	703

The G code has extracted the first group up to the dash in each data value, taken only one group, and then the extracted groups have been SORTed from low to high.

For the next Group Extraction take the second group in the item-id of the VENDOR file. This means we must skip the first group. Break the code into the required parts:

G   the code
1   skip 1 group before extracting
.   the separator character between groups
1   take 1 group

Together the parts are

```
G1.1
```

Type in the code on line 7 of the Descriptor ID.CHECK replacing whatever was on the line. Enter

```
>LIST VENDOR ID.CHECK <return>
```

Response

```
VENDOR     ID.CHECK

ACE.99     99
ACME.66    66
TOPS.55    55
  .
  .
  .
```

The output is the second group as you can easily see by comparison with the item-ids in the first column. The size of the group does not matter in the G code; the separation character, which can also be a blank, determines what is extracted.

The two examples worked because each time all of the data is in the same general format. G is not successful in a situation such as extracting the last names in the values for CONTACT in the VENDOR file because there are different formats. All of the values start with a two letter title but the next group varies because some data has one initial, some have two, and some have a first name. The last group in all cases is the last name but how can it be specified? In

```
Mr. J. J. King
```

the last name is the fourth group. In

    Ms. Ellen Van

the last name is the third group. The code executes from left to right and cannot go backwards. In order to use the G code with CONTACT there would have to be a uniform format such as title, first name, and last name for all the data values. This is an example of why you should decide what you want to produce from the data before setting up the file. And yet, if you do not anticipate your needs, you can restructure the file by adding a new attribute and Descriptor, and then rearranging the data values.

7.4.4 TEXT EXTRACTION OR TEXTRACT: T

The complete code name is Text Extraction which we have shortened to Textract. It outputs a specified number of characters starting from one end of a string. The simple form of T is

    T the number of characters to extract

It works according to the justification on line 9 of the Descriptor with the Textract code in it. When justification is L, the extraction starts with the left-most character in the string and proceeds toward the right for the given number of characters. When justification is R, the extraction starts with the right-most character in the string and proceeds to the left for the specified number of characters. The data values for ZIP in the VENDOR file are all the same length and will give uniform results. To extract three characters the code is

    T3

In these exercises test the code on line 7 of the Descriptor ZIP.TEST in the VENDOR file replacing whatever was previously on that line. Leave the R on line 9. In order to compare the output from the code T3 with the original complete data, specify both attributes to be output. Enter

    >LIST VENDOR ZIP.TEST ZIP <return>

The response follows.

VENDOR	ZIP.TEST	ZIP
ACE.88	456	23456
ACME.66	345	12345
ACE.99	A67	34A67
.		
.		

Inspect the output: T3 extracts 3 characters. The justification in ZIP.TEST is R therefore the code extracts the first 3 characters beginning at the right end of the string. Note that T works only on the number of characters and not the type of data as evident in the output for ACE.99.

To see the difference when the justification is changed replace the R on line 9 of ZIP.TEST with L. Enter the same command as before:

>LIST VENDOR ZIP.TEST ZIP <return>

Response

VENDOR	ZIP.TEST	ZIP
ACE.88	234	23456
ACME.66	123	12345
ACE.99	34A	34A67
.		
.		
.		

T3 extracts 3 characters just as it did before but this time the data is Left justified and T starts from the left end of the string. Change line 9 in ZIP.TEST back to R, which is proper for numeric data.

Next we come to an expanded format for T where processing can start from any position in the string (the simple form started from one end or the other) and extract the specified number of characters. This code consists of four elements:

1. T
2. the character position at which to start extracting
3. a comma

Changing the Output via the Descriptor 217

    4. the number of characters to extract

Parts 1 and 4 are what we have already used; Part 2 and the comma make it possible to start from any point in the string. The 4 part version of the T code <u>always</u> works from left to right regardless of the justification in the Descriptor.

As an application of the 4 part version of T output the second and third digits of the values for ZIP. To do so Textract must start with the 2nd character position and extract 2 characters. Thus the code is

    T2,2

It goes on line 7 in ZIP.TEST taking the place of whatever was on that line. Enter

    >LIST VENDOR ZIP.TEST ZIP <return>

Response

VENDOR	ZIP.TEST	ZIP
ACE.88	34	23456
ACME.66	23	12345
ACE.99	4A	34A67
.		
.		
.		

To review: both forms of the T code start with the letter T and extract the specified number of characters. However, using the simple form of T means that you must know the justification of the data because the extraction starts from that end of the string and proceeds in the opposite direction. In comparison, the long version always proceeds from left to right regardless of the justification in the Descriptor is and starts the extraction from any position in the string. For example, both forms of T can be used to output the same 3 left-most characters of the ZIP values. T3 was tested in the second Text Extract illustration and you saw the sample output. The same output is generated by

    T1,3

The results of T1,3 are the same whether the justification is L or R.

Place the code on line 7 of ZIP.TEST. Enter

>LIST VENDOR ZIP.TEST ZIP   <return>

Response

VENDOR	ZIP.TEST	ZIP
ACE.88	234	23456
ACME.66	123	12345
ACE.99	34A	34A67
.		
.		
.		

It is just a matter of using the code that outputs what you want to see. Leave ZIP.TEST with R on line 9 which is suitable for numeric data.

Consider also, as you learn new conversions and correlatives, that different codes can sometimes produce the same output. Group Extract requires uniformly formatted data values separated into parts; Textract is most effective when the data values are the same length. The values for PHONE in the VENDOR file are suited to both G and T. For instance, using the PHONE data values output the 3 digits for the exchange (the 3 numbers that follow the area code). The G code to do this must skip the first group, be given the dash separator, and extract 1 group:

G1-1

To save making a new Descriptor, temporarily put the G code on line 7 of the PHONE Descriptor. Replace the code with null after you see the ouput of the next command.

For T we must count each dash as a character, as well as the numbers, before directing where to start. Beginning at the left end of the string, extraction starts with the 5th character and 3 characters are to be taken. The code for Textract is

T5,3

Place this code on line 7 of the PHONE.TEST Descriptor. We name both of the Descriptors to compare their output, enter

>`LIST VENDOR PHONE PHONE.TEST` <return>

Response

VENDOR	PHONE	PHONE.TEST
PEAK.77	277	277
TOPS.55	890	890
ACME.66	123	123
.		
.		
.		

As expected, the output is the same for both codes in this particular example. Remember to remove the G code from PHONE or you will never see the complete data values.

So far we have been working with data values of uniform length. Textract can also be used with varied length data if part of the value is enough for you to see. Another application of T is to prevent wrapping when an oversized value continues on the next line. (This is not the same as T justification.) The T code takes the specified number of characters and ignores the balance. When the data is within the extraction number the complete value is output. To extract the first 15 characters in CO.NAME (which is left justified) the code is

    T15

For this illustration, temporarily put the code on line 7 in the Descriptor CO.NAME and remove it after seeing the results. Enter

>`LIST VENDOR CO.NAME` <return>

Response

VENDOR	CO.NAME
ACE.99	ACE TO TEST
TOPS.55	TOPS IN GADGETS
SUMMIT.33	THE SUMMIT FOR
.	

In the response:

ACE TO TEST	has 11 characters, falls within the 15 limit, and is output in full.
TOPS IN GADGETS	has 15 and just fits.
THE SUMMIT FOR	(including a blank after R) are the first 15 characters of THE SUMMIT FOR KITCHENWARE.

7.4.5 CONCATENATION: C

Concatenate is a common computer term that means link together. As a conversion/correlative it combines and outputs one or more attributes in the same file with optional user supplied text. For example the C (Concatenation) code can join the values for STREET, CITY, and STATE or output a word such as ATTENTION before the CONTACT person's name. Normally LIST uses a separate column for each attribute; with the C code the output is in a continuous stream.

We have been placing conversions/correlatives in either an A type Descriptor or an S type with the AMC of the A type on line 2. In both cases the AMC directed what raw data was to be used. Now we come to the first of three conversions/correlatives we cover that contain the attribute(s) to be referenced within the code itself. Thus the AMC on line 2 is of no importance with the C code. At this time we use a General Purpose Descriptor with the following conventions for each line; the format is

001	S	this is defined as an S type Descriptor
002	0	0 is generally used although this Descriptor does not reference the item-id. (Another AMC will not affect processing of the C code.)
003 through 006	null	
007	the line	on which the C code is placed
008	null	
009	L	Concatenation always works from left to right therefore justification is L or T
010	length	must allow for the Concatenated attributes as well as added text and so may be quite long

Attributes can be Concatenated in any sequence for output. They are referenced by their AMC numbers and output in the same order as in

Changing the Output via the Descriptor 221

the C code - from left to right. The system goes to the specified attribute, takes the raw data, and joins it with the next designated attribute or text. We cover Concatenating the results of conversions/correlatives in Section 7.4.8 Arithmetic.

The general format for Concatenation is

    C;

followed by any sequence of attribute number(s), and optional literal value(s) enclosed in double quotes. C and the elements in the code - attribute number(s) and literal(s) - must be separated by either the reserved semicolon ; which is not output, or any other non-numeric character which is output.

For the first application use the VENDOR file and Concatenate the value for STREET (attribute4), a comma, and the value for CITY (attribute5). The parts of the code are shown separately with explanations:

    C   the code to Concatenate
    ;   the reserved character used between the parts of the code. ; specifies that no character is to be printed in this position
    4   STREET is AMC 4 (attribute4)
    ,   the elements in the code must be separated. Use either the semicolon for no output character or some other character which will be output, such as the comma here
    5   CITY is AMC 5 (attribute5)

Put the parts together and the complete code is

    C;4,5

For demonstrating the code it is convenient to use an existing Descriptor; update STREET.UL as follows:

    001 S   remains as previously explained
    002 0   we are changing this to a General Purpose Descriptor
    003 through 006 null
    007 C;4,5   the concatenate Code defined above
    008 null
    009 L   justification; no change
    010 51   this is the total for the Concatenation:

STREET which is length 30
1 for the comma
CITY which is length 20

Enter

>`LIST VENDOR STREET.UL` <return>

Response

```
VENDOR     STREET.UL

TOPS.55    JANET LANE,CHARLES NECK
ACME.66    7 CHANDLER ST.,BILLINGS
PEAK.77    903 STEVENS AVE.,JOSEPH HARBOR
  .
  .
  .
```

The response has the item-ids in the first column, which is the normal default condition. The Concatenated data starts at the beginning of the column for STREET.UL and continues along the line: first STREET, then the comma, and last CITY as specified in the code.

To add an attribute to the output just add another separation character and the attribute number to the code. As separation character use a comma again. STATE is attribute2 so add

,2

to the code we already have, making line 7 in STREET.UL

C;4,5,2

By checking the test data we find that the length of 51 on line 10 allows for the additional 3 characters and need not be changed. Enter the same command as before to see how the change in the code alters the output.

>`LIST VENDOR STREET.UL` <return>

Response

```
VENDOR     STREET.UL

TOPS.55    JANET LANE,CHARLES NECK,MA
ACME.66    7 CHANDLER ST.,BILLINGS,IL
PEAK.77    903 STEVENS AVE.,JOSEPH HARBOR,IL
    .
```

The output is the three specified attributes with commas between.

For the next example combine text with an attribute. Let us insert the word (and a colon) ATTENTION: before the CONTACT person's name, also in the VENDOR file. Continue to use STREET.UL as a General Purpose Descriptor, but think how confusing it would be to keep a Descriptor with code that is totally unrelated to the name of the Descriptor. This is why Descriptors should be given logical names and set aside until their particular code is wanted.

The text is a literal value and must be enclosed in double quotes

```
"ATTENTION":
```

In the previous example the comma was the separation character, this time use the colon : which will be output. They will come before the value for CONTACT attribute7. Processing is from left to right and the sequence in the code is the same as for the output.

```
C;"ATTENTION":7
```

Place the code on line 7 and enter

><u>LIST VENDOR STREET.UL</u> <return>

Response

```
VENDOR     STREET.UL

ACE.88     ATTENTION:MS. C. MOORE
TOPS.55    ATTENTION:MS. ELLEN VAN
PEAK.77    ATTENTION.MR. R. M. DONALD
    .
    .
```

Blank spaces can also be Concatenated; they are treated as literal values and enclosed in double quotes. Each time the space bar is pressed you get one character space. Blanks can be alone as

```
" "
```

or combined with text as

```
"ATTENTION "
```

In any case, separation characters are necessary outside the quotes.

To output ATTENTION: followed by 2 spaces the entire literal must be inside the quotation marks

```
"ATTENTION:  "
```

Now the colon is no longer a separation character, so something else must be between the closing quote and the 7. The semicolon outputs no character and so we now have

```
"ATTENTION:  ";7
```

If you want the colon after the 2 spaces and before the CONTACT data value, the colon can be the separation character because it is outside the quotes as

```
"ATTENTION ":7
```

Place the code

```
C;"ATTENTION ":7
```

on line 7 and enter

```
>LIST VENDOR STREET.UL <return>
```

Response

```
VENDOR    STREET.UL

ACE.88    ATTENTION  :MS. C. MOORE
```

Changing the Output via the Descriptor 225

```
TOPS.55   ATTENTION  :MS. ELLEN VAN
PEAK.77   ATTENTION  :MR. R. M. DONALD
   .
   .
   .
```

Below is a review of Concatenation examples.

ATTRIBUTE NUMBER	DATA VALUE	CODE	OUTPUT
4	JANET LANE		
5	CHARLES NECK	C;4,5	JANET LANE,CHARLES NECK
4	JANET LANE		
5	CHARLES NECK		
2	MA	C;4,5,2	JANET LANE,CHARLES NECK,MA
7	MS. ELLEN VAN	C;"ATTENTION":7	ATTENTION:MS. ELLEN VAN

Always look for ways to combine procedures. As an illustration we might

1. SORT the VENDOR file BY STATE
2. output the CO.NAME Concatenated with ATTENTION: and the CONTACT name. The code for this will be placed in the Descriptor STREET.UL.
3. output the values for STREET, CITY, and STATE
4. suppress the column headings and the item-ids.

This is what we plan to do; now take one part at a time.

1. The verb is SORT, the filename is VENDOR, and the Sort key is BY STATE. So far we have

```
SORT VENDOR BY STATE
```

2. The C code requires these elements:

```
C
;
8                    (CO.NAME is AMC 8)
;
```

```
           " ATTENTION: "    (there are 2 spaces before the A and 1
                             space after the colon. For the length of
                             the literal count the blanks as well as the
                             characters. The total is 13 in this example.)
           ;
           7                 (CONTACT is AMC 7)
```

Together they are typed on line 7 of the Descriptor STREET.UL as

```
    C;8;" ATTENTION: ";7
```

The Descriptor with the code must have an output length that allows for all the Concatenated values. CO.NAME has a length of 35, the literal value length is 13, and CONTACT has 35. The total is 83 and must be on line 10 of STREET.UL; this attribute will be named for output in the command.

3. To output the values for STREET, CITY, and STATE just add them to the command sentence.

4. Column headings and item-ids are suppressed by the options (CI at the end of the command.

The complete command to enter is

```
>SORT VENDOR BY STATE STREET.UL STREET CITY STATE (CI <return>
```

Note that the format of the output is affected by the width of the screen which is generally 80 characters, or that of the paper which is generally 80 or 132. In this example the screen and the paper are not wide enough for the output to fit on a line horizontally, therefore it is forced into a vertical format.

```
    ZENITH   ATTENTION: DR. SIMON GUTH
    3-17 D ST.
    KENN CITY
    AR

    ACE TO TEST   ATTENTION: MS. JANFULCRO
    5 EXPERIMENT WAY
    TRYOUT
```

```
C4

ACME TECH INC.   ATTENTION: MR. J. J. KING
7 CHANDLER ST.
BILLINGS
IL

PEAK SUPPLY CO.   ATTENTION: MR. R. M. DONALD
903 STEVENS AVE.
JOSEPH HARBOR
IL

TOPS IN GADGETS   ATTENTION: MS. ELLEN VAN
JANET LANE
CHARLES NECK
MA

ACE BROS.   ATTENTION: MS. C. MOORE
3 KILGORE RD. SUITE 1202B
PETERBURG
NY

THE SUMMIT FOR KITCHENWARE   ATTENTION: MR. ROY POWELL
49 LINDA BLVD.
WARRENTON
SC
```

The response is SORTed by STATE in ascending order. Item-ids and column headings, which normally would be at the left end of each line in vertical format, have been suppressed. Since STREET.UL comes first in the command its output is first: the Concatenated elements - CO. NAME, the literal, and CONTACT. Each of the attributes is output one to a line, in the same sequence as in the command: STREET, CITY, and STATE.

Continue to experiment with combinations. Suppose we first Concatenate the raw data values for STREET and CITY, and then output the results in upper and lower case letters. This requires two codes: first to Concatenate the attributes and second to change the case with MCT.

In the C code this time use a blank as separation character between STREET (AMC 4) and CITY (AMC 5).

```
C;4 5
```

To show where one code ends and the next begins the system requires the same delimiting value that we used in a Tag exercise. Press

```
<control> ]
```

together. Only the bracket appears on the screen. Type in the second code

```
MCT
```

Line 7 of STREET.UL now has

```
C;4 5]MCT
```

Enter

```
>LIST VENDOR STREET.UL <return>
```

Response

```
VENDOR:SUMMIT.33
STREET.UL 49 Linda Blvd. Warrenton

VENDOR:PEAK.77
STREET.UL 903 Stevens Ave. Joseph Harbor

VENDOR:ZENITH.22
STREET.UL 3-17 D St. Kenn City

    .
    .
    .
```

The output above is in vertical format because STREET.UL has 83 on line 10 from the previous example.

Allowing space for all the Concatenated elements was advised earlier. To see what happens when the maximum length in the Descriptor does not provide enough room for the data assume that the code for line 7 is

Changing the Output via the Descriptor 229

```
C;"ATTENTION: ";7/8
```

with a slash as separation character. The literal value including the blank requires 10 spaces to which we must add 35 each for attribute7 and attribute8 making a total of 80 for the Concatenated values. When line 10 in STREET.UL has 45 for output length the command

```
LIST VENDOR STREET.UL
```

outputs

```
ACE.88      ATTENTION: MS. C. MOORE/ACE BROS.
SUMMIT.33   ATTENTION: MR. ROY POWELL/THE SUMMIT FOR KITC
            HENWARE
   .
   .
   .
```

The oversized Left justified value takes as much space as it can and then wraps to the next line. When line 10 is changed to allow for the longest value, the problem is eliminated.

7.4.6 RANGE: R

When a Descriptor is named in the command sentence, normally the data values for all of the items are output. In Chapter 5 selection criteria were introduced to output only those values that passed specified test(s); the values that did not meet the requirements were not output. Among the tests we used selection criteria to produce values that fell within a range: the relational operators >= specified the bottom of the range and <= defined the top of the range. Values below the bottom limit and above the top limit were ignored. neither the item-id(s) nor the value(s) for the attribute(s) were output.

The conversion/correlative R (Range) provides another way to extract values within a numeric range. R outputs all of the item-ids but only the attribute values that are within the specified range.

The term *parameter* specifies a limiting value. When used with Range, the minimum Range parameter is the bottom, or lowest value of the

Range; the maximum Range parameter is the top, or highest value of the Range. The format to specify one Range is

```
Rminimumvalue,maximumvalue
```

Note that there are no spaces between the numbers in the code but there must be a delimiter between them. A system delimiter cannot be used and the hyphen (minus sign) should be avoided since it may refer to the value, therefore the comma is a good choice. For example, to output values between 6 and 12 the R code is

```
R6,12
```

Can you guess what happens when the code is placed on line 7 of the A type Descriptor in the GADGETS file? QTY is as follows (unless you left the Tag on line 3).

QTY
001 A
002 2
003 through 006 null
007 R6,12
008 null
009 R
010 3

Enter

>LIST GADGETS QTY <return>

Response

GADGETS	QTY
50	
7	
20	
8	12
21	
9	10
42	
30	8
49	

The item-ids for the entire file are output. When there is no R code the QTY for each item is shown. But the QTY Descriptor now has a Range code which outputs only those QTY values that fall within the specified range i.e. between 6 and 12. Wherever a QTY value falls outside of the Range - less than 6 or more than 12 - a null value is returned (no value is output).

This is the same result as with Pattern: when the data does not meet the specifications it is not output. Again it is obvious that when these codes are placed in an A type Descriptor there is no way to see the data values that do not match the Pattern or fall within the Range.

You can use the A type Descriptor as we are doing purely to experiment and then remove the code after seeing how it works. In actual practice consider creating a Synonym Descriptor for the code if you will need it often. The alternative is to leave the A Descriptor as is and use a selection criteria phrase when necessary such as

```
WITH QTY >= "6" <= "12"
```

This accomplishes the same as the R code just illustrated and there is no risk of permanently walling in some of the data values. We continue to use QTY only because it is convenient.

It is a good idea to use a Tag in the Descriptor with the R code to define the output values. For example a column heading like

```
QUANTITY RANGE BETWEEN 6 & 12
```

better explains the output than QTY as in the preceding exercise. The Tag goes on line 3 in the QTY Descriptor and the output now becomes

```
GADGETS    QUANTITY RANGE BETWEEN 6 & 12

50
7
20
8                            12
21
9                            10
42
30                            8
49
```

By using a Tag you will remember why some of the items are displayed with null values.

You can also specify two Ranges to output data that falls within one or the other. Just place a semicolon ; after the first Range to delimit the parts of the code and define the minimum,maximum of the second Range. The complete format is

```
Rminimum,maximum;minimum,maximum
```

Suppose we expand our test code to output values that are either between 6 and 12, or between 20 and 25. The new code for line 7 is

```
R6,12;20,25
```

If you are working with a Tag it should be changed accordingly. Line 3 is now

```
QUANTITY RANGE BETWEEN 6 & 12]OR BETWEEN 20 & 25
```

Enter

```
>LIST GADGETS QTY <return>
```

Response

GADGETS	QUANTITY RANGE BETWEEN 6 & 12 OR BETWEEN 20 & 25
50	23
7	
20	
8	12
21	
9	10
42	
30	8
49	25

Replace the Tag on line 3 and the R code on line 7 with null values in the QTY Descriptor.

7.4.7 PUNCTUATE NUMERIC DATA: MR

For our purposes we use the MR code to format numeric data such as displaying a decimal, dollar sign, commas, and fill characters in the output. The data values for COST and SELL in the GADGETS file, entered as whole numbers, are appropriate test data for MR.

In many of the sample responses that follow, the column headings are not always extended to their full width. They serve only to identify the output.

Note that there are no spaces in any versions of the MR code. First let us output a decimal point with the COST values. The format is MR followed by the number of decimal places; up to 9 may be specified. Here we want the conventional two digits for cents, which means there are 2 decimal places. The code is

    MR2

Type the code on line 7 of the COST Descriptor. Always check the length on line 10 to allow for characters added by the code. When COST and SELL were created we anticipated adding the dollar sign and the period and so the length need not be changed at this time. Enter

    >LIST GADGETS COST <return>

Response

    GADGETS   COST

    50   1.10
    7   2.25
    9   0.75
    .
    .
    .

Item 9 with an original value of 75 (cents) now has a decimal point and a 0 printed to the left of it.

The next application of MR is to output a dollar sign at the left end of the string. The code for only a dollar sign is

    MR$

However the separate instructions can be combined. For a decimal with 2 digits to its right as above and also a dollar sign the code is

    MR2$

The sequence of the 2 and the $ must be as shown. Add the $ to the code on line 7 of COST. Enter

    >LIST GADGETS COST <return>

Response

```
GADGETS  COST

50       $1.10
7        $2.25
9        $0.75
.
.
.
```

MR can also insert a comma every three digits. For a comma only, the code is

    MR,

Sample output of MR, using a raw data value of 147550 is 147,550 (with no decimal). When there is no number after MR the system defaults to 0, which means there are no decimal places.

To output 2 decimal places and comma(s) the code is

    MR2,

The above raw data value is output as 1,475.50

The sequence of the symbols in the code must be correct but may be hard to remember at first. Take a moment and imagine any large number:

Changing the Output via the Descriptor   235

start at the right end of the string and count off the decimal places. Put in the decimal point and continue to the left, count three digits and add a comma as often as necessary. At the left end of the string add a dollar sign. This is the way to work with numeric data because it is right justified. Follow the same logic in setting out the code:

MR	names the code
2	count off 2 decimal places
,	insert commas
$	add $ at the left end

Combine the parts without any spaces between them:

    MR2,$

This code outputs the large test data string as

    $1,475.50

The MR code has other capabilities. You may have seen checks with dollar amounts printed like this:

    ***$23.45

The asterisk is called a *fill character* because it fills the unused positions in a specified number of places. For the first exercise use only the fill character and omit the dollar sign and the decimal. The values for the COST test data are 2 or 3 digits. Suppose we take a total of 6 character positions for output of the COST values and put an asterisk in each position that is not being used. If the value has 2 digits there will be 4 asterisks; if it has 3 digits there will be three asterisks. The total number of characters, in this case, is always 6.

The format for fill code is MR followed by parentheses enclosing the fill character and the total number of character positions. The code for the above is

    MR(*6)

Place this code on line 7 in COST. Note that line 10 with length 8 allows room for the total number of characters. Enter the following command.

>LIST GADGETS COST <return>

Response

GADGETS	COST
50	***110
7	***225
9	****75
3	147550
.	
.	
.	

Item 9 shows no leading 0 as it does with the decimal. A new item, 3, has been added. It has 6 characters for the data value, and so there is no space available for the fill character.

To figure output length start with the number on line 10 in the A Descriptor for the data in its original form. Each time you add to the output increase the length. For example, if you add a dollar sign and a decimal point add 2 to the length. If you want fill characters add the average number of fill characters to the original length to find the total positions. The test data values for COST are 3 or less characters. To this add an average of 3 fill characters, a $ and a decimal point making a total of 8. We already have 8 on line 10 of COST and there is enough space for the output. If allowance had not been made, line 10 would have to be changed.

Let us now write the code to output

    2 decimal places
    $
    * to fill 8 character positions:

MR2$(*8)

This replaces the previous code on line 7 of COST.

Enter

>LIST GADGETS COST <return>

Response

```
GADGETS        COST

   50        ***$1.10
    7        ***$2.25
    9        ***$0.75
    .
    .
    .
```

If you prefer to place the dollar sign at the left of the string move $ to inside the parentheses:

```
MR2($*8)
```

outputs

```
$****2.25
```

Here the $ is not considered in the number of character positions and so the output takes 9 places.

You may specify a blank as fill character by using the pound (or number) symbol #. The code

```
MR2($#8)
```

outputs 2 decimal places, blanks as fill characters for 8 positions and $ at the left end of the string.

Sample output is

```
$    1.10
$ 1475.50
```

As above, the $ is outside the number of character positions and the data requires 1 place more than the 8 specified.

Because line 10 has allowed for the increased length of the data with the MR codes or because the data had room to expand we have not had any problems. When line 10 does not provide enough space for the complete output you run into the situations outlined in Section 7.1 and 7.2 (Length and Justification). The data in COST is Right justified: oversized values would extend to the left and truncate whatever is in their path. If, for example, the item-ids are also Right justified they would be in the way of the oversized COST values and truncated by them. To illustrate, the COST Descriptor has

```
007 MR2($#8)
009 R
010 6
```

The GADGET item-ids have line

```
009 R
```

The command

```
LIST GADGETS COST
```

outputs

```
GADGETS...   COST
       $    1.10
       $    2.25
       $    0.75
       .
       .
       .
```

All of the item-ids have been truncated by the oversized COST values which do not fit in their column. This is because line 10 of the COST Descriptor has 6 and the data reqires 9 positions. The data for COST is output from right to left and overwrites the item-ids. As previously mentioned, allow for changes in output length when using conversions/ correlatives.

Data values that represent money are clearer with the dollar signs and the decimal points and so we make

```
MR2$
```

Changing the Output via the Descriptor

on line 7 part of the Descriptors for COST and SELL.

7.4.8 ARITHMETIC: A

A is the code for mathematical functions, which means that it performs calculations on numeric data. First we shall use it in a variety of arithmetic operations, and then explore its power to concatenate values. Up to now we have placed codes on line 7 making them conversions. In Section 7.4.11 we investigate the differences in processing lines 7 and 8 to decide where to put the code. The A code is generally used as a correlative and placed on line 8.

The arithmetic operators are expressed as symbols:

+ add
- subtract
* multiply
/ divide

Each of the operators dictates "what to do" (an action) and requires two *operands* or "what to do it to" (values to act upon) such as multiply two values or add one value to another. An operand can be either a value from a data file or a literal value. From using selection criteria phrases in Chapter 5, you recall how data values change with each item while the literal value (enclosed in double quotes) remains the same.

Begin our exercises with A by calculating the cost per dozen of the items in the GADGETS file. To do so take each data value for COST and multiply it by the literal value 12. The result is the cost for one dozen. The operation is translated into code as follows:

A	the Arithmetic code
6	take the value for COST which is attribute6 and
*	multiply it by
"12"	the literal 12

Combine the parts with no spaces between them:

A6*"12"

Create a General Purpose Descriptor to hold the code and give it a logical name like DOZ.COST.

```
    DOZ.COST
    001 S
    002 0
    003 through 006 null
    007 MR2$              the conversion to output 2 decimal places and
                          $
    008 A6*"12"           the A correlative goes on line 8
    009 R                 Right justification for numeric data
    010 10                allow for the results of the arithmetic, dollar
                          sign, and period
```

Enter

```
>LIST GADGETS COST DOZ.COST <return>
```

Response

```
GADGETS    COST    DOZ.COST

   7       $2.25   $27.00
   8       $1.00   $12.00
   9       $0.75   $9.00
   .
   .
   .
```

Keep in mind that multiplying any number by zero results in zero. Also, the system treats a null value as zero. In the example above, suppose an item had no value for COST. The output for DOZ.COST would be

```
$0.00
```

Never assume that you have written Arithmetic (or any other) code perfectly. Use some of the test data, perform the operation, and compare your results to the output. You may discover that your instructions are not quite what you want done and must be corrected.

The format of the Arithmetic code changes slightly when the attribute is referenced by name instead of number as above. Replace the attribute number 6 with

N   take the value for
(COST) the attributename

the balance of the code is the same as before

```
*"12"
```

Combine the parts to calculate the price per dozen into

```
AN(COST)*"12"
```

and type it on line 8 in DOZ.COST. How does the file look sorted on DOZ.COST in ascending order? Enter

```
>SORT GADGETS BY DOZ.COST DOZ.COST <return>
```

Response

GADGETS	DOZ.COST
9	$9.00
8	$12.00
50	$13.20
20	$18.00
42	$24.00
49	$25.20
7	$27.00
21	$30.00
30	$36.00

The A code, like C, specifies within the code itself the attribute(s) to be processed. However there are two important differences between C (Concatenation) and A (Arithmetic):

1. C code can reference any attribute and is independent of the Descriptor it is in. The A code references an attribute in two ways: either by the attribute number where the raw data value is used or by the N notation: N(Descriptor name). In the latter case, the Descriptor named within the parentheses is called and its correlative code is processed; this result is returned to the original A code. Thus A code cannot call itself and is therefore placed in a General Purpose Descriptor.

2. C code uses only the number of the attribute - the AMC on line 2 of the attribute's Descriptor. However, the A code uses either the number or the name of an attribute, such as 6 or COST.

Another useful calculation is multiplying the cost of each item by the quantity to produce the extended dollar amount at cost. This time both operands are data values; there is no literal value. Break the operation into parts:

A	the Arithmetic code
N	take the value for
(QTY)	the attributename
*	multiply it by
N	the value for
(COST)	the attributename.

Put the parts together without spaces and the code is

AN(QTY)*N(COST)

This correlative will be used often so create a General Purpose Descriptor for it as follows:

EXT.UNIT.COST
001 S
002 0
003 through 006 null
007 MR2$
008 AN(QTY)*N(COST)
009 R
010 10

Enter

>LIST GADGETS QTY COST EXT.UNIT.COST <return>

Response

GADGETS	QTY	COST	EXT.UNIT.COST
50	23	$1.10	$25.30

7	1	$2.25	$2.25
20	19	$1.50	$28.50
.			
.			
.			

A practical application of A code is to calculate the extended unit selling price for each item: multiply QTY by SELL. The only change in the code is to replace COST with SELL i.e.

    AN(QTY)*N(SELL)

Create another General Purpose Descriptor for this operation.

EXT.UNIT.SELL
001 S
002 0
003 through 006 null
007 MR2$
008 AN(QTY)*N(SELL)
009 R
010 11

The new Descriptor produces the results of the multiplication. By sorting the file on this calculation - the extended unit selling values - we can easily compare the dollar amounts for each item and see what makes up our GADGETS inventory. Enter

    >SORT GADGETS BY EXT.UNIT.SELL EXT.UNIT.SELL <return>

Response

GADGETS	EXT.UNIT.SELL
7	$4.50
9	$15.00
21	$20.00
8	$24.00
50	$51.75
30	$52.00
20	$61.75
42	$63.75
49	$100.00

Although we are using examples of business applications the arithmetic can be adapted for any purpose.

To illustrate subtraction using the test data, find the markup (mark-on) or the difference between the cost price and the selling price of an item. The calculation takes the SELLing price and subtracts from it the COST price. The result is the markup in cents; when the appropriate MR code is in the Descriptor, the output is in dollars and cents. The Arithmetic correlative is

>   A   the Arithmetic code
>   N   take the value for
>   (SELL) the attributename
>   -   subtract from it
>   N   the value for
>   (COST) the attributename.

Together

```
AN(SELL)-N(COST)
```

Before creating a new Descriptor for the code consider what else can be included in it. We can put a Tag on line 3 as a reminder of how the output was calculated

```
SELL-COST
= MARKUP $
```

The output represents money and will be clearer to read as suggested above when there are dollar signs and decimal points, and so add the conversion on line 7

```
MR2$
```

Create the Descriptor

>   MARKUP$
>   001 S
>   002 0
>   003 SELL-COST]= MARKUP $
>   004 through 006 null
>   007 MR2$

```
008 AN(SELL)-N(COST)
009 R
010 6
```

Enter

> `LIST GADGETS SELL COST MARKUP$ <return>`

Response

GADGETS	SELL	COST	SELL-COST = MARKUP $
7	$4.50	$2.25	$2.25
20	$3.25	$1.50	$1.75
8	$2.00	$1.00	$1.00
.			
.			
.			

Division is performed by the Arithmetic code but it returns only the integer (whole number) and not the remainder. For example, 3 divided by 2 is 1 and not 1.5; any result between 0 and 1 is output as 0. As an exercise in division let us calculate the markup percent on the GADGET items. The first operation has already been done by the correlative in MARKUP$ which figures the difference between the cost price and the selling price (the computing is on the data values which are in cents, the dollar signs and decimals are not added until the result is ready for output). The next procedure is to divide the markup amount by the selling price.

Let us review what happens when we figure percentages. Take a whole pie and cut it into portions of one half pie and 2 quarters. Separately each piece is a fractional part of the pie; together the pieces make the whole pie. When you express the fractions as hundreths the half pie is .50 and the two quarter pieces are each .25; the total is 1.00 pie.

Percent means parts to 100, therefore multiply each part by 100 and display the percent sign % with the results. The half was .50 and is now 50%, the quarter pieces were .25 and become 25% each. The total is 100% or the whole pie.

Break the markup operation into the same steps as the pie percents. Based on what we know of the A code so far it would seem that the code should start with

```
AN(MARKUP$)/N(SELL)
```

Do the work of the computer using test data values such as for item 49.

```
MARKUP$ 190
SELL    400
```

The arithmetic is 190/400 and the result is .475 As people we then multiply .475 by 100 to change the fraction to a percent. But the computer cannot do this; it changes a fraction that is less than 1 to 0. Processing stops because 0 cannot be multiplied by 100 (or any other number). Solve the problem by multiplying the value for MARKUP$ by 100 <u>before</u> dividing by the value for SELL.

```
AN(MARKUP$)*"100"/N(SELL)
```

Using the same test data the arithmetic is

190*100 = 19000
/400 and the result is the integer 47 (the remainder is not shown).

Thus we have checked the code and enter it on line 8 of the new Descriptor

    MARKUP%
    001 S
    002 0
    003 through 007 null
    008 AN(MARKUP$)*"100"/N(SELL)
    009 R
    010 3

Enter

```
>LIST GADGETS COST SELL MARKUP$ MARKUP%  <return>
```

Response

GADGETS	COST	SELL	MARKUP$	MARKUP%
50	$1.10	$2.25	$1.15	51
20	$1.50	$3.25	$1.75	53
49	$2.10	$4.00	$1.90	47
.				
.				
.				

The actual result of the arithmetic for item 49 was 47.5 but only 47 - the integer - was returned; the fractional part of the answer was ignored. When a numeric value has a fraction we often *round* it to the nearest whole number. A fraction of .5 or more is rounded up to the next integer thus 47.5 is rounded to 48. A fraction of less than .5 does not change the integer, for example 47.2 is rounded to 47. Those familiar with rounding do this quickly in their heads without a formula but what they actually do is add .5 to a value and then take the integer and drop the fraction as in the following examples.

```
the starting number is   47.2    47.5    47.8
add .5                   +.5     +.5     +.5
the total is             47.7    48.0    48.3
the output integer is    47      48      48
```
which is the starting number after rounding.

In short, the whole number after adding .5 is the same as the number we started with after it is rounded. This is the theory, but it cannot be executed by the system which works only with integers. Therefore we must change .5 to a whole number before the computer can add it. This is called *scaling* and we multiply .5 by 10 to get 5, a usable whole number. To maintain the relationship between the numbers in the operation we must also muliply 100 by 10. The very last step is to *descale* the calculation: in the example divide by 10 to offset multiplying by 10 earlier.

The code now has two distinct parts. The first steps are grouped for processing together within parentheses:

> A   the Arithmetic code
> (beginning of the processing segment, the operations within the parentheses are to be completed before continuing

N	take the value for
(MARKUP$)	the attributename
*	multiply it by
"1000"	1000
/	then divide the result by
N	the value for
(SELL)	the attributename
+	then add to the result
"5"	5
)	end of the segment

continue the code with the next calculation

/	divide the result of the first part by
"10"	10

Note that two pairs of parentheses are *nested* or lie within the outer pair. (SELL) is the name of the attribute whose value is to be used; (MARKUP$) is an attribute that contains other Arithmetic code whose results will be used in this calculation. MARKUP$ is being called by MARKUP%. Up to 7 calls or levels are permitted and they provide enormous flexibility when an operation must be split into parts. All of the Descriptors named in the code must be in the same file.

The code above is put together

    A(N(MARKUP$)*"1000"/N(SELL)+"5")/"10"

Walk through the operation using the data values for item 49. The first part is

    190*1000/400 = 475

next, round the result 475

    +5 = 480

last, descale the result 480

    /10 = 48

48 is the rounded number or integer for 47.5. Apparently the code works;

type it on line 8 in MARKUP%. Enter

>LIST GADGETS MARKUP% <return>

Response

GADGETS	MARKUP%
50	51
20	54
49	48
.	
.	
.	

Note that the data values for items 20 and 49 have changed as a result of the rounding by the new code.

As mentioned earlier the A code can also concatenate text. To output a % sign after the values in the MARKUP% column add to the existing code:

: the separation character is a colon
"%" the literal value % enclosed in double quotes.

The complete code on line 8 is now

A(N(MARKUP$)*"1000"/N(SELL)+"5")/"10":"%"

Enter

>LIST GADGETS MARKUP% <return>

Response

GADGETS	MARKUP%
50	51%
20	54%
49	48%
.	
.	
.	

Processing a combination of arithmetic operators is governed by *precedence* or an established sequence. Multiplication and division are performed first; addition and subtraction second. When two operations have the same precedence they are executed from left to right. Operations grouped together within parentheses are performed first and the result used for continuing the calculation.

Let us combine some of the procedures we have covered to output a practical report.

1. SORT the GADGETS file by NAME.
2. Output the EXT.UNIT.SELL value for each item and the subtotal amount for each NAME. Print the text SUBTOTAL FOR on the break line for NAME. To make room for the additional text, line 10 in the NAME Descriptor should be at least 25.
3. Print text on the GRAND-TOTAL line: TOTAL INVENTORY AT SELLING PRICE. The GADGETS Descriptor for the item-ids is Left justified; there will be no attribute value on the last line of the response and so it is not necessary to change line 10.
4. Underline the last value above the total.

The long command sentence requires continuation on the next line. Use

```
<control> <shift> _ <return>
```

where necessary. The colon prompt : appears on the next line for the balance of the command. Enter

```
>SORT GADGETS BY NAME BREAK-ON NAME "SUBTOTAL FOR 'V'" TOTAL <control> <shift> _ <return>
:EXT.UNIT.SELL  GRAND-TOTAL  "TOTAL  INVENTORY  AT  SELLING  PRICE  'U'"  <return>
```

Response

GADGETS	NAME	EXT.UNIT.SELL
50	FORK	$51.75
	SUBTOTAL FOR FORK	$51.75
20	LADLE	$61.75
21	LADLE	$20.00
	SUBTOTAL FOR LADLE	$81.75

```
42          SPATULA                    $63.75
49          SPATULA                   $100.00
            SUBTOTAL FOR SPATULA      $163.75

 7          SPOON                       $4.50
 8          SPOON                      $24.00
 9          SPOON                      $15.00
            SUBTOTAL FOR SPOON         $43.50

30          WHISK                      $52.00
            SUBTOTAL FOR WHISK         $52.00
                                      ------
     TOTAL INVENTORY AT SELLING PRICE $392.75
```

Thus far we have demonstrated the A code almost entirely for arithmetic operations. We used it once to concatenate the % sign to ouput. Calculations are not required for the A code; it can also concatenate the results of other processing by use of the N notation as in N(attributename). For example, output the second group of numbers in the PHONE value along with the first three digits in the ZIP. Three different Descriptors in the VENDOR file, each with the appropriate code are needed to do this.

1. Group Extract from the PHONE value
2. Textract from the ZIP value
3. Concatenate the above values for output.

1. Start with the Group Extract. The code must:

skip 1 Group
show the separation character a dash -
take 1 Group which combine as

G1-1

The Descriptor is

PHONE.TEST
001 S   no change
002 6   no change
003 through 007 null (remove old code from line 7)
008 G1-1

```
009 R          no change
010 13         no change
```

2. To Textract the first 3 characters of the ZIP value:

start with the first character
take 3 characters or

```
T1,3
```

The Descriptor is

```
ZIP.TEST
001 S          no change
002 3          no change
003 through 007 null (remove old code from line 7)
008 T1,3
009 R          no change
010 5          no change
```

3. The A code can concatenate the results of the two correlatives above with N(attributename) for each value. The first is

```
AN(PHONE.TEST)
```

The A code calls PHONE.TEST and takes the result after the G correlative has been applied. Before giving the next attribute consider making the output clearer by placing 2 blanks, a slash, and 2 blanks between the values. These are literal values and enclosed in double quotes as

```
"  /  "
```

The reserved character, the colon : separates the elements in the A code, therefore so far we have

```
AN(PHONE.TEST):"  /  "
```

The next value is from the ZIP.TEST Descriptor and it too must be separated by a colon

```
:N(ZIP.TEST)
```

ZIP.TEST is called by the A code and the result of the Textract correlative is taken for output. The complete A code is

```
AN(PHONE.TEST):" / ":N(ZIP.TEST)
```

and it goes on line 8 of

STREET.UL
001 S   as we already have
002 0   as we already have
003 through 007 null(remove old code from line 7)
008 AN(PHONE.TEST):" / ":N(ZIP.TEST)
009 L
010 12   this allows enough room for the Concatenated values

The complete instruction is in the A correlative in STREET.UL. It fetches the values from the other Descriptors, therefore is the only one to be named for output. Enter

```
>LIST VENDOR STREET.UL <return>
```

Response

VENDOR	STREET.UL
ACE.88	123 / 234
TOPS.55	890 / 678
PEAK.77	277 / 123
.	
.	
.	

7.4.9 TRANSLATION: TFILE

After creating the VENDOR file in Chapter 5 we noted that the data values for the attribute VENDOR in the GADGETS file are the same as the item-ids in the VENDOR file. The common data made it possible to travel from the GADGETS file to the VENDOR file. File Translation, or Tfile, uses the same common data values to move from an attribute in the original file to an item in another file. Once there it can "translate" any attribute value to the output. Using our test data, GADGETS is the original file and VENDOR is the translated file. The coincidence that VENDOR is the name of an attribute in the GADGETS file and also the name of a file is no problem as long as you are aware which one you are referring to.

The first step is to decide what attribute to translate from the VENDOR file; suppose we take STATE which is attribute number 2. From now on we work with the original file GADGETS. The instruction becomes the Tfile code which is placed in the VENDOR Descriptor.

Walk through these simplified processing steps and assume the system is reading item 21 in the GADGETS file. The Descriptor for VENDOR instructs it to:

> take the data value which is TOPS.55
> go to the VENDOR file
> go to the item-id for the same value: TOPS.55
> read across the row to attribute2 which is STATE
> the value is MA
> take this translated value back
> and output the translated value MA instead of the original value TOPS.55.

A diagram of the steps is below.

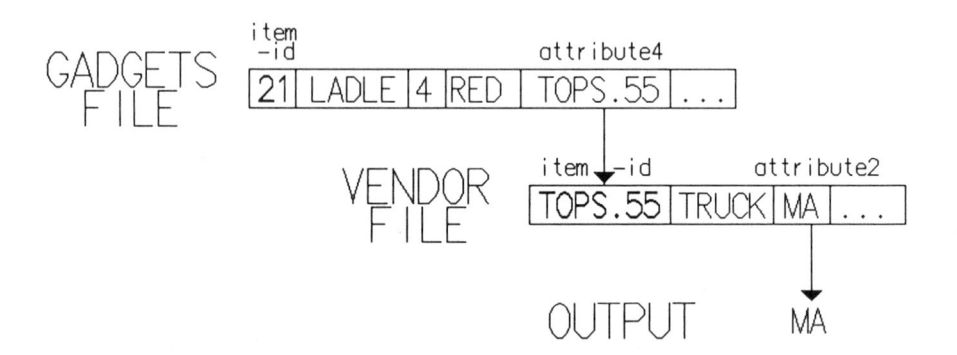

```
                    item
                    -id                    attribute4
GADGETS           |21|LADLE|4|RED|TOPS.55|...|
  FILE
                                  item -id          attribute2
                    VENDOR       |TOPS.55|TRUCK|MA|...|
                     FILE
                                                   |
                                                   ▼
                                  OUTPUT          MA
```

Any attribute value can be taken from the translated file to replace the original value as long as the original attribute in the original file is an item-id in the translated file. If an item in the GADGETS file has a null value for VENDOR or the item has a value but there is no equal item-id in the VENDOR file, the code returns a null value because it could not complete the translation.

Changing the Output via the Descriptor

Tfile, like C and A, specifies within the code which attribute to reference. The format is

T	Translate from
filename	translated file
;	separation character
X	return null if there is no value
; ;	this section is not used by us at this time
attributenumber	attributenumber to fetch from the translated file

There are no spaces between the parts; they are combined as

    Tfilename;X;;attributenumber

For the example under discussion the code is

    TVENDOR;X;;2

As you can guess we create a new Descriptor for the Tfile code to use when we want it otherwise we would always get the result of the Translation and never see the original data value. It is helpful to name the Descriptor with the combination of the translated filename VENDOR, a period because no embedded blanks are allowed, and the name of the attribute to be translated: STATE. This Descriptor called VENDOR.STATE with the Tfile code belongs in the original file GADGETS.

    VENDOR.STATE
    001 S
    002 4
    003 through 007 null
    008 TVENDOR;X;;2
    009 L   the same as in the translated attribute
    010 2   the same as in the translated attribute

To output the vendor's state, the system works through the VENDOR.STATE Descriptor in GADGETS. The Descriptor references the VENDOR file for us. Enter

    >LIST GADGETS VENDOR.STATE <return>

The response follows.

GADGETS	VENDOR.STATE
7	IL
8	NY
21	MA
.	
.	
.	

VENDOR.STATE outputs the translated values for STATE instead of the original values for VENDOR. Any other GADGETS file attributes can be output by naming them in the command.

Next translate a different attribute from the VENDOR file: the PHONE attribute6. The new Descriptor, VENDOR.PHONE, is another Synonym for attribute4 VENDOR in the GADGETS file. Translations always start from the attribute value in the original file and so the AMC on line 2 is 4 again.

The previous Tfile code referenced attribute2 STATE; this time reference attribute6 PHONE. Only the last part of the code with the attribute's number has to be changed from 2 to 6; the rest of the code is the same as before.

```
TVENDOR;X;;6
```

The Descriptor is

```
VENDOR.PHONE
001 S                    this is an S Descriptor for
002 4                    VENDOR attribute4
003 through 007 null
008 TVENDOR;X;;6 the Tfile code
009 R                    the same as the translated attribute
010 13                   the same as the translated attribute
```

Enter

```
>LIST GADGETS VENDOR.PHONE <return>
```

Response

Changing the Output via the Descriptor 257

```
GADGETS      VENDOR.PHONE

8            516-123-8911
21           703-890-1234
9            215-277-0123
 .
 .
```

Tfile can be combined with another code. For example, translate the value for PHONE and then use Group Extract to output the area code. In essence the instruction in the VENDOR.PHONE Descriptor is

> first go and fetch the value for attribute6 PHONE (apply the Tfile code) then apply the G code:
> extract the first group (do not skip any groups)
> the separator character is a dash -
> take 1 group. The code is either G0-1 or G-1 (default to skipping 0 groups)
> output the results.

The Tfile code remains the same. Before adding the G code type in the delimiter

```
<control> ]
```

Only the bracket] shows on the screen. The two codes for line 8 are

```
TVENDOR;X;;6]G0-1
```

Enter

```
>LIST GADGETS VENDOR.PHONE <return>
```

Response

```
GADGETS      VENDOR.PHONE

8            516
21           703
9            215
 .
 .
```

In summary, always work through the attribute in the original file to reference the item-id in the translated file. The Synonym Descriptor is in the original file and has the Tfile code. This is the only reference to the translated file.

7.4.10 DATE: D

The Date code is very different from all of the other codes. We are used to seeing dates written in formats like 11/25/86, or 11-25-86, or 25 NOV 1986. These are examples of *external format*, which we normally use. This form takes up too much storage space and is cumbersome for date comparisons. By storing date values as integers, the system saves space, provides an easy method of comparing dates, and also gives us a variety of formats for outputting date values. The numbers we entered as DATE data values in the GADGETS file were in internal format. Note that the attribute named DATE is in no way related to the Date code.

All dates are reckoned from the base date DEC 31 1967 which is date 0. Dates before then are negative numbers such as DEC 30 1967 which is date -1 in internal format. All dates after the base date are positive numbers (the + sign is omitted); JAN 1 1968 is date 1. For example, the external date 11/25/85 is internal date 6539. Dates must be changed from external to internal format before they can be entered as data to be used with the Date code. Some systems have a special utility program to change external to internal format and vice versa. To see if your system has this utility enter

>DATE 0 <return>

If the response is

31 DEC 1967

you have the Date utility; you entered internal date 0 and the output is the external format of the date. Skip to Output Options and omit the next instructions.

If the response to the command above is similar to

[3] VERB?

you do not have the Date utility. The following steps create a short BAS-

Changing the Output via the Descriptor

IC language program which will serve as a substitute for the Date utility. For those who do not have the utility and do not wish to use the program an alternative for handling dates is suggested at the end of the section, however this does not permit use of the Date code.

The following procedure must be copied exactly as shown. Enter

>CREATE-FILE BP 1,1 1,1 <return>

Response

[417] FILE 'BP' CREATED; BASE = 43493, MODULO = 1, SEPAR = 1.
[417] FILE 'BP' CREATED; BASE = 43675, MODULO = 1, SEPAR = 1.

As noted in Chapter 3 the BASE numbers will be different for each user. On any system except Microdata (McDonnell Douglas) continue as below. Those with Microdata omit the next four steps and skip to the command ED BP DATE.

Enter

>ED MD BP <return>

Response

TOP
.

Enter

001 <return>

Response

D
.

Enter

R/D/DC/ <return>

The response follows.

```
001 DC
.
```

Enter

```
FI <return>
```

Response

```
'BP' FILED.
```

Enter

```
>ED BP DATE <return>
```

Response

```
NEW ITEM
TOP
.
```

Enter

```
I <return>
```

You are now in Input mode in the Editor and will see consecutively numbered lines with the + sign appear, one after another as you go. Enter the following for each line of the program:

```
001+PRINT "ENTER DATE IN INTERNAL OR EXTERNAL FORMAT" <return>
002+INPUT DATA: <return>
003+IF NUM(DATA) THEN <return>
004+PRINT "EXTERNAL FORMAT IS ": OCONV(DATA,"D2/") <return>
005+END ELSE PRINT " INTERNAL FORMAT IS ": ICONV(DATA,"D2/") <return>
006+END <return>
007+END <return>
008+<return>
```

Response

```
TOP
.
```

Changing the Output via the Descriptor

Enter

    <u>FI</u> <return>

Response

    'DATE' FILED.
    >

Enter

    <u>BASIC BP DATE</u> <return>

Response

    ******
    [241] PROGRAM 'DATE' COMPILED! 1 FRAMES USED.

or

    PROGRAM 'DATE' COMPILED. 1 FRAME/S USED.

Enter

    ><u>CATALOG BP DATE</u> <return>

Response

    [244] 'DATE' CATALOGED!

The program is ready to use. We test it twice, first typing in a date value in external format to be changed to output format. Enter

    ><u>DATE</u> <return>

Response

    ENTER DATE IN INTERNAL OR EXTERNAL FORMAT
    ?

Enter the following response.

5/17/86 <return>

Response

    INTERNAL FORMAT IS 6712

Next change the internal to external. Enter

>DATE <return>

Response

    ENTER DATE IN INTERNAL OR EXTERNAL FORMAT
    ?

Enter

6712 <return>

Response

    EXTERNAL FORMAT IS 05/17/86

The date values that were entered for the GADGETS items had already been changed to their internal format when they were given earlier in the chapter. If they had not been changed we would have used the above DATE command to figure the internal format before typing in the date values.

OUTPUT OPTIONS

Either the built-in utility or the program you have just created make it possible to choose a Date conversion for the output format of the date values. The decision whether to place the code in the A type Descriptor or to create a Synonym Descriptor is based on the same considerations as before. Code to output day, month, and year is probably all right in the A type; code for day and month, or year only may be more suited to an S type. The Date code must be a conversion on line 7 in the Descriptor; for the test data it goes in the Descriptor DATE in the GADGETS file. The output length of 11 allows enough space for the codes illustrated. A list of frequently used Date codes is below. For other variations see your user reference manual.

CODE	OUTPUTS	EXAMPLE
D	2 digit day 3 letter month 4 digit year	01 JAN 1987
D/	2 digit day/2 digit month/4 digit year	01/01/1987
D2/	2 digit day/2 digit month/2 digit year	01/01/87
D-	as D/ above with a dash instead of a slash	01-01-1987
D0	2 digit day-2 digit month (no year)	01-01
DY	4 digit year	1987

Simple commands with LIST and SORT output the date according to the code. For example when line 7 of the Descriptor DATE has D the command

```
LIST GADGETS DATE
```

outputs

```
GADGETS   DATE

7         09 JAN 1986
9         03 OCT 1985
49        19 SEP 1985
.
.
.
```

Dates stored in external format require more storage space and do not permit use of the Date code. You must treat the values for date as we did those for PHONE and make a standard pattern. Let each part of the date value consist of 2 numbers separated by a symbol such as the slash for clarity. The sequence must be:

year as 2 numbers/month as 2 numbers/day as 2 numbers

which becomes

```
YY/MM/DD
```

or a data value like

```
86/01/16
```

Note that leading zeroes are used in this format.

The 4 digit date values that were entered earlier in this chapter will be of no value to those without the utility or the program. Change the values to the slash format described above. The Descriptor DATE does not have to be altered. Handle the data as you would any other with LIST and SORT.

7.4.11 PROCESSING WITH SELECTION CRITERIA

Conversion and correlative codes and what they output have been shown, but all we know so far is that a correlative is applied before a conversion. To see the differences in execution sequence let us walk through the processing steps.

Start with a simple LIST command. Assume that the Descriptor for the attribute ZIP.TEST has Textract code T1,3 to extract the first 3 characters of the data values for ZIP.TEST.

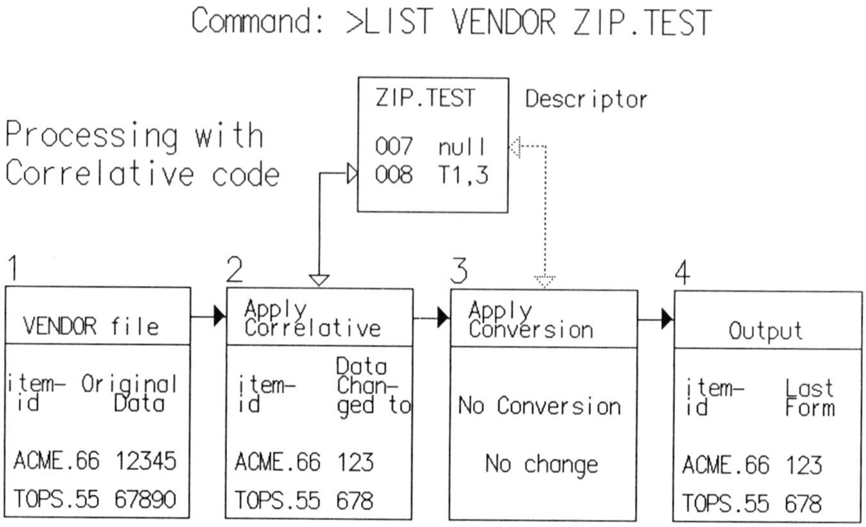

FIGURE 7.1A: PROCESSING WITH A CORRELATIVE AND NO SELECTION CRITERIA

Changing the Output via the Descriptor

The sample command is

```
LIST VENDOR ZIP.TEST
```

Follow across the correlative code diagram 7.1A where the code is a correlative on line 8 in the ZIP.TEST Descriptor.

1. Read the item: item-id ACME.66 and the raw data value for ZIP is 12345.
2. Apply the correlative: the data value is changed to 123 by the code.
3. Apply the conversion: there is none (null on line 7) and therefore the value is not changed, it remains in its last form 123.
4. Output the most recent form of the data: item-id ACME.66, data value 123.

Each item in the file is read and processed in the same way.

Next go to the conversion code diagram 7.1B. Here we have the same code but it is now a conversion on line 7 and line 8 has a null value. Follow the steps as before.

Command: >LIST VENDOR ZIP.TEST

Processing with Conversion code

ZIP.TEST Descriptor
007 11,3
008 null

1 VENDOR file	2 Apply Correlative	3 Apply Conversion	4 Output
item-id Original Data	No Correlative	item-id Data Changed to	item-id Last Form
ACME.66 12345	No change	ACME.66 123	ACME.66 123
TOPS.55 67890		TOPS.55 678	TOPS.55 678

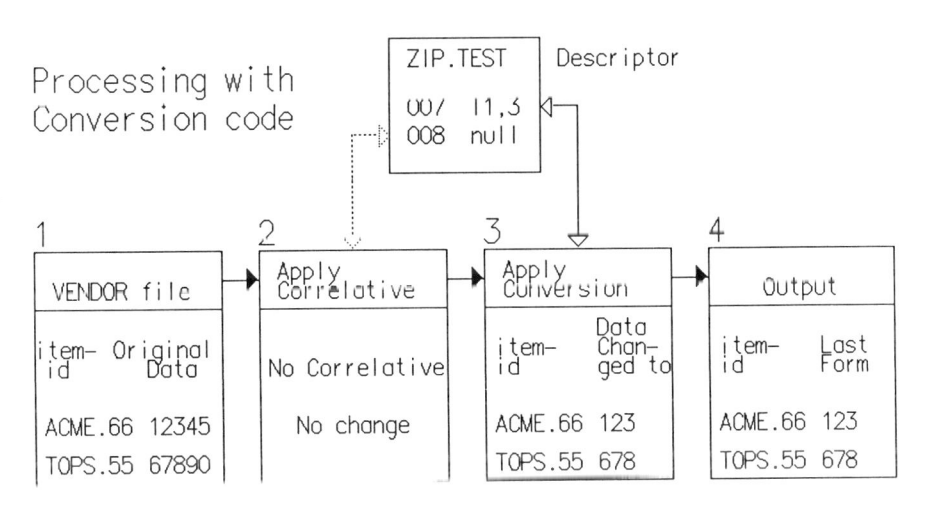

FIGURE 7.1B: PROCESSING WITH A CONVERSION AND NO SELECTION CRITERIA

1. Read the item: item-id ACME.66, raw data value 12345.
2. Apply the correlative: there is none (null on line 8) and the data stays as it was.
3. Apply the conversion: the data is changed to 123.
4. Output the last form of the data: item-id ACME.66, data value 123.

As you see the output in both examples is the same. When there are no selection criteria it does not matter whether the code is applied as a conversion or a correlative.

Carefully examine what happens when a selection criterion phrase is added to the command sentence. Now another step is inserted in the middle of the processing sequence. Note that we are concerned only about selection criteria that refer to Descriptors with codes in them; other attributes are processed in the usual way. Normally selection criteria are applied <u>after</u> the correlative on line 8, and <u>before</u> the conversion on line 7. However, three of the codes we have tried are exceptions to the general rule: MC, MR, and D and they are covered separately. The following processing sequence applies to all of the other codes we have discussed.

For the next illustration continue to use the ZIP.TEST Descriptor with the code to output the first 3 characters of the data value as above. Use the same command sentence but add the selection criterion phrase

```
WITH ZIP.TEST > "500"
```

The complete command is now

```
LIST VENDOR WITH ZIP.TEST > "500" ZIP.TEST
```

We want the system to apply the code to each data value for the zip and then compare the results to 500. The last step is output those values that are greater than 500; ignore those less than 500. What difference does it make if the code is on line 7 or line 8? With selection criteria in the command the position of the code is vital to produce valid output.

Walk through the processing steps. The code and the data are exactly as they were, the only change is the addition of the selection criterion. First examine the correlative code diagram 7.2A where the code is on line 8.

Changing the Output via the Descriptor

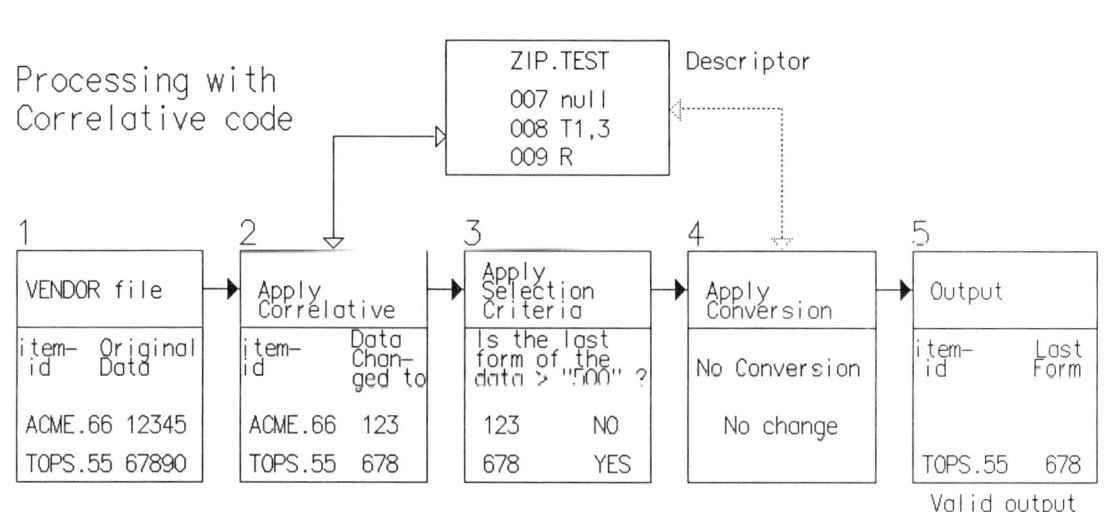

Command: >LIST VENDOR WITH ZIP.TEST > "500" ZIP.TEST

```
Processing with                ZIP.TEST      Descriptor
Correlative code               007 null
                               008 T1,3
                               009 R
```

```
1                2                 3                  4               5
VENDOR file      Apply             Apply              Apply           Output
                 Correlative       Selection          Conversion
                                   Criteria
item-  Original  item-   Data      Is the last        No Conversion   item-     Last
id     Data      id      Chan-     form of the                        id        Form
                         ged to    data > "500" ?
ACME.66 12345    ACME.66   123     123       NO       No change
TOPS.55 67890    TOPS.55   678     678       YES                      TOPS.55   678
                                                                      Valid output
```

FIGURE 7.2A: PROCESSING SEQUENCE FOR TEXTRACT CORRELATIVE WITH SELECTION CRITERIA

1. Read the item: item-id ACME.66, raw data value 12345.
2. Apply the correlative: the data is changed to 123.
3. Apply the selection criterion: is the last form of the data (123) greater than 500? No. The data does not pass the test and is ignored. Go to the next item and follow the same steps.
1. Read the item: item-id TOPS.55 and the value 67890.
2. Apply the correlative: the value is changed to 678.
3. Apply the selection criterion: is the last form of the data (678) greater than 500? Yes. Continue processing.
4. Apply the conversion: there is none therefore the value remains the same.
5. Output the latest form of the data: item-id TOPS.55, data value 678.

The results are valid for the items shown and will be for all the items in the file. This is true because the correlative changes the original data value first, such as 12345 becomes 123. Then this changed value is compared to the literal value in the selection criterion phrase, here 500. Both values are in the same format and there is a possibility that some value(s) will pass the test and be output as 678 was.

Compare these results to those in the conversion code diagram 7.2B. Here the code is a converion on line 7 and line 8 is null. Go through the processing sequence and carefully observe the data in steps 3 and 4.

1. Read the item: item-id ACME.66, raw data value 12345.
2. Apply the correlative: there is none therefore the value stays as it was: 12345.
3. Apply the selection criterion: is the last form of the data (12345) greater than 500? Yes. Continue processing.
4. Apply the conversion: the data value is changed to 123.
5. Output the last form of the data: item-id ACME.66, data value 123.

Take a good look at the output. Is 123 greater than 500? The results are not valid here because the values are not in the same format when they are compared. The literal value of 500 is in the changed format. But the raw data value has not yet been changed by the code when it is compared to the literal. Thus the results can never be valid because all the original ZIP values are greater than 500 and will be output.

Command: >LIST VENDOR WITH ZIP.TEST > "500" ZIP.TEST

Processing with Conversion code

ZIP.TEST — Descriptor
007 T1,3
008 null
009 R

1. VENDOR file
   item-id   Original Data
   ACME.66   12345
   TOPS.55   67890

2. Apply Correlative
   No Correlative
   No change

3. Apply Selection Criteria
   Is the last form of the data > "500" ?
   12345   YES
   67890   YES

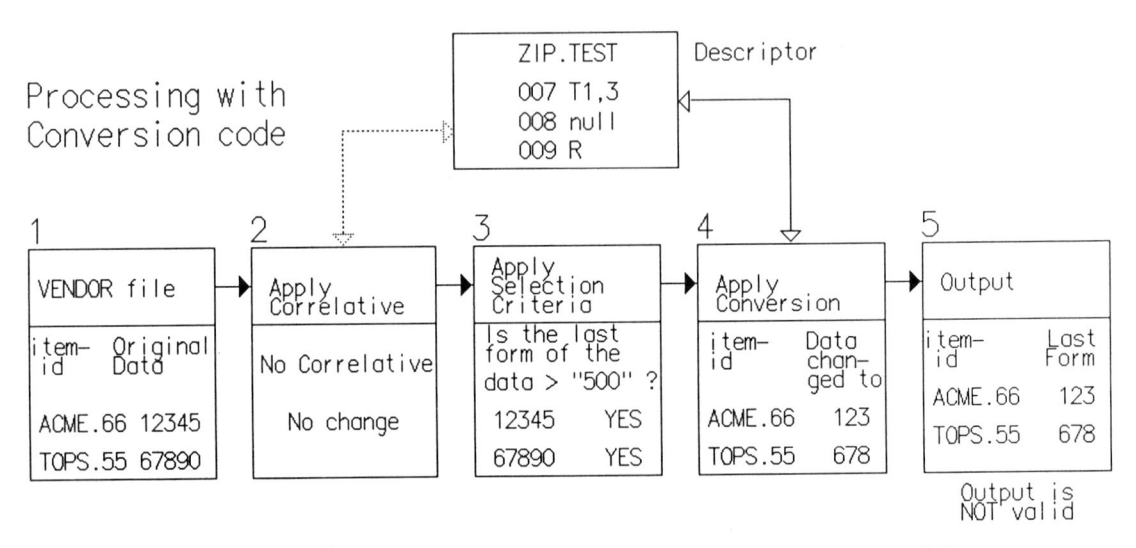

4. Apply Conversion
   item-id   Data changed to
   ACME.66   123
   TOPS.55   678

5. Output
   item-id   Last Form
   ACME.66   123
   TOPS.55   678

   Output is NOT valid

FIGURE 7.2B: PROCESSING SEQUENCE FOR TEXTRACT CONVERSION WITH SELECTION CRITERIA

Changing the Output via the Descriptor 269

In Section 7.4.9 we used Translate file code but without selection criteria in the command sentence. Now examine Tfile code, first as a correlative, and then as a conversion, with a command containing selection criteria. As before, note the relationship between the step where the code changes the original data form and the literal value to which the data is compared. Here the Tfile code translates the data into an attribute from another file.

For example suppose we take the GADGETS file and the Descriptor VENDOR.STATE with the Tfile code that we used earlier to output the values for STATE:

```
TVENDOR;X;;2
```

The command is

```
LIST GADGETS WITH VENDOR.STATE "IL" VENDOR.STATE
```

Follow the processing in the correlative diagram 7.3A where the code is on line 8.

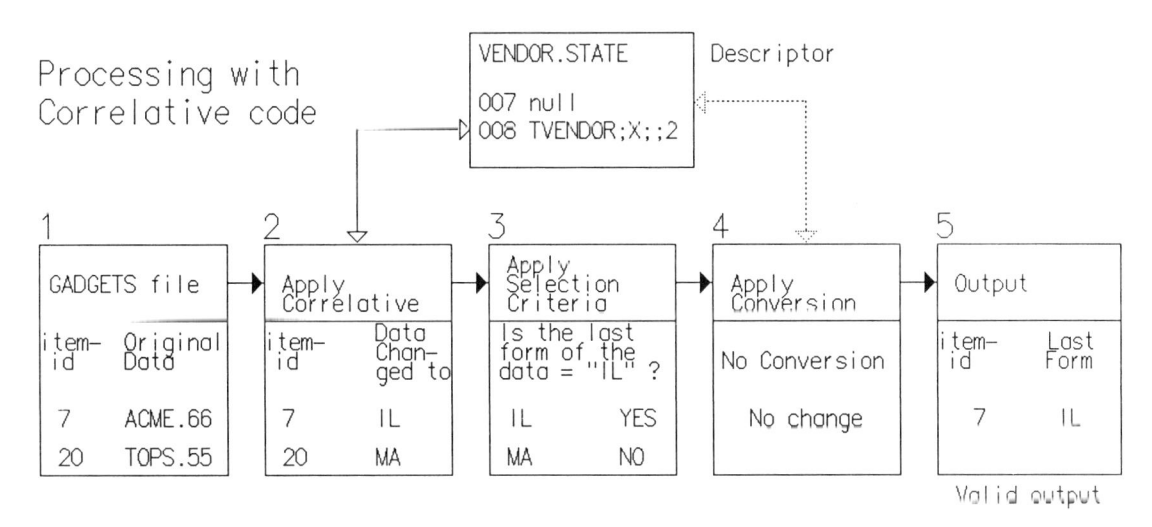

FIGURE 7.3A: PROCESSING SEQUENCE FOR TFILE CORRELATIVE WITH SELECTION CRITERIA

1. Read the item: item-id 7, original data value ACME.66.
2. Apply the correlative: the data value is changed to IL.
3. Apply the selection criterion: is the last form of the data (IL) equal to IL? Yes. Continue processing.
4. Apply the conversion: there is none, the value remains IL.
5. Output the last form of the data: item-id 7, data value IL.

Repeat the procedure with item 20. As you see, each time the data value is compared to the literal they are in the same format. The item(s) that pass the test are valid output.

In the conversion code diagram 7.3B the code is on line 7 and line 8 is null. Note the differences using the same test data.

1. Read the item: item-id 7, original data value ACME.66.
2. Apply the correlative: null value, no change.
3. Apply the selection criterion: is the last form of the data (ACME.66) equal to IL? No. The data does not pass the test and is ignored. Go to the next item.

Command: >LIST GADGETS WITH VENDOR.STATE "IL" VENDOR.STATE

Processing with Conversion code

VENDOR.STATE   Descriptor
007 TVENDOR;X;;2
008 null

1. GADGETS file
   item-id   Original Data
   7   ACME.66
   20   TOPS.55

2. Apply Correlative
   No Correlative
   No change

3. Apply Selection Criteria
   Is the last form of the data = "IL"?
   ACME.66 NO
   TOPS.55 NO

4. Apply Conversion
   No items have passed the test

5. Output
   [401] NO ITEMS PRESENT.
   No items will ever pass the test

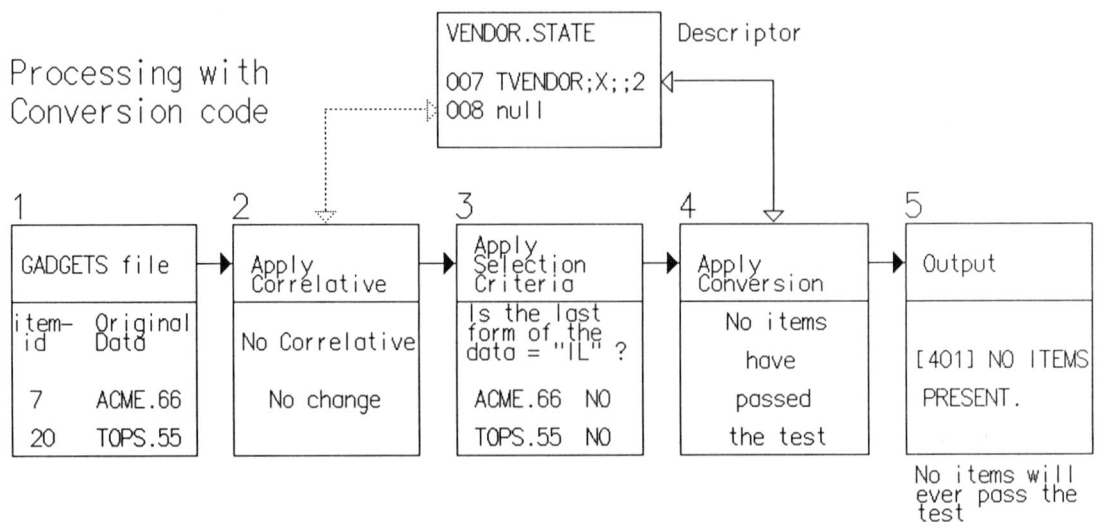

FIGURE 7.3B: PROCESSING SEQUENCE FOR TFILE CONVERSION WITH SELECTION CRITERIA

1. Read the item: item-id 20, original data value TOPS.55.
2. Apply the correlative: there is none, therefore no change and the data is still TOPS.55.
3. Apply the selection criterion: is the value (TOPS.55) equal to IL? No. And the same thing happens to each data item because the values being compared are not in the same format. The literal value is in the changed form but the data value is in its original form. There is no chance that any data in the file will ever pass the test and the response will always be

```
[401] NO ITEMS PRESENT.
```

But we know that this is not true. If we look at the test data in the VENDOR file we find that both ACME.66 and PEAK.77 have IL as their value for STATE. Therefore any item in the GADGETS file that has either ACME.66 or PEAK.77 as its value for the attribute VENDOR will have IL as its value for VENDOR.STATE, namely items 7, 9, and 30. The crux of the problem is the relationship between the line with the code and the form of the literal value in the selection criterion phrase: what are you testing against? For all codes except the three exceptions - MC, MR, and Date - put the code on:

line 8: when the literal in the selection criterion phrase is the changed form
line 7: when the literal is in the raw or unchanged form of the data.

When in doubt walk through the processing steps using sample data to be sure of getting valid results.

Let us examine an application of a code and a selection criterion phrase. Back in Section 5.3 it required two separate commands to find the quantity of SPOONs that came from suppliers in IL. By using the Tfile code which we already have on line 8 in VENDOR.STATE we can get the same information from only one command with selection criteria phrases:

```
WITH NAME "SPOON"
AND WITH VENDOR.STATE "IL"
```

On which line in the Descriptor VENDOR.STATE does the code go? The literal value IL is in the changed form and so the original data value must also be in its changed form in order to compare them properly. Follow the rule above and keep the code on line 8 as a correlative. The complete command is

```
LIST GADGETS WITH NAME "SPOON" AND WITH VENDOR.STATE "IL" QTY NAME
VENDOR VENDOR.STATE.
```

The response is the same as when two stages were necessary:

GADGETS	QTY	NAME	VENDOR	VENDOR.STATE
7	1	SPOON	ACME.66	IL
9	10	SPOON	PEAK.77	IL

Combinations of code and selection criteria offer many different possibilities for output. As another example consider Pattern match. In Section 7.4.2 we used P code to output the original data values that matched a Pattern; a null value was returned for a value that did not match. One of the exercises tested the PHONE values against the code

```
P(3N-3N-4N)
```

which was in the Descriptor PHONE.TEST. The code worked as selection criteria and output only the values that passed the test and ignored those that did not. When checking against a Pattern it may be easier to do the opposite: output the item-ids with phone numbers that do not match the Pattern and overlook those that do match the P code. So far we have used some form of NOT EQUAL as a relational operator in phrases like

```
WITH NAME NOT "FORK"
WITH STATE NE "MA"
```

In these phrases we specified the attribute to be tested, the relational operator, and the literal value. With P code the test is against the Pattern and takes the place of a literal value.

To disregard items that match the Pattern and output those that do not meet the requirement calls for new relational operators:

```
NO            (used after WITH), or
WITHOUT
```

For example

Changing the Output via the Descriptor

```
WITH NO PHONE.TEST
```

Process in the normal sequence.

1. Read the item.
2. Apply the correlative which is the P code on line 8 in PHONE.TEST.
3. Apply the selection criterion. Here we want the item-ids whose phone numbers do not match the Pattern; these are the items that continue processing.
4. Apply the conversion: there is none.
5. Output the data in its most recent form.

The Descriptor is PHONE.TEST as below.

```
001 S
002 6
003 through 007 null
008 P(3N-3N-4N)
009 R
010 13
```

Enter

```
>LIST VENDOR WITH NO PHONE.TEST PHONE.TEST PHONE <return>
```

Response

```
VENDOR     PHONE.TEST     PHONE........

ACE.99                    184-279-80041
```

The output is the opposite of what we are used to seeing. The response consists of the item-id(s) as normal; PHONE.TEST outputs a null value for any item with a non-matching phone number. To see the raw data value we also specified PHONE for output. The advantage is that we get only those items with a problem. ACE.99 has a null value for PHONE.TEST because it does not match the P code. PHONE outputs the raw data value. As you see the telephone number for item ACE.99 has one digit too many in the last part. This item is no longer needed and should be deleted from the file.

EXCEPTIONS TO THE RULE

MC, MR, and Date are the three codes where the previously defined relationship between the line with the code and the form of the literal value in the selection criterion phrase does not always apply. Examine each of the codes in turn.

MC

The MC (Mask Character) family is made up of

```
MCL MCA MCT MCU MCN MC/A MC/N
```

These codes follow the general rule only when they are on line 8 as a correlative and the literal is in the changed form. For example this produces valid output:

imagine that the Descriptor VENDOR has MCA on line 8 (output only alphabetic characters) and the command is

```
LIST GADGETS WITH VENDOR "ACME" VENDOR
```

The literal "ACME" is the changed form of the value ACME.66. The correlative processes the raw data values and compares each one to "ACME". The response is valid:

```
GADGETS    VENDOR
7          ACME
```

Remember that the general rule does <u>not</u> apply when the MC codes are a conversion and the literal is in the original form. Do not use selection criteria when one of the MC codes is on line 7. Neither form of the literal works with MC as a conversion.

MR

The MR code follows the general rule when the code is a correlative on line 8 and the literal is in changed form. For example, Descriptor COST has MR2$ on line 8 and the command is

```
LIST GADGETS WITH COST > "$2.00" COST
```

"$2.00" is the changed form of the literal and the response is valid:

GADGETS	COST
7	$2.25
21	$2.50
30	$3.00
49	$2.10

When the MR code is on line 7 as a conversion, show the literal as a decimal without a dollar sign or commas. For example, if the Descriptor COST has MR2$ on line 7, the above command must be changed to

```
LIST GADGETS WITH COST > "2.00" COST
```

to produce valid output.

D

When the Date code is combined with selection criteria the system has a unique processing method. As previously mentioned, every date value is stored as a number in internal format. Yet it is much easier for people to express date in external format. Normally there would be no way to compare data in two different formats. However with Date, the system has an efficient solution to the problem. Note that the Date code must be a conversion on line 7. First the literal value in the selection criterion phrase is automatically converted from external to internal format. Next, each data value in the file for Date is compared to the literal in its newly changed internal format. This is possible because both values are in the same format - internal. The results of the test are as normal: data that passes continues processing, data that does not meet the requirement is overlooked. The conversion is then applied to the data that passed the test and the data is output in the external format dictated by the Date code in the Descriptor. Thus

1. We express the literal value in the form most convenient for us.
2. The system changes the literal value to internal format and tests it against each data value, which is also stored in internal format.
3. Only the values that meet the selection criteria are changed to external format and output.

Use test data and walk through the processing sequence. The conversion on line 7 in the Descriptor controls only the output form of the data; here we have D2/. The sample command is

```
LIST GADGETS WITH DATE > "12/1/85" DATE
```

Note that the external date in the literal can be in any of the allowed Date code formats; it need not be the same as the conversion code in the Descriptor. The change from external to internal format is made automatically for us. The use of leading zeroes such as 01 in the literal is optional.

Command: >LIST GADGETS WITH DATE > "12/01/85" DATE

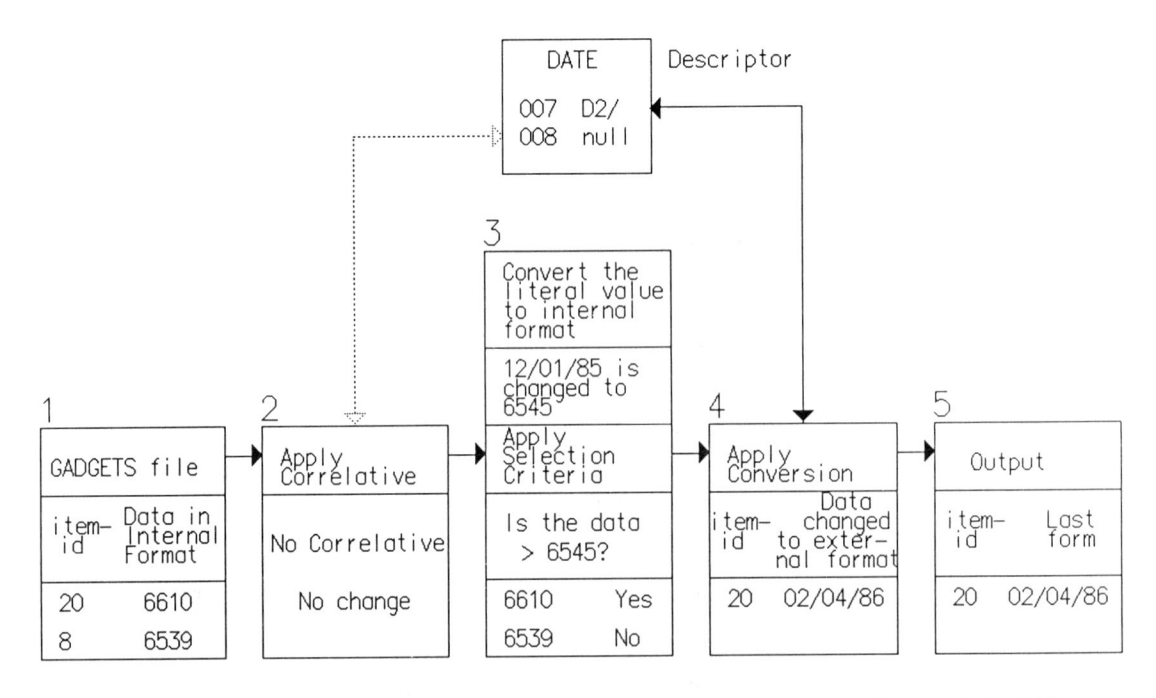

FIGURE 7.4: PROCESSING SEQUENCE FOR DATE CONVERSION WITH SELECTION CRITERIA

1. Read the item: item-id 20, the Date value in internal format is 6610.

2. Apply the correlative: null value, no change.
3. Since this is a Date conversion we have an extra step to convert the literal value "12/1/85" to its internal format which is 6545. Apply the selection criterion: is the data value (6610) greater than 6545? Yes. Continue processing.
4. Apply the conversion: change the internal format of the date to the external form as directed in the Date code in the Descriptor, here D/. Data is changed to 02/04/1986.
5. Output the last form of the data: item-id 20, DATE 02/04/1986.

Follow across for the next item which is item-id 8. 6539 is not greater than 6545 therefore item 8 does not pass the test and is not output.

You may prefer using the relational operators

AFTER instead of GT or >
BEFORE instead of LT or <

To find dates within a period such as a calendar year use selection criteria like

    WITH DATE >= "1 JAN 1985" AND WITH DATE <= "31 DEC 1985"

Although only part of the date is output with the codes

    D0   e.g. 16 JAN
    DY   e.g. 1986

the complete internal date is tested when the selection criteria are applied. For example when the conversion code is D0 and the command is

    LIST GADGETS WITH DATE AFTER "01/09/86" DATE

the output is

    GADGETS   DATE

    50   16 JAN
    20   04 FEB
    42   09 FEB

The preceding discussion of the Date conversions and selection criteria applies to systems where date values have been stored in internal format. For users who store and manipulate date values in the external format, selection criteria are processed in the usual way. Follow the format of the data values

    YY/MM/DD

e.g.

    85/09/22

for the literal in the selection criterion phrase. A variety of information can be produced from a command such as

    LIST GADGETS selection criteria phrase(s) DATE

To find dates equal to a particular date use

    WITH DATE "85/01/16"

Prior to a certain date use

    WITH DATE BEFORE "84/09/19"

After a cutoff date use

    WITH DATE AFTER "83/10/03"

Output all the dates that have 85 as the year by using placeholders as

    WITH DATE "85/^^/^^"

or with a bracket as

    "85]"

With September as the month

    WITH DATE "^^/09/^^"

Pattern, Group Extract, and Textract codes are all suited to data in this kind of format. The important thing to remember is when one procedure cannot be used look for an alternative.

7.5 ERROR EXAMPLES

DESCRIPTOR and LINE(S) WITH CODE	COMMAND and RESPONSE
PHONE.TEST 007 (P3N-3N-4N)	>LIST VENDOR PHONE.TEST [705] ILLEGAL CONVERSION CODE : '(P3N-3N-4N)'

COMMENT: P for Pattern code belongs outside the parentheses as P(3N-3N-4N).

PHONE.TEST 002 8 007 P(3N-3N-4N)	>LIST VENDOR PHONE.TEST VENDOR PHONE.TEST ACE.88 TOPS.55 etc.

COMMENT: line 2 references attribute 8 which is CO.NAME therefore no values match the Pattern and null is output for each item.

COLOR.LC 007 MCL]C;3 1	>LIST GADGETS COLOR.LC GADGETS COLOR.LC 50 TAN FORK 21 RED LADLE etc.

COMMENT: The result of MCL was superseded by the result of the C;3 1 code. MCL should be applied after Concatenation. The sequence should be C;3 1]MCL

QTY 007 R6,12	>LIST GADGETS WITH QTY < "12" GADGETS QTY 7 1 9 10 30 8

COMMENT: item 7 with QTY 1 and item 21 with QTY 4 meet the selection criteria. However they are not output because the Range code passes only values between 6 and 12. The Range code should be in a Synonym Descriptor.

```
COST                    >LIST GADGETS COST
007 MR(!8)              GADGETS         COST
                        8               !!!!!!!!
                        30              !!!!!!!!
                        etc.
```
COMMENT: ! is not a legal fill character; use * or the # for a blank.

```
COST                    >LIST GADGETS COST
007 MR$,2               GADGETS         COST
                        50              MR$,,
                        8               MR$,,
                        etc.
```
COMMENT: the code is in the wrong sequence. For 2 decimal places, commas, and a dollar sign the code should be MR2,$.

```
QTY                     >LIST GADGETS QTY
008 AN(QTY)*"12"        RTN STACK FORMAT ERR ABORT @ 7.
```
COMMENT: the Arithmetic code cannot call itself: the code calls QTY and is also in the QTY Descriptor. Use a General Purpose Descriptor for the A code in this situation.

```
DOZ.COST                >LIST GADGETS DOZ.COST
008 AN(COST) * "12"     [168] ILLEGAL A-CORRELATIVE.: 'AN(COST) * "12"'
```
COMMENT: no blanks are permitted in Arithmetic code; it should be AN(COST)*"12"

```
VENDOR.PHONE is in      >LIST GADGETS VENDOR.PHONE
the VENDOR file         [24] THE WORD "VENDOR.PHONE" CANNOT BE IDENTIFIED
```
COMMENT: the Descriptor VENDOR.PHONE with Translation file (Tfile) code was incorrectly placed in the VENDOR file. It belongs in the original file GADGETS.

```
COLOR.LC              >LIST GADGETS WITH COLOR.LC "RED" COLOR.LC
007 MCL               [401] NO ITEMS PRESENT.
```
COMMENT: the MC codes are exceptions to the general rule when used with selection criteria. Place MCL on line 8 and use the changed form of the literal value "red".

```
COST                  >LIST GADGETS WITH COST > "$2.00" COST
007 MR2$              GADGETS           COST
                      50                $1.10
                      7                 $2.25
                      20                $1.50
                      8                 $1.00
                      21                $2.50
                      9                 $0.75
                      42                $2.00
                      30                $3.00
                      49                $2.10
```
COMMENT: the whole file has been output and some of the data values are less than $2.00 showing that the selection criteria have not been applied. MR like MC is one of the exceptions to the general rule when used with selection criteria. Place the code on line 8; the literal value here is correct in its changed form.

7.6 REVIEW QUESTIONS

1. *What does Pattern code test? What does it output?*
2. *What are the advantages and disadvantages of Range code?*
3. *Explain the functions of Arithmetic code and where it is placed.*
4. *Can the first four lines of the Descriptor for the item-id (D type) be altered? Why?*
5. *Describe the difference in processing between a conversion and a correlative. Where are the codes placed?*
6. *How does the Date code differ from the other codes?*
7. *Illustrate what happens when an oversized Right justified item-id or attribute is output.*
8. *What is a General Purpose Descriptor? When is it used?*
9. *How is an attribute value translated from one file to another for output?*

10. Explain the difference between Group Extraction and Textract (Text Extraction). Can they ever produce the same output? How?
11. What is the normal relationship between the form of the literal in a selection criterion phrase and the line with conversion/correlative code? Which codes are exceptions to the general rule?
12. How are attributes referenced by Concatenation code? Literals?
13. Give the MR code to output a comma, a dollar sign, and a decimal point in numeric data.
14. What determines the maximum length of the space reserved for outputting a value?
15. Give 5 examples of MC code and what each outputs.

Chapter 8

Word Processing with JET

FOREWORD

As author of the JET Word Processor, I am particularly impressed with this chapter. The style is clear and the material is presented in an easy to understand format. I am also happy to see how well it ties in with the Pick Operating System.

This guide to JET will prove invaluable to the beginning user. The steps are carefully ordered from simple to complex, and the examples are so relevant to everyday use.

My thanks to the authors for a job well done and for including this section in their book.

> John E. Treankler
> Author of the JET Word Processor
> President, JET Software

8.1 WHAT IS JET?

JET is a general name for the word processing software routinely included by computer manufacturers with the Pick Operating System. Most versions of JET are called JET I or II; examples of other names are *Wordmate* on Microdata, *Ulti-Word* on Ultimate, and *Documentor* on the ADDS Mentor.

Unlike a word processor, a typewriter prints each character as it is pressed; you can correct an error with the backspace on correcting typewriters, but major changes call for retyping the page, possibly the entire document. The only record of the text is on the paper. A word processor is either a *dedicated* (single purpose) computer with a printer, or special software on a multipurpose system as we have here. The document is displayed while you work and not printed until you give the command. Meanwhile all kinds of manipulation are permitted such as moving blocks of text from one position to another, searching for a string, making corrections, inserting, deleting, and adding instructions to output headings, footings, and page numbers. At any point you can stop working on the document, discard or save all or part of it and/or print it as many times as you wish.

JET is capable of all of these operations and many more. As a processor it has its own unique procedures and vocabulary. This chapter covers the most commonly used procedures. All versions of JET have word processing capabilities, but there are variations among them. Therefore, consult your user's manual when necessary, particularly with "The Works" version, which has the most features.

Although you may notice similarities to the EDITOR in the Pick Operating System it is not essential to be familiar with the material in the preceding chapters to use most JET operations. However the user must be able to Logon and off to the system and recognize the TCL prompt (Chapter 3).

First, a few general remarks about JET. As with any computer, entries are made through the keyboard. Each key - letter, number, or symbol - is considered one character. All the text characters and some commands, such as headings, appear on the screen, but many do not. You will see how each command works as we try it. Remember you must give the system time to execute a command. Do not be impatient and enter another command to speed things up. The computer follows the sequence as it is given and must complete one instruction before starting on the next.

You probably already know that the cursor on the screen is a rectangular block or underline that may or may not blink. Thus far it has indicated the place that the next typed character would take and we could not move the cursor from one location to another. In word processing the cursor occupies your current position, which can be anywhere between the beginning and the end of the document; all commands are executed from the cursor position. For example, to insert a word within the text the cursor must be where the word is to go. Therefore, we use special keys to *position* the cursor to move it around.

JET follows the same conventions as the Pick Operating System and stores all data as an item within a file (Chapter 2). The manuscript for this book was created on JET and given the filename BOOK. Each chapter was an item in the file and given an item-id like 1, 2, and so on. The maximum size of an item is the same as before: 32,267 bytes (newer versions of JET do not have the limitation). This is equivalent to approximately 7 single spaced or 14 double spaced standard pages. When the text will be longer, it must be divided into as many items as necessary and can be identified accordingly. For example 4.EXT was the item-id for the extension or second part of Chapter 4. Later we cover how to check the length of an item in order to stay within the limit (Section 8.6.1) and also how to link items so that they are printed together as one whole unit (Section 8.9).

Most screens display 23 lines. When this text is printed, single spacing takes between 1/3 and 1/2 of an 8 1/2 by 11 inch page depending upon the width of the margins and the spacing between the lines.

JET works with two types of documents: continuous line text like reports, letters, and books; and single line text like computer programs. The JET-IN command for continuous lines has optional embedded instructions for text alignment, underline, headings, paging, and so on. We shall use JET-IN to create and modify a document and then JET-OUT to output it. Note that on the ADDS Mentor DOC-IN is equivalent to JET-IN and DOC-OUT to JET-OUT. JET-EDIT is for single lines; it has the same basic commands as JET-IN but no embellishments. Since it is not suited to our purpose of general word processing it is not covered here.

As you recall, there are two modes for the EDITOR; we moved from Command mode into and out of Input mode depending on the kind of job to be done. This is only a comparison because the JET software and the EDITOR cannot be used interchangeably.

From here on, we refer to the JET-IN software as JET. JET has three modes and each specializes in a particular activity. We enter JET from TCL; when the item is not new, we go into Command mode which is the base mode. It is called Edit mode in other guides, but this is confusing for a beginner because of the similarity to JET-EDIT and the EDITOR, therefore the name Command mode is used here. In JET Command mode we change, delete, search, replace, and move text; all of these operations are far more extensive than those allowed in the EDITOR Command mode. JET Insert mode is similar to Input mode in the EDITOR: input text and return to Command mode when finished. The EDITOR has nothing comparable to Ruler mode which permits us to set up the controls for alignment such as margins, tab stops, and centering. At any time we can leave one mode and enter another by pressing special keys called *mode transitions*, all of which we cover as they are needed.

The functions of some keys vary according to the mode in which they are used. In Insert mode a letter is the letter on the key, but in Command mode the same letter may be a command. For example in Insert mode Q is Q; in Command mode Q deletes a word.

JET helps you by displaying a *status line* (message) across the bottom of the screen to show what mode you are in and/or other information.

8.2 BEGIN THE ITEM

The first step is to create a file. Items in the word processor, like all data in the Pick system, are stored in a file. Let us write a form letter to our housewares store suppliers to notify them that we are moving. In the future there may be other letters and so we can keep them together in one file called LETTERS. Each different letter will be an item in the LETTERS file. Since this particular letter is about moving, we give it the logical item-id MOVE. When choosing names for the file and the item check the constraints in Chapter 2.3.

Before we start on MOVE, we create the LETTERS file. The command to set up a JET file is the same as for a Dictionary and Data File: we instruct the system to allocate space for the new file. The general command format is

```
>CREATE-FILE your.filename dict.mod data.mod
```

Before we type in the command note that:

1. > or : is the TCL prompt displayed on the screen.
2. Commands from TCL are entered in upper case letters.
3. The numbers given for modulo and separation are suggested for this exercise.
4. The line completion or carriage return key is not marked the same on all keyboards. You will probably see either SEND LINE, NEWLINE, ENTER, RETURN, or an arrow pointing down and left. Find out how yours is identified. In this text <return> indicates carriage return.

For our example enter

```
>CREATE-FILE LETTERS 1 17,10 <return>
```

if the response is similar to

>	IMPROPER MODULO OR SEPARATION

try

>	>CREATE-FILE (LETTERS 1,1 17,10) <return>

A sample response that indicates successful execution of the command is

>	[417] FILE 'LETTERS' CREATED; BASE = 9458, MOD = 1, SEP = 1
>	[417] FILE 'LETTERS' CREATED; BASE = 10390, MOD = 17, SEP = 10

Your BASE numbers will not be the same as above. Whatever they are, the response shows that space has been reserved for the file LETTERS. If the message is

>	[413] THE FILE NAME ALREADY EXISTS IN THE MASTER DICTIONARY.

it means that the file has been created; this step is not necessary.

The general command format to get to a JET item is

>	>JET-IN filename item-id

When you try to JET-IN to a filename that is spelled wrong or has not been created the response is

>	[201] 'filename' IS NOT A FILE NAME

Spell the filename exactly as originally given to the system. In our test data:

> the filename is LETTERS
> the item-id is MOVE

The command is

>	>JET-IN LETTERS MOVE <return>

If you omit the item-id (here MOVE), most systems ask for it:

    ITEM ID:

Enter the

    item-id <return>

which in our example is

    MOVE <return>

Both the filename and the item-id are necessary for the system to find the proper item.

When we start a new item that has never been worked on before, JET makes it easy by automatically taking us directly into Ruler mode. When going into an existing item, we travel from JET-IN to Command mode. You know you are in Ruler mode (called the Ruler Editor in some manuals) by the screen display: a ruler strip with marks for 80 columns (characters) that fit across on one line and a *menu* or list of Ruler functions. The Ruler status line across the bottom of the screen is

    change ruler or hit ? for help "item-id" View on

The message "View on" indicates that JET is displaying the item including Rulers and output instructions, which we shall cover.

Every document should have a Ruler at the Top (beginning) to align the text. The first task with the new item is to set up the Ruler after deciding on the format. When you do not want to design your own Ruler, you can use the default Ruler which is available and already set up with margins and tab settings. This is advisable for first time operators of the word processor. After becoming more familiar with JET, you will learn to customize Rulers in Section 8.5. Press the ESC key to leave Ruler mode.

As mentioned earlier, at all other times we go from Ruler mode to Command mode; when working for the first time on a new item, JET takes us directly from Ruler mode into Insert mode so that we can enter text. The screen clears and then we see the default Ruler across the top showing the positions of the L (Left) and R (Right) margins and < for paragraph indentation. Always use the tab key and not the space bar to move the cursor to the indent location. L, R, and < will do for starters; A, C, and Z are covered in Section 8.5.3. The cursor is just below the Ruler and the page is blank because there is nothing in the document as yet. The Insert mode status line is across the bottom of the screen:

```
insert text, then press ESCAPE "item-id"     View on
```

The word "text" here includes characters, spaces, tab stops, and blank lines - anything that is placed into the item except a Ruler.

A few points before entering the text. Keep typing to the end of the paragraph; the words *wrap* (flow) automatically to the next line. This is called "automatic word wrap." Press the <return> key only when the text must start on a new line such as for a paragraph. You then see the arrow pointing left < after the last character on the line. This indicates that what follows starts on a new line; the < does not show in the output. The cursor moves to the next line; if an indent is required, press the tab key. If your keyboard has no tab key, press the control key and I together to indent.

The backspace key moves the cursor to the left one space at a time, erasing the character(s) it passes over. Backspace to the proper place and retype or else leave an error and correct it later when editing. Change the caps lock key to type lower case and use the shift key when necessary as on a typewriter.

The first two lines of the letter are below. Before typing press the tab once to move the cursor to the indent position. As you work, watch how the "h" in "has" appears briefly on the first line under R (Right margin) and then wraps to the line below. Do not use the <return> for continuous text. Note that there are many errors in MOVE to provide test data for editing later on. Alignment with the L and R margins, and the indent are indicated in the sample below.

```
L    <    A                    C                         Z    R
        Thanks to our reliable Suppliers likeyou, our businesss
    has grown SUBSTANTIULLY over the last five years,
```

We want the text after "years," to start on a new line at all times; therefore, we press the <return> key. The symbol < indicates the end of the line on the screen and is not printed; the cursor moves to the Left margin of the next line. No matter how the document is altered, whatever follows an end of line indicator is placed on the next line.

The default Ruler which was recommended for this exercise contains a hyphenation zone. All we need to know for now is that when a full word does not fit on a line and would extend past the Right margin, the word must be hyphenated. This will occur with the word "facilitate" below. As you type, the bell rings to alert you to the problem and part of the status line changes to

```
backspace, hyphenate this word
```

Press the backspace key one position at a time until the cursor is where the hyphen should be between the first "i" and "l". Press the hyphen - key. The last part of the word shifts down to the next line and the cursor moves to the position of the next typed character. This is called a *soft hyphen* and may not necessarily appear again either on the screen or in output if the text or margins are changed. If you do not want the word hyphenated at any time, backspace to the blank before the word and the entire word moves down. In contrast, a *hard hyphen* is entered along with the characters in the word and is always shown such as in life-giving.

Type in the next sentence of the letter without a tab at the beginning:

```
On September 19 th we are moving to bigger quartres to faci-
litate expanded operations.
```

The complete item as it looks on the screen is below; if you have additional mistakes you can correct them later.

```
        Thanks to our reliable Suppliers likeyou, our businesss
has grown SUBSTANTIULLY over the last five years,<
On September 19 th we are moving to bigger quartres to faci-
litate expanded operations.
```

Assume that you are ready to leave Insert mode. Follow the instruction in the status line and press ESC. We move into Command mode and see its status line:

```
move cursor or press ? for help "item-id"  View on
```

The item-id is in quotes; here it is "MOVE", the item that was specified in the JET-IN command. Also note that the symbol < has been added automatically to indicate the end of the item.

Working with JET involves moving from one mode to another via the mode transition keys. As you become familiar with them, you will find it easy to get around. You can leave JET at any time by using the proper command(s) to return to TCL and continue with other operations or log off. It is up to the user to decide what to do and when.

This item will be needed for other procedures; therefore it must be filed. The first step is press

    F   Do not press <return>. The status line changes to

```
press I to file, S to save, or D to delete
```

Since we are keeping the item we have two choices: either go from the item and JET immediately and return to TCL, or save what we have so far, remain in the item to continue working, and quit later. Decide which you want to do. To leave now press

    I   No <return>. The response confirms that the item was FIled:

```
'item-id' FILED.
```

and displays the TCL prompt. For example

```
'MOVE' FILED.
>
```

Stay on the system as long as you like and then log off (see Chapter 3.7). To return to the item you will have to log on and use the JET-IN command format

```
JET-IN filename item-id
```

or as we did

```
JET-IN LETTERS MOVE
```

The other way is to save the item and stay within JET. In the preceding step, we pressed F and I to FIle the item to disk and leave JET. The alternative is to press F and S to save the item to disk and also remain in JET to continue editing. It is wise to save the document every so often. Otherwise, if the system malfunctions, you could lose all the changes made during the JET session. If you FS frequently, you are "checkpointing" the item and the most you could lose is changes made since the last FS command.

8.3 CURSOR POSITIONING

Whatever the operation when working in JET, decide first which mode is required for what you want to do, and then which mode you are currently in. The status line messages are a big help; get into the habit of reading them. Then if you must change modes you can give the appropriate instruction. Each of the three modes - Command, Insert, and Ruler - has its own type of cursor movement. When we were in Insert mode, the cursor automatically moved forward into the position of the next character as we typed. The extent of the cursor control in Insert mode is the tab key to move forward, the backspace to go backward, and <return> to start a paragraph. Section 8.5.2 covers cursor movement in Ruler mode to set up the Ruler alignment characters.

This section applies to the cursor in Command mode only. The screen displays:

    the ruler across the top
    the text
    and the Command mode status line:

        move cursor or press ? for help ...

Since the position of the cursor is the place where commands are executed, it is essential to learn how to control its movement. In Command mode the cursor is positioned in four directions primarily by the numeric 10-key pad to the right of the main bank of characters on the keyboard. All cursor movement is within the boundaries of the document.

Find the numeric pad on your keyboard. The arrangement may not be exactly like the diagram but the keys have the same functions:

```
7  8  9
4  5  6
1  2  3
   0  .
```

The obvious question is, why are there eleven keys to move the cursor in four directions? Each key has a direction - back, forward. up, or down

- and also a distance - a character, a word, a sentence, a line, or a page. Note that words are recognized as starting with a letter or a number; symbols are skipped when cursor movement is to a word. For maximum control avoid holding down a key.

Advance by these keys:

    6 to the next character
    9 to the next word
    3 to the next sentence
    2 down one line
    . to the bottom of the page. If the item is longer than one screen press . again to get to the next page.

When the cursor is at the Bottom (end) of the item, it can go no further forward and stops, no matter which of these keys you press.

To move backward use:

    4 to the preceding character
    7 to the preceding word
    1 to the previous sentence
    8 to the line above. When the cursor is at the top of the screen, 8 moves back one screen.
    5 to the top of the screen
    0 to the page before.

When the cursor reaches the Top (beginning) it cannot travel further back and halts if positioned by this group of keys.

Below is the numeric key pad with the functions of each key.

7	8	9
<WORD	^LINE	WORD>
4	5	6
<CHARACTER	^PAGE TOP	CHARACTER>
1	2	3
<SENTENCE	DOWN A LINE	SENTENCE>
0		.
<PAGE		PAGE BOTTOM

In addition to the above, the following keys on the main key bank also control cursor movement in Command mode; the case of the letters does not matter.

PRESS	TO MOVE THE CURSOR TO
T	the Top (beginning) of the item which is the Ruler above the opening text. Note this is not necessarily the current page.
B	the Bottom (end) of the item, probably the < end of line symbol after the last character. Note that this is not necessarily the current page.
}	the next paragraph
{	the preceding paragraph
^	the end of the line. The cursor will not move past the end of line indicator on any line; if you are at the end of the line on < and press the caret, the cursor moves to the next line.
<return>	the first character at the beginning of the line. If you are already there, the cursor moves down one line.
tab	the next tab stop

SUMMARY: THE COMMAND MODE CURSOR POSITIONING KEYS

1. BY KEY

The Numeric Key Pad
0	back a page
1	back a sentence
2	down a line
3	forward a sentence
4	back a character
5	to page top
6	forward a character
7	back a word
8	up a line
9	forward a word
.	bottom of page, press again for next page

The Main Key Bank
B	Bottom (end) of item
T	Top (beginning) of item

```
}          forward a paragraph
{          back a paragraph
^          end of line or next line
<return>   beginning of line or next line
tab        next tab stop
```

2. BY DISTANCE AND DIRECTION

Distance	Forward	Back
character	6	4
word	9	7
sentence	3	1
end of line	^	
beginning of line	<return>	
line	2	8
next tab stop	tab	
paragraph	}	{
page top		5
page bottom	.	
page	.	0
end of item	B	
beginning of item		T

Practice moving around within the text. The easiest route to the target may require a combination of keys such as moving first to the sentence, then to the word, and last to the character. Familiarity with the cursor positioning keys makes the job of editing go faster.

As mentioned these keys function as described <u>only</u> in Command mode; they also move the cursor off the Ruler after you JET-IN to an existing item. You may be in Insert mode and press 6, expecting to see the cursor move forward one character; instead the 6 appears in your text. Erase the 6 by pressing the backspace and decide whether to stay in Insert mode or leave via the ESC key to go to Command mode. Errors like this are quickly corrected and part of learning a new operation.

8.4 EDIT THE TEXT: INSERT, CHANGE, AND DELETE

In Chapter 4 we broke the update procedure into three types of data activity and covered each one separately: add, change, and delete. *Editing* with the word processor is made up of the same operations, but when working on a document we usually move through it and make all kinds of corrections as we go. We start at the Top of the item and deal with a variety of text manipulations one after another.

Unless you are already in the item you must get to it from TCL and the JET-IN command. Some editing, such as deleting and changing case, is done in Command mode; inserting calls for Insert mode. Each mode has its own transition commands to enter or leave and we cover them as they are needed. Remember that instructions are executed from the position of the cursor and the cursor is controlled from Command mode. Check the status line to see what mode you are in. If you are in Command mode and see the status line

    move cursor or press ? for help

you are ready to use the cursor positioning keys; if you are in Insert mode, press ESC to return to Command mode.

The test data provides an assortment of editing operations for a start. If you make mistakes, look on the corrections as practice in improving your skill with JET. Most of the commands do not require the <return> key; do not use it unless directed to do so.

While you are working, part or all of the screen may fade. Sometimes it is to provide a place to see what you are typing, other times to display rearranged text. The item is changed with each edit operation. Note that some terminals blank the screen when no keys have been pressed for five minutes or more. Simply press <control> and R together to re-display the screen.

As you are working, you may want to see just what is on the screen. The command C Clears the screen and re-displays the item at the current location. Do not use C in the middle of another operation.

In the exercises below, the operation is described first and then the text is shown before editing, with the cursor position as a shaded box. Next the command is given and followed by the new version of the text. Note that the case of the letter in the command may be either upper or lower.

Delete the tab stop.

BEFORE   ▓Thanks to our reliable Suppliers likeyou, our businesss
                has grown SUBSTANTIULLY over the last five years,<

PRESS   D

AFTER   Thanks to our reliable Suppliers likeyou, our businesss has
                grown SUBSTANTIULLY over the last five years,<

The tab stop was deleted and so the word "Thanks" was shifted to the Left margin; all that follows was moved along with it up to and including the end of line indicator.

Delete a word. The cursor can be on any character in the word when the entire word is being deleted.

BEFORE   Thanks to ▓ur reliable Suppliers likeyou, our businesss

PRESS   Q

AFTER   Thanks to reliable Suppliers likeyou, our businesss has

Change the case of one letter. The cursor must be on the letter being changed.

BEFORE   Thanks to reliable ▓uppliers likeyou, our businesss has

PRESS   :

AFTER   Thanks to reliable suppliers likeyou, our businesss has

Insert a space between two characters. Added characters, spaces, tab stops, and blank lines as well as words etc. are considered new text. They are inserted from Insert mode immediately before the cursor position. There is no limit as long as the total item size does not exceed the maximum.

BEFORE   Thanks to reliable suppliers like▓ou, our businesss has

PRESS the following keys:

    I   (for Insert mode)
    the space bar
    ESC   (to return to Command mode)

AFTER   Thanks to reliable suppliers like you, our businesss has

Delete a character. The cursor in this case can be on any "s" in the word "businesss" for deletion. The text that follows whatever is deleted is shifted to take up the newly available space.

BEFORE   Thanks to reliable suppliers like you, our businesss has

PRESS   D

AFTER   Thanks to reliable suppliers like you, our business has

Change the case of a word. Here the cursor can be on any letter in the word (as compared with changing only one letter when the cursor must be on the letter being changed). The asterisk * alters case as follows

from	to
CASE	case
case	Case
Case	CASE
cASE	Case

BEFORE   grown SUBSTANTIULLY over the last five years,<

PRESS   *

AFTER   grown substantiully over the last five years,<

Replace a character. The command R Replaces existing text. This is a Replacement operation, character for character including blanks, until you press ESC. Note that tab stops and end of line indicators are not affected by R and remain in their original positions. Delete them when in Command mode if necessary. R is not the same as I.

BEFORE   grown substantially over the last five years,<

PRESS   R

The status line changes to

   replace text, then press ESCAPE ...

Next press the Replacement character, here the letter

a

and then

>   ESC

AFTER   grown substantially over the last five years,<

Replace the comma with a period.

BEFORE   grown substantially over the last five years<

PRESS R (as above)

>   .

to replace the comma

>   ESC (as above)

AFTER   grown substantially over the last five years.<

Note that when the Replacement reaches the end of a line, JET takes you into Insert mode as shown by the status line

>   insert text, then press ESCAPE ...

Check the end of line symbol; it should be next to the last character for the line, here the period just typed in. If there is a space between the . and the < such as

>   . <

position the cursor on the space and press D to delete it.

Insert a blank line. We must move into Insert mode for a new line just as we did when we added a space earlier.

BEFORE   grown substantially over the last five years.<
              On September 19 th we are moving to bigger quartres to faci-

PRESS the following keys:

>   I   (for Insert mode)
>   <return> (for a new line)
>   ESC   (to return to Command mode)

AFTER grown substantially over the last five years.<
       <
       On September 19 th we are moving to bigger quartres to faci-

The entire new line is blank therefore, the end of line indicator is at the Left margin.

Delete a space just as you delete a character.

BEFORE   On September 19 th we are moving to bigger quartres to faci-

PRESS D

AFTER   On September 19th we are moving to bigger quartres to faci-

Replace a word. As when replacing a character, first we give the command, then we are taken to Insert mode; the new replaces the old, and we press ESC to return to Command mode.

BEFORE   On September 19th we are moving to bigger quarters to faci-

PRESS W

the status line changes to

    retype the word, then NEWLINE

or

    insert text, then press ESCAPE

type in the new word

    larger

whichever of the above status lines you have, press ESC

AFTER   On September 19th we are moving to larger quartres to faci-

Transpose two characters. Position the cursor on the first of the two to be transposed.

BEFORE   On September 19th we are moving to larger quarties to faci-

PRESS   z

AFTER   On September 19th we are moving to larger quarters to faci-

Insert the word "our" between "facilitate" and "expanded." Earlier we inserted a space between two characters; use the same procedure to add any kind of new text. Move the cursor to the position for the new material, press I for Insert mode, type in whatever is necessary staying within the item size limit of 32,267 bytes, and press ESC to return to Command mode. When the page is re-displayed, the inserted text may have caused what follows it to shift.

BEFORE   litate expanded operations.<

PRESS   I

type in the word to be inserted

    our

press the space bar for the space between "our" and "expanded"

    ESC

AFTER   litate our expanded operations.<

When you are in Command mode, you might press I by mistake without planning to enter Insert mode. Just press ESC to leave; it is not necessary to insert text.

The edited version of MOVE is now:

    Thanks to reliable suppliers like you, our business has
    grown substantially over the last five years.<
    <
    On September 19th we are moving to larger quarters to faci-
    litate our expanded operations.<

End of line indicators may be deleted by positioning the cursor on <

and pressing D in Command mode. The text that had started on a new line moves up, fills the line, and wraps.

SUMMARY: EDITING IN COMMAND MODE

The Operation	Character	Word	Sentence	Line
change	:	*		! (from the cursor)
transpose characters	Z			
replace	R	W		

    Note that R is for one or more characters but not tab stops or end of line indicators.
    Automatic entry to Insert mode, press ESC to leave.

| delete | D | Q | Y | K |

                                                                 (from cursor)

Warning: holding down a key can repeat the command.

The last time we finished working on MOVE, we FIled it to disk. When we started this session with JET-IN, we found MOVE just as we had previously FIled it. During the current work session many changes were made and we now have two versions of the item: the one displayed on the screen and the earlier one that was FIled. Every time we are ready to leave a JET item, which can be at any point in Command mode and not necessarily when editing is complete, we must decide what to do with the item as it now stands. First press F. You have already seen the status line

```
press I to file, S to save, or D to delete
```

Let us look at the operations in more detail.

    I   FIles the current version of the item. This replaces the previously FIled form when there is one. Thus the newly corrected MOVE takes the place of the old error filled one, which is discarded. The response is

```
      ...'item-id' FILED.
```

        and the TCL prompt is displayed. For our example it is

```
...'MOVE' FILED.
>
```

You have left the item and JET, and gone to TCL as shown by the prompt.

S   Saves the item but you remain in it. You will eventually leave the item by one of the other keys.

D   Deletes the entire item - this version along with the previously FIled one if such exists. After an item is deleted, there is no way to get it back and so the system gives you a chance to reconsider. It beeps and displays

```
press "Y" to delete item
```

If you decide not to delete the item, press N or ESC. The delete is cancelled and the usual Command mode status line is displayed.

If you are sure that you want to delete, press Y and the item is deleted. You move from JET to TCL as shown in this sample response

```
'item-id' DELETED.
>
```

The next procedure discards the present version of the item and does not file it. If there is an earlier form on file - in our case it would be MOVE with all the mistakes - it remains exactly as it was. The edited version of MOVE which we just completed is erased as if it were deleted. The command is

X

to eXit the item. The response is a reminder that changes may have been made since the previous version was FIled:

```
item has changed: press "Y" to exit
```

If you want to discard the current version (the one we have just edited), press Y and the response is

```
'item-id' EXITED
```

followed by the TCL prompt. The latest form of the item is discarded, you have left JET and gone to TCL. The alternative is to to cancel the X command and continue working in the item; press

```
<return>
```

SUMMARY: WHAT TO DO WITH THE ITEM

COMMAND   ACTION

    FI   FIle the item and go to TCL
    FS   File the item; stay in it and in JET
    FD   Delete all versions of the item; go to TCL
    X   eXit the item; do NOT file this version, go to TCL

As above, many procedures are summarized immediately after they are completed. All of the operations covered up to Section 8.7 are consolidated into two guides to JET functions. You may find it helpful to refer to 8.7.1 THE JET MODES, and 8.7.2 FUNCTIONS OF THE KEYS IN JET, before reaching them in the text.

8.5 ALIGN THE TEXT: RULERS

8.5.1 OVERVIEW

A Ruler controls the alignment of the text that follows until there is another Ruler or the item ends, both on the screen and in the printed output. The first line of every item is generally a Ruler. One Ruler may be enough for the entire document but if special formatting is required, such as for columns or blocks of text, a new Ruler can be embedded wherever it is needed. There is no limit to the number of Rulers in an item; they are not shown in the printed output. You can arrange the text exactly as you want by changing or adding Rulers. Activities related to Ruler manipulation are performed in Ruler mode.

When it comes to specifying the locations for margins, indents, and so on, JET offers two choices: take the default Ruler which is set up and ready to use or design your own.

In Section 8.2 we used the JET-IN command to go to the newly created - and at that time empty - item MOVE. Whenever a new item is entered for the first time, the system automatically takes us into Ruler mode. This is because we must give instructions on how to align the material before typing in the actual text. At that time we chose to use the default Ruler as displayed across the Ruler mode screen without going into details about it. We pressed ESC to embed the Ruler and left Ruler mode. Because this was the first time in the item MOVE we were put directly into Insert mode (at all other times ESC from Ruler mode takes us to Command mode). The text was typed in, FIled, and then edited. With this experience we are better able to investigate how Rulers function.

Start from Command mode. As with the other commands, the position of the cursor is where the instruction is carried out. Therefore, you will probably not want to be in the middle of a sentence. First we examine the default Ruler and then make a new Ruler to change the alignment of the last two lines in MOVE. Position the cursor on

    On September 19th we are moving to larger quarters to faci-

Press

    E   Do not press <return>

The most recent embedded Ruler with the locations of the alignment characters is displayed across the screen. The status line is

    change ruler or hit ? for help ...

From here you can press X to return to Command mode. However we want to see the Ruler help screen, press

    ?   Do not press <return>

The Ruler help screen is a one page guide to Ruler terms and cursor movement. The default Ruler is across the top of the screen with all its symbols in fixed places that cannot be changed. Below is the current Ruler which is adjustable. The two Rulers are not necessarily the same. The lower is the most recent one and they are alike now only because we used the default Ruler when starting the item.

A conventional size page 8 1/2 inches wide has 8 inches for text and about 1/2 inch for margins. There is room for 80 characters on a line; thus the page is described as 80 columns wide, each column the width of one character. Instead of a measuring ruler marked in inches, the JET Ruler is divided into columns from 1 to 80. The column positions are shown on the Ruler diagram displayed in Ruler mode, generally 10 columns to 1 inch. Note that some terminals can display more than 80 columns but this special case is not covered here. The cursor is at the left end of the adjustable Ruler; numbers mark the columns by sections of 10 and also individually from 1 to 80. The balance of the screen lists the command keys and how they:

1. position the cursor along the adjustable Ruler
2. control alignment: some keys are unique, others can be used more than once
3. delete
4. Save and Get a Ruler
5. and leave Ruler mode.

The status line is unchanged.

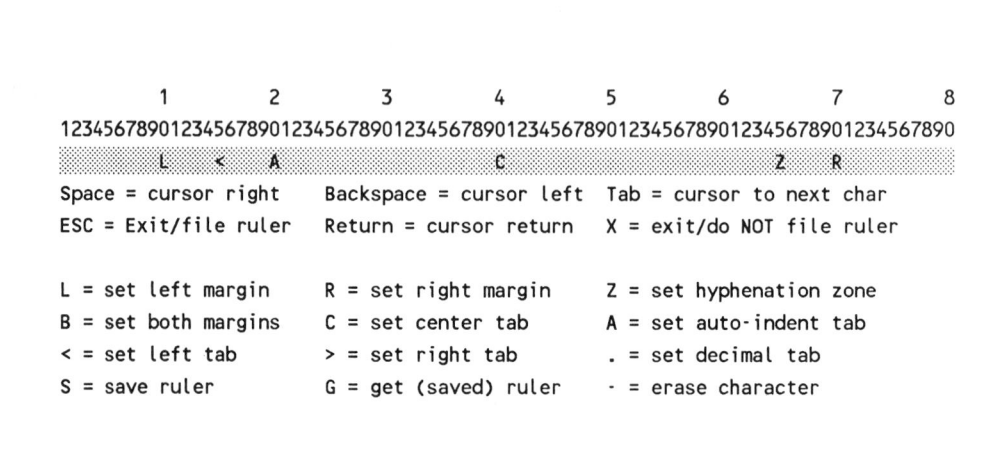

```
                   L   <    A                 C                              Z    R

                       1         2         3         4         5         6         7         8
              12345678901234567890123456789012345678901234567890123456789012345678901234567890
                   L   <    A                 C                              Z    R
```

Space = cursor right   Backspace = cursor left   Tab = cursor to next char
ESC = Exit/file ruler   Return = cursor return   X = exit/do NOT file ruler

L = set left margin   R = set right margin   Z = set hyphenation zone
B = set both margins   C = set center tab   A = set auto-indent tab
< = set left tab   > = set right tab   . = set decimal tab
S = save ruler   G = get (saved) ruler   - = erase character

change ruler or hit ? for help

THE RULER HELP SCREEN

We shall group the keys according to operation and examine them one at a time. Systems do vary; on some terminals you may have to regulate the contrast to see the characters on the Ruler because the display is the reverse of the screen.

8.5.2 CURSOR POSITIONING

In Command mode we move the cursor anywhere within the item. In Ruler mode we move the cursor only along the Ruler to reach the positions of the alignment characters. Movement is controlled by the following keys:

space	moves the cursor one position at a time to the right, at column 80 the cursor wraps to column 1
tab	moves the cursor to the next tab stop or margin, one tab at a time; after the last tab the cursor wraps to the left end of the Ruler
backspace	moves the cursor one column at a time to the left; on some terminals the backspace temporarily erases the character it passes but this character is not removed
<return>	moves the cursor to column 1.

The fastest way to reach the target location may be with a combination of keys such as the tab and then the space bar, but you cannot move off the Ruler.

8.5.3 ALIGNMENT CHARACTERS

UNIQUE KEYS

L and R indicate the Left and Right margins; there can be only one of each on a Ruler. Text starts at L and continues across to R. Margins can be equal or not, each as many columns wide as the item requires.

Note the locations of L and R on the adjustable Ruler, which at this time are the same as on the default Ruler. L is at column 10, leaving columns 1 through 9 for the Left margin. R is at 70, reserving columns 71 through 80 for the Right margin. The two margins are considered to be equal. Text is output between L and R generally at 10 characters per inch. The words are arranged to fit across the line and extra spaces are inserted automatically between words to keep the margins even.

Let us make the text line wider by making the margins narrower. By moving L to column 5 from column 10 we add about 1/2 inch on the left. Move the cursor along the Ruler to 5. Note that the alignment letters can be typed in as either upper or lower case but they appear on the Ruler as upper case. Press

    L

L is a unique key. There can be only one, therefore it moves from the old place into the new. If you leave Ruler mode without making an L, the system assigns L to column 1.

Make the Right margin about 1/2 inch smaller. Position the cursor at 75 and press

    R

R is also unique and the new replaces the old.

When both margins are to be the same width, you can set them with one command. Position the cursor however many columns from the Left end of the Ruler you want L, and press

    B   (for Both margins)

L is set at the cursor position; R is automatically placed the same number of columns from the Right end of the Ruler.

A setting for the R margin permits automatic word wrap to the next line during Insert mode. It is possible to work without R but this is not recommended. As a convention place R at column 78 or before.

The last of the unique keys is Z, which marks the beginning of the hyphenation (or "hot") zone. If a word starts before Z and would extend past R, a bell rings and the status line instructs us to backspace and insert a hyphen in the proper place. This happened as we typed in the word "facilitate." When a word starts after Z, the whole word wraps to the next line. The less space between Z and R, the more hyphens will be needed; the more space between Z and R, the fewer hyphens. When B is used to set up equal margins, Z is automatically moved the same distance from R that it was before. If Z is deleted from the Ruler, there is no hyphenation zone and consequently no soft hyphens. Leave Z where it is on the Ruler for now.

NON-UNIQUE KEYS

The balance of the characters for alignment are five different kinds of tab stops. They are not unique and you may use as many of each as required. A Ruler may have several of one type and none of another, depending on how the text is to be set up. When the tab key is pressed in Ruler and Insert modes, the cursor moves to the next stop as specified on the Ruler. Anticipate where tabs will be required in the item and design the Ruler accordingly. In this way the text will be aligned as it should be, but you can always change a Ruler if the need arises. Remember to use tab stops when entering text from Insert mode; never use the space bar for alignment.

The tab keys are shown below along with their functions and examples.

    <   the left tab indents as for a paragraph. It should not be confused with the Left margin.

```
       10   15                                                    65
       L    <                                                     R
```

        The left tab < starts the text at < such as for an indented paragraph, continues to the R margin, and then wraps to L on the next line.

    A   the auto tab

```
       10        20                                               65
       L         A                                                R
```

        The auto tab is used to indent an entire block of text. The material starts at the A and wraps from R to A on the next line. When the block is complete press <return>
to move to the Left margin on the next line.

Note the difference between < and A:

    <   indents the first line only and then wraps to L on the next line
    A   indents every line at A until <return> is pressed.

    C   centers text around it. The location of C on the Ruler determines the center of the text. For centering on the page, C must be at

40. But there can be as many C tab stops as necessary and at any column(s) between L and R. When inserting text simply press the tab key to reach the C and the text will be positioned with C at the center.

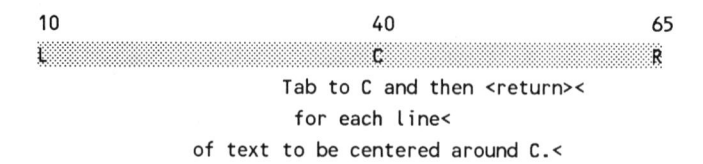

```
10                      40                      65
L                       C                        R
            Tab to C and then <return><
                   for each line<
          of text to be centered around C.<
```

> the right tab is the right edge of the text on the line.

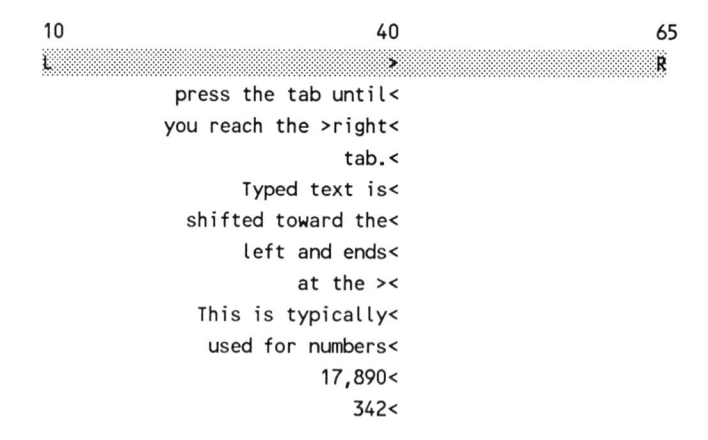

```
10                      40                      65
L                       >                        R
                     press the tab until<
                     you reach the >right<
                                      tab.<
                              Typed text is<
                           shifted toward the<
                               left and ends<
                                 at the ><
                             This is typically<
                             used for numbers<
                                     17,890<
                                       342<
```

Press <return> for each line before the text passes the limit of the Left margin. Note that on some terminals there may be a delay in the screen display: a character does not appear until the next one is typed.

the decimal tab (a period) aligns the numbers below it. If there is no decimal point, its place is understood.

```
10                              52      65
L                                .       R
                                7.2
                                438
                              65.394
                             $910.50
```

Knowing how each tab functions, you can use those that are necessary to align your document. Simply move the cursor along the adjustable Ruler to the location and press the appropriate alignment character.

8.5.4 DELETE

An accumulation of tab stops on a Ruler can be very confusing. Keep the ones that you need and delete the rest. With a bit of practice it is easy to add a tab or embed a new Ruler, if necessary, as you work.

The delete procedure is the same for all the alignment keys. To delete a character:

1. move the cursor to the character using the Ruler mode cursor positioning keys
2. press the - hyphen
3. and the character is erased from the Ruler.

To delete all of the characters on the Ruler at one time:

1. press the _ underline (this requires the <shift> and - keys pressed together). The Ruler is blank.

The preceding operations are performed in Ruler mode. Note that to delete an embedded Ruler you must be in Command mode: position the cursor on the Ruler and press K to Kill the line, which in this case is the Ruler.

8.5.5 SAVE AND GET A RULER

At times it may be convenient to save and re-use Rulers during a work session (after you JET-IN to an item and until you leave it; up to 9 Rulers can be saved). This kind of Save does not embed the Ruler in the document but instead saves it outside where it is available for copying into the item. If you expect to use a Ruler again, set up the adjustable Ruler the way you want it. While in Ruler mode press

    s

The response is

    save which ruler (1 to 9)

Assign a number from 1 through 9 to identify this Ruler. Each number can be used for only one Ruler. If you give a number that has already been used during the current session, the most recent Ruler takes the number and replaces the previous Ruler which can no longer be retrieved by that number. Press a number. The Ruler is saved and displayed below the default Ruler at the top of the screen. Each time you Save a Ruler it is added to the Ruler help screen but the cursor always remains on the adjustable Ruler. In this way you could set up a Ruler to be used later, Save it, and return to the adjustable Ruler to design another Ruler. When ready to leave Ruler mode, press ESC as normally done.

Later on in the work session, embed a Saved Ruler by first positioning the cursor in Command mode where the Ruler is to go. Enter Ruler mode via E and press

    G   (Get the Ruler)

The response is

    get which ruler (0 to 9)

0 is reserved for the default Ruler, 1 through 9 are user assigned. Type in the number of the Ruler to be embedded in the item. Press ESC to leave Ruler mode and return to Command mode; you will see the Saved Ruler embedded in the item. When you press X, the Ruler is not embedded and you return to Command mode.

If you enter a number that has not been assigned to a Saved Ruler, the response is the usual Ruler status line

    change ruler or hit ? for help

Either press X to leave, or remain in Ruler mode, set up the required Ruler, and leave via ESC.

When you end the work session and leave the item from Command mode by FI or X, in early versions of JET Saved Rulers are discarded. The next time you JET-IN to the item the Save routine may start all over again. In Section 8.6.4 Merge there is a method of making a Ruler available indefinitely.

Note that you must be in Ruler mode to Get a Saved Ruler. If you press

G from Insert mode, you see G entered as a character. Backspace to remove it and ESC to Command mode, then E to enter Ruler mode. If you are in Command mode and type G, the response asks

    Go To which Line #

We are not using line numbers, therefore press ESC and then E to enter Ruler mode.

8.5.6 LEAVE RULER MODE

When you are ready to leave Ruler mode, you must make the same decision regarding the adjustable Ruler as you do regarding the text when leaving the item from Command mode: file this version or discard it?

> ESC   embeds the Ruler in the item just above the line the cursor was on when you entered Ruler mode. You are taken from Ruler mode into Command mode.
>
> X   (eXit) discards the adjustable Ruler in its present form, and takes you from Ruler mode into Command mode. Thus the text continues to be aligned by the same Ruler as before you went into Ruler mode.

We have used E and ? to see the Ruler help screen but the ? is not always necessary. In Command mode, press E to enter Ruler mode and the Ruler strip is displayed with the alignment characters in their positions but not the column numbers. This information is often all you need, press X to return to Command mode without embedding a duplicate of the current Ruler. If you want to change the Ruler and do not need the Ruler help screen, follow the normal procedures for cursor positioning and adding or deleting alignment characters. Press ESC to embed the Ruler and return to Command mode. Saved Rulers can be inspected in the same way. Enter Ruler mode, press G and the Ruler number. When you have finished, X Ruler mode and the Saved Ruler is not embedded in the text.

Note that the same command, X, is used for transition from two modes. In both cases the most recent version (of Ruler or text) is not kept.

> X   eXits Ruler mode and takes you to Command mode
> X   eXits Command mode and takes you to TCL

Some time ago we changed the Right and Left margins on the adjustable Ruler to see how MOVE would look with narrower margins - L is at 5, R is at 75. Press ESC to embed the new Ruler. Once back in Command mode we see the new Ruler that was just embedded and the text as re-aligned below it.

The item starts with the opening Ruler:

```
10                                                          70
L                                                            R
```
Thanks to reliable suppliers like you, our business has grown substantially over the last five years.

```
5                                                              75
L                                                               R
```
On September 19th we are moving to larger quarters to facilitate our expanded operations.

The soft hyphen in "facilitate" is no longer necessary and does not show. The new Ruler has served its purpose and should be removed. Position the cursor on the lower Ruler and press K to Kill the line. The text that followed the deleted Ruler is now re-aligned by the closest preceding Ruler; in this case it is the opening Ruler at the Top of the item. Always delete Rulers that are unnecessary to avoid cluttering the document. Press FI to FIle the item and go to TCL.

The information on the Ruler help screen is regrouped by function below.

SUMMARY: THE RULER MODE COMMAND KEYS

CURSOR POSITIONING   DELETE

space bar: move right   - (dash): one character
tab: to next tab   _ (underline): all characters
<return>: to the left end of the Ruler
backspace: move left

ALIGNMENT CHARACTERS   SAVE AND GET A RULER

unique
   L: Left margin   S: Save this Ruler
                              G: Get a Saved Ruler

R: Right margin
B: Both margins
Z: hyphenation zone

non-unique
   <: left tab
   A: Auto tab   LEAVE RULER MODE
   >: right tab   ESC: embed (save) this Ruler
   C: center tab   X (eXit): do not embed this Ruler
   .: decimal tab

8.5.7 APPLICATIONS

Most of the editing in Section 8.4 was on text characters. Knowledge of the Ruler enables you also to make changes in alignment, which is governed by the alignment characters on the most recently embedded Ruler. Some operations do not call for a new Ruler; for example, tab stops are inserted from Insert mode and deleted from Command mode. In comparison, changing one or both margins or adding new tab stops requires altering the adjustable Ruler from Ruler mode.

Rulers can be added to existing text at any time but it is logical to design the Ruler before starting the item. Be guided by how you plan to arrange the output. Continuous text may need a minimum of alignment characters; more detailed formatting, such as data in columns or the summary above, involves more thought. Consider the number of characters in the data and also the amount of space needed between the printed columns. You may find it helpful to work out the design first, using pencil and paper with vertical lines numbered to represent the 80 columns across the page. If coding forms such as for COBOL are available, use them for designing the layout. They have columns numbered from 1 to 80 and make it easy to block in the text. When the layout seems right, copy it to the adjustable Ruler and then test it. JET makes it easy to change the Ruler and re-align the material as necessary.

We have now moved into and out of all three JET modes. As you see there is no secret to mastering JET; decide what you want to do and then go to the appropriate mode to do it. In the sections that follow, new procedures are introduced but they all fall within this basic framework. Below are a summary and a diagram.

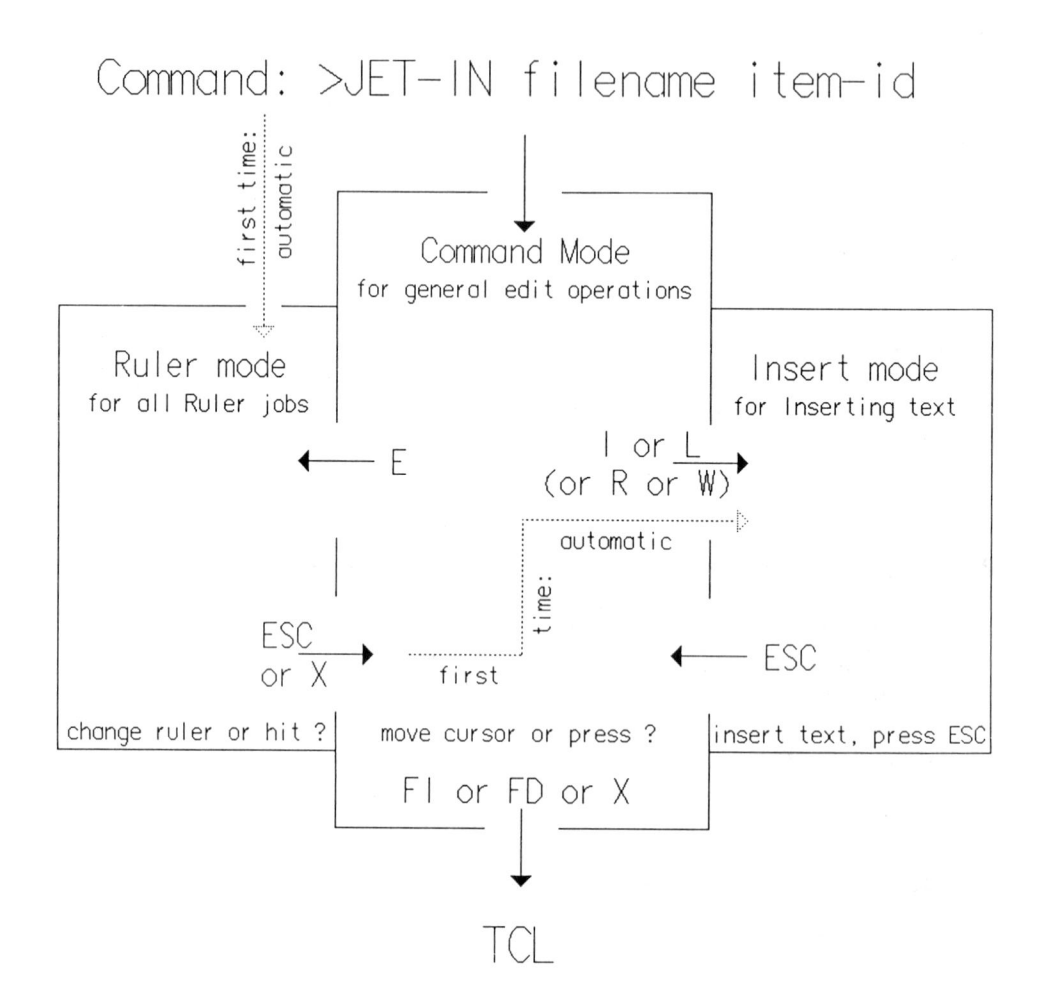

FIGURE 8.1: THE JET MODES: MOVING IN, AROUND, AND OUT

MOVING AROUND IN JET

Reach all items by `>JET-IN filename item-id <return>`

MODE	ENTER VIA	LEAVE VIA	GO TO
COMMAND main status line: move cursor or press ? for help	the JET-IN command except for first time in a new item when you go directly to Ruler mode	FI (FIle) or FD (Delete) or X (eXit do not file)	TCL
RULER main status line: change ruler or hit ? for help	E except for first time in a new item when you enter automatically	ESC (embed Ruler) or X (eXit do not embed Ruler)	Command mode except for first time in a new item when you go to Insert mode
INSERT main status line: insert text, then press ESCAPE	I except for first time in a new item when you enter automatically	ESC	Command mode

8.6 ADVANCED EDITING

8.6.1 ABOUT FILES AND ITEMS

Before you try the editing techniques in this section, here are a few tips on files and items in general. JET uses the same framework as the Pick Operating System to store all data in the format of files, each with one or more items. We created a file called LETTERS and then the item MOVE in that file. The names have been easy to remember so far because they are all we have. Eventually there will be other files and items and it will be difficult to recall the exact spelling of the names and the contents of each file and item. How can you find out the names of the files in your account? Use the same command as in Chapter 4:

>LISTFILES <return>

The response is a listing of all the files in the account. The files created by the user, such as our LETTERS, have a D code and are shown together; these are the JET and also the Data Files. A sample response in part is

```
GADGETS   D   ...
VENDOR    D   ...
LETTERS   D   ...
   .
   .
   .
```

You will recognize the name(s) of your file(s) in this group. Always spell the filename exactly as it appears here. The display probably requires more than one screen. Press <return> to continue. At the end of the listing, you automatically have the TCL prompt. If you prefer to leave the display before the end, press <control> X and you will see the TCL prompt.

After you know the filename, you can get the item-ids that are in it. Use the same formats of LIST and SORT to output the items in the file as we have done in the past. For example

>LIST filename

outputs the items in their internal stored order. Using the test data the command is

>LIST LETTERS <return>

The response is

MOVE

See Chapter 4.2 for expanded forms of LIST.

>SORT filename

outputs the items sorted in ascending order by item-id. See Chapter 5.6 for the SORT verb.

We have been using

```
>JET-IN filename item-id
```

to take us to the item named in the command. Although we do not have other items in the LETTERS file now, there will be a time when you want to work on several items in the same file. Instead of entering and leaving the JET file for each item separately, use an explicit item list as we did in Chapter 4: specify the item-ids in the sequence that you want to see them. The format is

```
>JET-IN filename item-id1 item-id2 item-id3 ...
```

Both existing and new items may be given in the command. Each item is presented in the same order as in the list, starting with item-id1. Perform the operations just as you normally do. When you leave the item via FI or FD or X, instead of going to TCL you go to the next item on the list until you have reached the last item. Then the above commands take you to TCL as they do when there is only one item.

To return to TCL before reaching the last item in an item list, press

```
FK
```

It acts like a multiple X in that it:

1. exits the item
2. does not file the current version
3. Kills the rest of the list without displaying any more items and takes you to TCL.

As mentioned, the maximum size of an item is 32,267 bytes (characters). How can you check the size of an item in order to stay within the limit? Depending on your system, you can do one of the following:

1. After JET-IN to the item, you have seen the Command mode status line part of which is

    ```
    press ? for help
    ```

    When you do so the Command mode help screen is displayed On all systems there is a listing of the cursor positioning and text editing keys and how each functions in Command mode.

We have covered many of the keys and continue with the balance, one at a time. Some systems also show the item-id and its current size in bytes. Leave the help screen by pressing

    N <return>

If you have this information, you can check at any time by pressing ?. Omit procedures 2 and 3 below.

2. When you FI or FS an item larger than 32,267 bytes, the message is

    Document too big. Type the extension document name:

JET will break off part of the item and make it another item. Enter the item-id for the extension. If the name has been assigned, the message is

    Extension document already exists:

Choose another name and type it in. Since JET cannot decide on a logical place to break, it is wiser if you maintain control.

3. Type in this short procedure starting from TCL and you will be able to get the number of bytes in any item whenever you wish.

    >ED MD SIZE <return>

If SIZE already exists the response is

    TOP
    .

Type in

    EX <return>

and skip to the commands starting with LIST. If SIZE does not exist the response is

```
            NEW ITEM
            TOP
```

We are going to create a new Descriptor called SIZE. The procedure is the same as for creating a Data File Descriptor as summarized in Chapter 3 CREATE THE DICTIONARY DESCRIPTOR. The Descriptor for SIZE is as follows:

```
Line
001 S
002 9999
003 through 008 null
009 R
010 6
```

After you have completed all the steps, FIle the item.

Note that 9999 has special meaning to the system here: it does not reference attribute 9999, but instead refers automatically to the size of an item, in bytes. One command format is

```
>LIST filename SIZE
```

to output all the items in the file and their size. For the test data use

```
>LIST LETTERS SIZE <return>
```

When you do not want all of the items in the file, use an explicit item list; the format is

```
>LIST filename "item-id" SIZE
```

or, using the test data

```
>LIST LETTERS "MOVE" SIZE <return>
```

The SORT verb can also be used in the formats covered in Chapter 5.6. For example SORT the file in ascending order on item-ids and output the size of each item. Note that there is no Sort clause - BY attributename - in JET because we are not using attributes, only filenames and item-ids. The format is

```
>SORT filename SIZE
```

When working on a long item, check the size from time to time. As it nears 20,000 to 25,000 bytes, plan to end it at a logical break point, such as at a section boundary, and create a new item to continue. In Section 8.9 we cover how to link the items and print them as one unit.

8.6.2 THE SPELLING CHECKER

Once again, note that there may be slight differences among versions of JET in the editing procedures that follow, particularly in "The Works." Consult your reference manual when necessary.

The Spelling Checker compares the words in your text to those in a WORDS file of approximately 48,000 entries that comes with most versions of JET. When the Checker is turned on, it inspects each word in the text, one at a time; the case of the letters does not matter. The cursor moves forward and stops at the first word that has no match in the WORDS file. This means that the text word is not in the file: either the word is misspelled or it has not yet been entered. You may then change your word or leave it as written and, if you wish, add it to the file. Thus a misspelled word can be added inadvertently to the file. The word could again be spelled wrong but as long as it matches a word on the list it is passed as correct. There is another reason not to rely blindly on the Spelling Checker. As mentioned in Chapter 1, the computer cannot deal with the context in which a word is used. Suppose you type in "sail" instead of "sale", and "sail" is on the WORDS list. You will not be alerted by the Checker. Making sense is your responsibility not the computer's.

The Spelling Checker requires at least 1 megabyte on the disk and so may not have been loaded on your system. You can find out shortly for yourself when we try to use it. There is a choice between checking the words in existing text from the cursor position to the end of the item or as the text is typed in during Insert mode. In both cases remember that when the Checker stops at a word, it is not necessarily spelled wrong but only that it is not in your WORDS file. Start the exercise from Command mode.

CHECK EXISTING TEXT

Here we check the words already in MOVE and position the cursor at the beginning of the item. Press

    | No \<return>

If you do not have the Spelling Checker the system beeps and displays

```
"WORDS" file not available
```

Press ESC and plan to check your own spelling. Continue reading and enter the new text in the section CHECK INSERTED TEXT.

When there is a WORDS file the check starts from the cursor position and the cursor stops at the first word that is not on file. This varies with each user's WORDS list. The terminal beeps and the status line displays

```
word spelled correctly? (Y/N/ESC)
```

The choices are:

    ESC leaves the word as it is and continues the check
    N   (No) gives you a chance to change the word and displays the Command mode status line. Perform the required editing and press | to resume the check
    Y   (Yes) allows you to add the word to the file if you wish by displaying

```
enter it in the dictionary? (Y/N)
```

Press either

    N (No, do Not add this word and continue), or

    Y (Yes, enter this word. The response is)

```
retype word with dots at syllable breaks:
```

Follow the instruction and press the \<return> key. The word is entered in the file and the check goes on.

CHECK INSERTED TEXT

In order to check words as they are typed in from Insert mode, we add a few lines of text to MOVE. While in Command mode and before entering Insert mode, position the cursor at the Bottom of the item. (The word "facilitate" was hyphenated on the preceding line.)

```
litate our expanded operations.
```

Turn on the Checker by pressing

    U   No <return>

If you do not have the WORDS file, the response is the same as before. Press ESC and continue. If you have the Checker the status line is

```
Spelling checker on!
```

U is like a toggle switch: it turns the Checker ON from OFF, or OFF from ON.

Whether you have the Checker or not, enter Insert mode:

Press	I	
Press	<return>	to go to the next line
	<return>	for a blank line.

If you are using the Checker, any of the inserted words that are not in your WORDS file will be flagged as you type them in. Follow the same procedures as with | . Note that to make a correction you are taken into Command mode and then returned to Insert mode automatically.

Enter the first line to be added:

```
The new address is
```

Press <return> once for a blank line and then again so that the street address starts on a new line. Press the tab key for the indent. Type in

```
123 Tain Street
```

To start the city on a new line press <return> and the tab. The text to

Word Processing with JET 325

enter is

    Aceville NY 34567

We are now ready to leave Insert mode, press ESC. Back in Command mode turn off the Spelling Checker (if you have been using it) by pressing U. The status line is

    Spelling checker off!

If you do not press U to turn off the Checker, it will be on the next time you go into Insert mode.

8.6.3 INSERT ON A NEW LINE

There is only one way to become familiar and comfortable with all of these editing techniques - practice. Try them. Repeat a new procedure. Change the item and then change it again. Plan a revision and use the proper commands to make it. The time is well spent because we also learn from mistakes.

Up to now we have pressed I in Command mode to enter Insert mode and then inserted the new text from the cursor position. When we wanted the new material to start on a new line, we had to press the <return> key first. Thus two keys were required. One command - L - combines I and <return>. L takes you to Insert mode and also to a new line.

As always be sure that you are in Command mode before starting to edit. Let us use L first to add a blank line at the end of MOVE. The cursor is at the end of the item:

    Aceville NY 34567

Press

    L

The cursor moves to the Left margin on the line below. Press ESC and the end of line indicator is on the new line.

    Aceville NY 34567
    <

Now add a new line with text. Press L and the cursor moves down to the next line. Add the following sentence to MOVE starting at the left margin where the cursor is. The complete sentence does not fit on one line. Instead of hyphenating "loyalty" after the beep, backspace to the space between "continued" and "loyalty"; and "loyalty" wraps to the next line. Finish typing the word and the period.

```
As our major vendor you can be assured of our continued
loyalty.
```

When the insert is complete, leave Insert mode by ESC.

8.6.4 MERGE

The M (Merge) command copies material into the item you are working in. For our purposes the Merge can be part of the item we are in such as the opening Ruler, or another item from the same or a different file. When text is Merged it is only copied; the source remains exactly as it was and can be Merged unlimited times. Always use the Merge command when you are in the item that is to receive the Merge. The procedure is the same wherever the Merge is coming from; first cover the general steps and then specific exercises.

Position the cursor where the Merge is to go. For clarity you may want to insert a blank line for the cursor to rest on and delete extra space later. All Merges are initiated by

```
       M           do not press the <return> key unless so instructed.
```

The same four questions are always asked so that the material can be found, copied, and Merged into the new location:

1. From what file are you Merging text? Spell the filename exactly as when it was originally created.
2. From what item? Once the file has been found, the proper item must be reached. Spell the item-id correctly.
3. Where in this item does the Merge begin? Generally we start at the Top of the item.
4. Where does the Merge end? Most of the time we Merge the entire item and go to the end or last line.

After the questions are answered, the specified material is copied into the current item at the cursor position. The Merged text becomes part of the item. In the following examples we are using a Ruler as illustration because a document frequently requires new alignment and Merging a Ruler is convenient. However the same procedures apply to Merging a large or small text item.

SAME FILE, SAME ITEM

As the first exercise, Merge the Ruler from the Top of the file named LETTERS, item-id MOVE into the end of the same file and item. Actually this is not necessary at this time because the opening Ruler here aligns all of the text that follows it. Since a document can have multiple Rulers, you may want to use the Ruler at the Top instead of creating a duplicate.

First add a new line at the Bottom of MOVE and position the cursor on it. Next, in Command mode, press

    M

The response is

    File-name or RETURN for current:

This Merge is from the current file (the one we are in which is LETTERS); RETURN indicates the carriage return <return>. Press

    <return>

The next response is

    Item-ID or RETURN for "MOVE"

The name of the item you are in is enclosed in double quotes. Since this Merge is from the same item press

    <return>

The response is

    First line# (RETURN for 001):

This means, where do you want the Merge to start, from a particular line number or from the beginning of the item? JET does not automatically generate line numbers. The only line we know is the first line 001 which is the Ruler at the Top of the item. The easiest course is to Merge from line 001 and take either the entire item (deleting text later if necessary) or Merge only the Ruler at line 001. Although you can determine line numbers within the item, it is not practical. A line in JET consists of one of the following:

1. A paragraph, which terminates with the < indicator.
2. An embedded Ruler.
3. Backslash lines (covered in Section 8.8).

In order to find the line numbers within an item you must count starting from the Top with the opening Ruler on line 001. We eliminate the need for counting lines by Merging from line 001. Press

    <return>

The last of the prompts is

    Last line# (RETURN for E-O-Item):

E-O-Item means the end or the last line of the item. In this particular example we are Merging only the Ruler from line 001 therefore the last line to be Merged is 1. Type in

    1 <return>

After the last question is answered, you see the Merged text - here the Ruler - copied to the line below the cursor position. When a Ruler has no lines below it, you can move the cursor off it by pressing I. The cursor moves down to the next line. Press ESC. You then have room to move the cursor around.

When Merging from the item being edited, the Merged text is copied from the previously filed version of the item. This means that until changes are filed via FS (or FI) they do not appear in the Merge.

You may find that extra lines were Merged along with the Ruler. To delete an unwanted line, position the cursor anywhere on the line and press K.

In this example the Ruler from the Top was used to illustrate a Merge from the same file, same item. The item as it now stands does not require a duplicate embedded Ruler and so position the cursor on the line with the Ruler and press K to delete the line.

SAME FILE, DIFFERENT ITEM

Any text material can be Merged from one item into another. One practical application is to Merge a Ruler. As mentioned earlier, Rulers can be Saved and Gotten, and embedded in the item. In early releases of JET, Saved Rulers vanish when you leave the item. By creating an item that consists only of a customized Ruler, you always have that Ruler available to Merge into another item in the same or another file whenever that particular alignment is required. The steps to do this are outlined below:

First create a new item in an existing file. The general format is

>JET-IN filename new.item-id

Using our file LETTERS and the new item named RULER.A the command is

>JET-IN LETTERS RULER.A <return>

You automatically enter Ruler mode because this is a new item. Set up the Ruler to align the text the way you want it. ESC to embed Ruler in the new item and leave Ruler mode. You are taken directly to Insert mode since this item is entered for the first time. We want only the Ruler in this item and no text is to be added. ESC to leave Insert mode and go to Command mode. The last step is to FI (FIle) the item. RULER.A is now ready to be Merged into any other item as often as necessary. The contents of this new item could just as easily have been text that we anticipated needing.

At some point we may want to align the text in MOVE, using the Ruler we have set up in RULER.A. All we have to do is Merge RULER.A in the place we want it.

JET-IN to LETTERS MOVE if you are not there. Position the cursor in MOVE to the place for the Merge and press M to start. As mentioned, the series of responses is the same for all Merges:

```
file-name or RETURN for current:
```

Press <return> because MOVE is in the file LETTERS and so is RULER.A. The response is

```
Item-ID or RETURN for "MOVE":
```

This time the Merge is from another item. Type in the item-id of the item being Merged, here RULER.A, and the <return> key

```
RULER.A <return>
```

If the item does not exist - either it was not created or you have spelled the name incorrectly which is the same thing to the computer - what you typed in is erased and the question remains until a valid name is given. The Merge procedure can be cancelled at any time by pressing ESC as answer to any of the questions.

```
First line# (RETURN for 001):
```

Press

```
<return>
```

to Merge from line 001 of item RULER.A. The response is

```
Last line# (RETURN for E-O-Item):
```

The last line is the end of the Merge therefore press

```
<return>
```

The contents of RULER.A are copied and displayed in the item MOVE. In this example it happens to be a Ruler but whatever the item contains, it can be copied into its new location. Here the Merged material is not of any value. Position the cursor on the Ruler that was just Merged and press K to Kill the line. After Merging, decide if the original item will be needed again. We shall be using the item RULER.A. Otherwise we would JET-IN to RULER.A and delete it by pressing FD from Command mode.

Another application is to Merge RULER.A at the Top of a new item instead of setting up the same Ruler again. The normal sequence after first entry to a new item is leave Ruler Mode via the ESC key, embed the Ruler, and automatically enter Insert mode. When we plan to Merge a Ruler for the Top of the item the procedure is slightly different: press X to leave Ruler mode without embedding a Ruler. Because there is no Ruler at the Top, we are taken to Command mode; the item is totally blank with only the cursor at the Top and the status line at the bottom of the screen. Follow the Merge above to copy RULER.A into the new item and then press I to enter Insert mode.

DIFFERENT FILE

Eventually there will be more than one JET file (review Section 8.2 when you are ready to create a file). The same Merge procedure is used to copy material from an item in one file into an item in another file. For example, suppose there is a file named PROCEDURES with an item in it called ACCOUNTING. You could Merge the item ACCOUNTING into the item MOVE. Position the cursor in MOVE where the item ACCOUNTING is to be copied and press M. The answers to the four questions in this instance are as follows:

For the filename:

    PROCEDURES <return>

For the item-id:

    ACCOUNTING <return>

For questions 3 and 4:

    <return>

to Merge the entire item. ACCOUNTING remains exactly as it was but is copied into and becomes part of MOVE.

8.6.5 SEARCH (AND REPLACE)

FORWARD SEARCH

S Searches for a specified target called the *search string*. Search can also replace the search string with a replacement string. All searches take place in Command mode after a series of questions have been answered. The Search can be cancelled during the questions by pressing ESC once or twice depending on the question.

The first step in all types of searches is to position the cursor. The following examples, except for the last one, are searches that go forward from the cursor position starting with the next word. In this exercise be sure that you are in Command mode and position the cursor at the Top of the item MOVE. The key S gets things started; press

    S   No <return>

The response to S is always the same: what do you want to look for?

    Search for:

The search string can be a symbol, a word, one or more numbers, or whatever you choose to have the system find except the automatic < indicator. Let us search for the first occurrence of the word "our" in MOVE. Type in

    our

and press

    <return>

to show the end of the search string. The next response is also displayed with all searches:

    replace with (or ESC for search only):

Here you indicate whether you want only to search for the string and go to its location or search for it and replace it with another string. In this example we are searching only, therefore press

    ESC   No <return>

The next question asks whether or not to compare the case of the search string to that in the text. This prompt appears only when the search string contains alphabetic characters which could be upper or lower case, or a combination:

```
Compare case (Y/N):
```

Press either

| Y | (Yes, both strings must be the same. For example search string "our" matches the text "our" but not "Our"), or |
| N | (No, the case does not matter). |

Enter

```
N          No <return>
```

JET searches through the item until it finds the first occurrence of the search string "our" and positions the cursor on the target:

```
Thanks to reliable suppliers like you, our business has
```

This ends the Search and the status line changes to the normal one for Command mode.

Start the next Search again from the beginning of MOVE by pressing T to get to Top of the item. As always, initiate the Search by pressing

```
S
```

This time when the prompt asks for the search string, enter the word

```
aardvark <return>
```

We are searching and not replacing so again press

```
ESC
```

There is no need to compare case so the next prompt is answered by

```
N          No <return>
```

The system tries to find the search string in the item but cannot which is no surprise to us. The response is

```
String not found...
```

or

>   cannot find "aardvark"

Leave the Search by pressing

>   ESC

and the usual Command mode status line is displayed.

SUMMARY: SEARCH FOR THE FIRST OCCURRENCE OF THE SEARCH STRING

Press S	No <return>
Enter the search string	<return>
Press ESC for Search only	No <return>
Compare case? Press Y or N	No <return>

Just as you use a bookmark to keep your place in a book you can mark your place in an item in order to return to it quickly whether you go out to lunch or look for the place three days later. When in Insert mode type an odd symbol or string - anything that is not in the text such as @ or ??? - at the proper spot. When you are ready to work, simply Search for the string and then delete it after you get to the location. This is also helpful for flagging the place for a Merge.

Next we Search for all occurrences of the search string "our" and replace each one with the replacement string "my"; the operation becomes Search and Replace. Position the cursor at the Top of MOVE. The first two steps are the same for all Searches

>   S   No <return>

Enter the search string

>   our <return>

The response is the same as before

>   Replace with (or ESC for search only):

Now we enter the replacement string; type in the following.

my <return>

The response gives you the choice of having every occurrence of the search string replaced automatically or not.

    all occurrences (Y/N):

At this point we want every occurrence of "our" to be replaced with "my". Press

    Y   No <return>

Note that when we typed in the word "our" we did not think about the possibility that the search string might be part of another word such as "detour." There will be no problem of this sort in MOVE, but consider the likelihood whenever ordering replacement of all occurrences. You could use a blank space on each side of the word " our " to eliminate this problem. In any case, be very sure that you want every occurrence replaced before pressing Y. The example that follows the next Summary shows the alternative. The response is familiar

    compare case (Y/N):

Press

    N   No <return>

JET goes through the item and each time it finds the search string "our" it replaces it with "my". The operation ends at the last replacement and the Command mode status line appears.

SUMMARY: SEARCH AND REPLACE ALL OCCURRENCES

Press S	No <return>
Enter the search string	<return>
Enter the replacement string	<return>
all occurrences? Press Y	No <return>
compare case? Press Y or N	No <return>

Instead of automatically replacing every occurrence of the search string, JET can be instructed to stop at each one and ask whether to replace or not. Again go to the Top of MOVE and press S. We shall search for the string "my" and at each occurrence decide if it should be replaced with "our" or left as is. The responses and our replies are:

```
Search for: my <return>
Replace with: our <return>
```

The next query is where we instruct JET to stop at each occurrence and give us the option of replacing:

```
all occurrences (Y/N):
```

Here we press

    N   No <return>

The response is familiar

```
compare case?
```

Enter

    N   No <return>

The cursor stops at the first occurrence of "my" and the response is

```
replace (Y=yes N=no Q=quit):
```

Press one of the following keys:

- Y (Yes, replace this occurrence of the search string; the change is shown on the screen. Continue the Search and stop at the next occurrence.)
- N (No, do not replace here; leave the search string as it is and continue to the next occurrence.)
- Q (Quit the Search; the usual Command mode status line is displayed.)

Each time the search string shows up you can replace or not, or quit the Search. After the last occurrence the message at the bottom of the screen is

```
String not found...
```

Press

```
ESC        or
<return>
```

and the Command mode status line appears.

You can also replace a string with nothing which is the same as deleting it. Instead of typing in a replacement string, press <return> only. Follow the choice of procedures from that point on.

SUMMARY: SEARCH FOR ALL OCCURRENCES AND DECIDE AT EACH ONE TO REPLACE OR NOT OR QUIT

Press S	No <return>
Enter the search string	<return>
Enter the replacement string	<return>
all occurrences? Press N	No <return>
compare case? Press Y or N	No <return>

at each occurrence press either
    Y   (Yes, replace and continue.)
or N   (No, do not replace, continue.)
or Q   (Quit the Search.)

BACKWARD SEARCH

All of the examples thus far are for forward Searches. A Search can also be made backward from the cursor position to the Top (beginning) of the item. Instead of S use the semicolon ; to start a backward Search. The same series of questions are asked and you have the identical procedures from which to choose.

SEARCH AGAIN

The most recent Search can be repeated during a work session. Start as always by positioning the cursor where the Search is to begin. Instead of S or ; press A (for Again). Whatever answers you gave for the Search that preceded A become the instructions for the repeat. There may be no change in the status line after you press A, but the Search is initiated. Wait. If there is no previously defined search string from the current session, the response is

```
No search string!
```

Leave the Search by ESC or <return> and start from S.

An application of A is to repeat a Search that found the first occurrence of the search string. The command A will find the next occurrence after the cursor position, if there is one.

8.6.6 CUT AND PASTE

It is often necessary to duplicate a block of text or move it from one place to another or to delete it. If you are working with paper, you use scissors and glue or scissors only. The *Cut* and *Paste* operations in JET do the same, but with no mess. The procedures have separate parts: first define the boundaries of the cutout text, then delete it, or save it to be Pasted whenever you wish. At the cursor position indicate the beginning of the material to cut. Move through the item to the location for the end of the cut and mark it. The specified text is "cut" or removed from the item. The cut can be deleted immediately or assigned an identifying number and saved as a "Paste". Once saved, the material can be "pasted" (copied) unlimited times into the item from which it came or into another item in the same file. The Paste is available until its number is assigned to a new cut which *overrides* (takes the place of) the old one. A Paste can also be deleted. The system allows 10 Pastes for each file at a port (terminal). (Reminder: "The Works" has added modifications to the Cut and Paste procedure such as unlimited paste items.)

CUT

As an exercise, let us move the first sentence in the item MOVE and re-position it after the second sentence. This involves cutting the segment, saving it, and then pasting it in a new location. In Command mode, position the cursor at the start of the cut as below:

```
▓hanks to reliable suppliers like you, our business has
```

To make the beginning cut press the left square bracket [and do not press <return>.

```
[            No <return>
```

Note that if you wanted to type this bracket into the text you would be in Insert mode. The status line reads

    position cursor for 2nd cut.

After you initiate a cut you must move the cursor through the item to the place for the second cut without performing any other operation along the way. Position the cursor at the end of the sentence:

    substantially over the last five years.

The right square bracket] marks the end of the cut. Press

    ]   No <return>

The response is

    save as paste # (0 - 9) or - to delete text

This is where you give the instruction on what to do with the cut text. If you press the hyphen - you delete the cut and it is gone forever. You can save the cut by giving it a number from 0 to 9 (ten numbers). If the number selected has already been assigned, the new cut takes the number and overrides the old cut. Since this is the first cut to be saved, any number can be chosen. Later in this section we cover how to find which numbers have been assigned and what each number contains. For the example press

    1   No <return>

The material within the brackets has been *cut out* of the item and disappears from the screen. The cut is saved as a Paste item and identified by the number just given to it. A Paste item can be copied in any location in the item from which it was taken, here MOVE, or into any other item in the same file, here LETTERS.

PASTE

The Paste item is stored and available whenever you are ready to copy it. Position the cursor where the Paste is to go, perhaps on a new line or within a line. Move the cursor to the following position.

litate our expanded operations.▓

Type in the Paste command which is

    P   No <return>

If you are in Command mode and hit P by mistake and do not want to Paste a cut, press ESC to cancel P. The response to P is

    which paste # (0 - 9)

Type in the number of the Paste, here

    1   No <return>

This is a valid Paste number; it has been assigned. The Paste is copied to the item and the Command mode status line is displayed. When there is no Paste item with that number, the message is

    cannot find that paste item!

Then press ESC to leave the Paste operation.

The item in part is now

    On September 19th we are moving to larger quarters to faci-
    litate our expanded operations. Thanks to reliable suppliers like you,
    our business has grown substantially over the last five years.<

The letter looked better the way it was originally; suppose we change it back to the first version. The sentence starting with "Thanks" is Paste 1 and we can paste it again where we want it. Delete the sentence from its new place by the command Y. Insert a new line above the sentence "On September...".

The screen in part showing the cursor position is

    ▓
    On September 19th we are moving to larger quarters to faci-

The cursor is at the place for the Paste. Press P and then 1 to put the first sentence back where it was. Insert a blank line after the word "years.". Always check to see if editing is required such as removing extra line(s) or punctuation. The item should be as follows:

```
Thanks to reliable suppliers like you, our business has
grown substantially over the last five years.<
<
On September 19th we are moving to larger quarters to faci-
litate our expanded operations.<
```

The location for a Paste can be flagged in the same way as suggested for a Merge. Insert one or more unique characters to mark the place, Search for the marker, then delete it and Paste in the addition.

To save storage space when a Paste is no longer needed, create a small amount of text, make the cuts, and assign the old paste number to the new cut. The alternative is to delete the Paste from TCL which is described shortly. Another suggestion is to use Paste 0 for temporary cuts that can be discarded after they are pasted, and reserve numbers 1 through 9 for those you may want for the future.

It is impossible - and unnecessary - to remember what Paste numbers are in use and their contents. There are two ways to get this information about the Pastes in a particular file. The first is convenient when you are in JET Command mode. The position of the cursor does not matter when displaying a Paste. Press the double quote " to call for a Paste

    "   No <return>

The response asks which Paste number you want:

```
which paste # (0 - 9)
```

For our example, type in the number

    1   No <return>

You may want to see the contents of a particular Paste displayed or only to find a number that has not yet been assigned.

If the Paste number exists, it is displayed. Note that editing cannot be done at this time; the Paste can be altered only after it has been copied to an item. A small Paste fits on one screen. When you are ready to leave it, press ESC or <return>. A long Paste requires multiple screens. Press <return> to display it, a page at a time; to leave at the end of the display press ESC or <return>. You can leave the Paste before the last screen is displayed by pressing the control key and X together

    <control> X

and return to the Command mode status line.

If the Paste number has not been assigned, the response is

    cannot find that paste item!

This may be exactly what you want to know - a number that is available. Press ESC to return to the Command mode status line.

The item MOVE should be FIled; leave JET and go to TCL.

As just shown, JET saves Pastes by their user-assigned numbers. The limit is 10 Pastes for each file per port and the Pastes can be copied into any item within its file. You cannot Paste a cut from one file to another file.

More than one terminal (port) can be connected to a CPU and each port is identified by its port number. In addition to their Paste number and file, Pastes are also stored by port. If you are always at the same work station, there is no problem in retrieving your Pastes. But, if you change to another port, you cannot get the Pastes you had stored previously. To find your port number use the command WHO at TCL

    >WHO <return>

The response is the port number at which you are working and your account name, such as

    0 JAN

or

    37 SALES

The other method of getting to Pastes is directly from TCL. To do this you must understand that the Paste is saved as an item in the file and the system automatically provides a 3-part item-id:

1. PASTE* is the beginning of all Paste item-ids
2. Port.number* is the port at which the Paste was created, usually 2 or 3 digits
3. Paste.number is the number assigned by the user when the cut was saved.

For example, if the port is 0 and the Paste is 2, the item-id for that Paste is

```
PASTE*00*2
```

Note that the system uses a leading zero. You could figure out a Paste item-id for yourself knowing the elements but you need not bother.

In Section 8.6.1 the verbs LIST and SORT were mentioned to output the items in a file. Now that there are several items in the file LETTERS it makes sense to use the SORT verb. The command

```
>SORT LETTERS <return>
```

outputs

```
MOVE
PASTE*00*1
RULER.A
```

Note that your Paste may not necessarily have the port number 00. As you see, the output is arranged in ascending order on the item-ids. The item-id for the Paste provides the means to reach it from TCL as with any JET item if you wish to do so. The format to enter the Paste item is

```
>JET-IN filename paste.item-id
```

Although the second part of your Paste item-id is probably different, an example of the command is

```
>JET-IN LETTERS PASTE*00*1 <return>
```

The response is a display of the Paste item. As with any long item continue the display by pressing <return>.

When a Paste is displayed from within JET by double quotes " you can only inspect it and leave. In contrast, a Paste entered from TCL can be treated as any JET item: edit and leave via FI, X, or FD. FD deletes the Paste entirely as compared to assigning the number again to over-write the previous contents. Press X to leave the Paste and return to TCL.

To practice Pasting to another item in the same file we can copy Paste 1 into RULER.A. The procedure is the same as before: we must be in Command mode in the item which is to receive the Paste.

>JET-IN LETTERS RULER.A <return>

This item has only the Ruler in it so far. If there is a blank line below the Ruler, move the cursor to it; if not, press I to move the cursor off the Ruler to a new line and then ESC to leave Insert mode.

In Command mode we give the instruction

P   No <return>

The response asks for the Paste number, type in

1   No <return>

The Paste is copied into RULER.A but continues to exist as Paste 1 until 1 is assigned to another cut in the LETTERS file. Leave RULER.A via FI.

If you JET-IN to a Paste item-id that has not been assigned, the system treats it as a new item taking you directly to Ruler mode and then to Insert mode in the usual sequence.

The Cut and Paste operation as shown has saved the cut and removed it from the source item. There may be occasions when you want to have the material available as a Paste item without taking it out of the original and then having to Paste it back in. The procedure to duplicate a segment of an item (without removing it) is as follows:

>JET-IN filename item-id <return>

Generally we would perform several edit tasks while in the item, this time confine the activities to these four:

1. Position the cursor for the first cut and press [
2. Position the cursor for the second cut and press]
3. Assign a number to save the cut as a Paste. The cut is saved.
4. Press X to eXit the item. X instructs JET to ignore the changes made during the current work session and retain the former version of the item. Therefore the cut text is copied to the Paste and stored but not removed from the item. The next time you JET-IN to the item you will find it unchanged.

A COMPARISON OF MERGE and CUT AND PASTE

	MERGE	CUT AND PASTE
The source text is:	an entire item (or part if line numbers are used)	any part of an item as defined by the cuts
saved as:	original filename and item-id at any port	a Paste number within one file for each port
limited to:	no limit	10 Pastes per file per port
copied into:	any file, any item	same file, any item
The specified text:	remains in the source item	normally is removed from the source item and deleted immediately or saved as a Paste
To delete:	use normal procedures for all or part of the item	delete the Paste item from TCL or over-write the Paste by assigning the number to another cut

SUMMARY: FILES AND ITEMS IN JET

TO DISPLAY	USE THE COMMAND	THE OUTPUT IS
filenames	>LISTFILES	JET and Data Files are listed together
item-ids in one file	>LIST filename or >SORT filename	all items including Pastes
a JET item including a Paste	>JET-IN filename item-id	the item specified
several JET items including Pastes	>JET-IN filename item-id1 item-id2 ...	the items specified in the order given
a Paste item	>JET-IN filename PASTE*port*paste.number or from Command mode in an item in the same file press the double quote "	the Paste specified; it can be edited the Paste specified is displayed only; it cannot be edited
item size	from Command mode in the item by pressing ? or from TCL via the Descriptor SIZE such as >LIST LETTERS "MOVE" SIZE	the item size in bytes

8.7 SUMMARY GUIDES

8.7.1 THE JET MODES

Note the exceptions as listed below for first time entry to a new item.

RULER MODE

ENTER   from Command mode E
Exception: when you JET-IN to a new item for the first time you automatically enter Ruler mode.

FOR   all Ruler activities, mainly to inspect, create, and alter a Ruler

CURSOR   OCCUPIES the place of the next typed character
POSITIONING along the Ruler only
    space bar: move right
    tab: to the next tab stop
    <return>: to the beginning of the Ruler
    backspace: move left

FUNCTIONS Alignment characters
    Unique
        L: Left margin
        R: Right margin
        B: Both margins
        Z: hyphenation zone
    Non-unique
        <: left tab
        A: Auto tab
        >: right tab
        C: Center tab
        .: decimal tab
    Delete
        - (dash): one character
        _ (underline): all characters
    S: Save a Ruler during the current session
    G: Get a Saved Ruler

USUAL STATUS LINE   change ruler or hit ? for help

LEAVE   ESC (embed the Ruler)
X (eXit, do not embed the Ruler)

GO TO   Command mode
Exception: when you are in a new item for the first time
    ESC takes you to Insert mode.

INSERT MODE

ENTER from Command mode
I
L
(or R Replace a character or W replace a word with restrictions)
Exception: the first time you JET-IN to a new item you are automatically taken by ESC from Ruler mode into Insert mode.

FOR inserting all text

CURSOR OCCUPIES
the place of the next typed character
POSITIONING
tab: to the next tab stop
backspace: back one character
<return>: to the next line (the end of line indicator is automatically entered in the item)
Note that the cursor moves along the line and wraps to the next line until the <return> is pressed.

FUNCTIONS
type in all "text"

USUAL STATUS LINE
insert text, then press ESCAPE

LEAVE ESC

GO TO Command mode

COMMAND MODE

ENTER >JET-IN filename item-id1 {item-id2} <return>
Exception: when you JET-IN to a new item for the first time you automatically enter Ruler mode.

FOR editing operations excluding Ruler activities and Inserting text

CURSOR OCCUPIES the place from which the command is executed
POSITIONING is in 4 directions via
  the Main keypad
    B: Bottom (end) of item
    T: Top (beginning) of item
    ): forward a paragraph
    (: back a paragraph
    ^: end of line
    <return>: beginning of the line or to the next line if you are already at the beginning of the line
    tab: next tab stop
  the Numeric keypad
    0: back a page
    1: back a sentence
    2: down a line
    3: forward a sentence
    4: back a character
    5: to page top
    6: forward a character
    7: back a word
    8: up a line
    9: forward a word
    .: to page bottom and again for the next page

FUNCTIONS
  Cancel
    Merge, Paste, Search, Spelling checker if there is no WORDS file: ESC
    balance of items on an explicit item list: FK
    multi-screen display before the end: <control>X

Change case
   letter: :
   word: *
   line: !
Cut [to start
   ] to end
Delete
   character: D
   word: Q
   line: K
   sentence: Y (from the cursor position to the end of the sentence)
   item: FD
Display
   the Command mode help screen: ? (leave by N)
   the next page of a multi-page item: <return>
   output format: O
   a Paste item: "
File the item
   FI (leave the item)
   FS (stay in the item)
Merge M
Paste P
Redisplay the screen C
Replace
   character: R
   word: W
Search (and Replace)
   forward: S
   backward: ;
   Again: A (repeat the previous Search in the current item)
Spelling checker
   existing text: | (from the cursor position to the end of the item)
   Inserted text: U (toggle)
Transpose characters Z
View V (toggle)

USUAL STATUS LINE   move cursor or press ? for help

LEAVE   Command mode and remain in the item
        E to enter Ruler mode
        I or L to enter Insert mode

LEAVE   the item
          FD (Delete the item)
          FI (FIle this version of the item)
          X (eXit, do not file this version of the item)

GO TO   TCL (or the next item if there was an explicit item list in the JET-IN command)

8.7.2 FUNCTIONS OF THE KEYS IN JET

Most of the keys are commands and the mode in which the key is pressed determines its function. Therefore each of the command keys listed below is followed by an abbreviation for the mode where that function occurs:

(C) Command mode
(I) Insert mode
(R) Ruler mode

THE MAIN KEYPAD

KEY	MODE	FUNCTION
A	(C)	Search Again
	(R)	Auto tab
B	(C)	move the cursor to the Bottom (end) of the item
	(R)	Both margins
C	(C)	Re-display the screen
	(R)	Center tab
D	(C)	Delete a character
E	(C)	display the current Ruler. Next press either ? for the Ruler help screen or X to return to Command mode
F	(C)	FD Delete the item and leave it
FI FIle the item and leave it
FK cancel the remaining items in a multiple item list
FS File the item and remain in it
G	(R)	Get a Saved Ruler
I	(C)	enter Insert mode
K	(C)	delete a line
L	(C)	enter Insert mode and start on a new line

	(R)	Left margin
M	(C)	Merge
O	(C)	display output format
P	(C)	Paste
Q	(C)	delete a word
R	(C)	Replace a character
	(R)	Right margin
S	(C)	Search forward
	(R)	Save a Ruler
T	(C)	move the cursor to the Top (beginning) of the item
U	(C)	(toggle) invoke or disable the Spelling checker for Inserted text
V	(C)	(toggle) View the embedded Ruler(s) and output format instructions
W	(C)	replace a word
X	(C)	eXit the item, do not save this version
	(R)	eXit Ruler mode, do not embed this Ruler
Y	(C)	delete a sentence
Z	(C)	transpose characters
	(R)	hyphenation zone
ESC	(C)	cancel Merge, Paste, Search, or the Spelling checker when there is no WORDS file
	(I)	leave Insert mode, go to Command mode
	(R)	embed this Ruler, go to Command mode
!	(C)	change the case of the line
^	(C)	move the cursor to the end of the line
*	(C)	change the case of the word
-	(R)	(dash) delete a character
_	(R)	(underline) delete all characters
<backspace>	(I)(R)	move the cursor one position to the left
<tab>	(C)(I)(R)	move the cursor to the next tab stop
[	(C)	start a cut
]	(C)	end a cut
}	(C)	move the cursor forward a paragraph
{	(C)	move the cursor back a paragraph
:	(C)	change the case of a letter
;	(C)	search backward
"	(C)	display a Paste item
<return>	(C)	move the cursor to the beginning of the line or to the next line if already there
	(I)	defines the end of the line
	(R)	move the cursor to the beginning of the Ruler

| (C) | invoke the Spelling checker for existing text starting from the cursor position
< | (I) | appears automatically after <return> is pressed and indicates the end of the line
 | (R) | left tab
> | (R) | right tab Note: most systems also use this symbol as the TCL prompt.
. | (R) | decimal tab
? | (C) | display the Command mode help screen or E ? enter Ruler mode
<space> | (C)(I)(R) | move the cursor one position to the right
<control>I | (C)(I)(R) | used if there is no tab key
<control>R | (C) | re-display a blank screen
<control>X | (C) | terminate the display of a multi-screen item

THE NUMERIC KEYPAD

Cursor movement in (C) Command mode is as follows:

0: back a page   6: forward a character
1: back a sentence   7: back a word
2: down a line   8: up a line
3: forward a sentence   9: forward a word
4: back a character   .: to the page bottom, press again for
5: to page top   the next page

8.8 FINISHING TOUCHES

8.8.1 OVERVIEW

The item so far has been aligned by Rulers with margins and tab stops; new lines have been indicated. This section covers additional regularly used format instructions that give the item a more finished appearance. All of them can be edited i.e. inserted and removed from the item as required. Some deal with the page as a whole: headings, footings, and page numbers. Others, like underline and highlight (hilite), can be applied to smaller segments of text. It is possible to preview most of the instructions and display the item in output format from Command mode by pressing

o   No <return>

As before, when there are multiple screens press <return> to continue, or <control> X to leave the display before the end of the item.

All format instructions are entered in the item from Insert mode and perform special operations at output. We use the terms "set" to turn on, and "disable" to turn off an instruction. Choose the operations from this section that are required for your individual needs.

BACKSLASH LINES

Start by examining the instructions described as *backslash lines*, so called because each has the backslash \ as the first character. The instructions vary according to the operation but all must be alone on a line without any additional characters. A backslash line affects the text that follows it until another backslash line cancels or disables it. Enter all backslash lines as follows:

1. Position the cursor at the Left margin
2. Press I to enter Insert mode
3. Press \ and the backslash automatically moves to the left edge of the screen
4. Type in only the backslash instruction on the line and press <return>
5. Continue with normal operations. Note that \ can be inserted in text at any other location as an ordinary character.

8.8.2 HEADINGS AND FOOTINGS

HEADINGS

A common requirement for output is a heading like those covered in Chapter 6.2 under the ACCESS modifier HEADING. JET also provides for headings, but the procedure is not the same. In JET the heading command is logically placed immediately after the opening Ruler and consists of three parts:

1. The backslash line that indicates a heading follows
2. One or more lines of heading text
3. The backslash line that marks the end of the heading

The first line is always one of the following.

```
\HEADING    or
\heading    or
\h
```

It defines the next line(s) as the heading text; each separate line becomes one line in the output heading. An example of a 1 line heading is

```
Sales Report
```

a 2 line heading is

```
Sales Report
Northeast Territory
```

A separate line consisting of

```
\*
```

indicates the end of the heading command.

The alignment of the heading text is controlled by the Ruler that precedes it. If the Ruler is not suited to the heading, change the Ruler. After the heading command is completed, embed another Ruler for the body of the text if necessary.

The system can furnish specific information for the heading. All of the options below can be used alone or combined with user supplied text; most are like those in Chapter 6.

HEADING OPTIONS

TO OUTPUT	USE	SAMPLE OUTPUT
time and date	'T'	14.31.18 03 FEB 1987 Time is in 24 hour format Date is DD MMM YYYY
date	'D' without text: 'D' with text: As of 'D'	as above without time 03 FEB 1987 As of 03 FEB 1987

consecutive page numbers	'P'	the number is printed as right justified in a space for 4 digits
	without text: 'P'	1
	with text: Page 'P'	Page 1 (the unused spaces show when there are less than 4 digits)
	or	
	'PN'	the number is printed as left justified and there are no gaps
	without text: 'PN'	1
	with text: Page 'PN'	Page 1
the name of the item	'I'	MOVE

Always use the tab stops on the Ruler to align the heading text. For example, to print the page number on the right side of the page, define a tab stop where the number is to go and type in the instruction such as 'PN' at that position. To output centered text, put C on the Ruler at the column around which the text is to be centered. Use the tab stop to reach the location for the text.

The following are examples of complete heading instructions and their output.

INSTRUCTION

    \heading
        Sales Report as of 'D'
*

OUTPUT

        Sales Report as of 03 FEB 1987

INSTRUCTION

    \h
                JET Example of A Centered Heading
Item-id is 'I'   Page 'PN'
*

OUTPUT

                JET Example of A Centered Heading

Item-id is MOVE   Page 23

Note that blank lines can be specified in the heading instruction by using the normal JET end of line indicator. For example, we can specify a blank line between two lines of text:

INSTRUCTION

```
\h
NORTHEAST TERRITORY 'D'
<
Page 'PN'
\*
```

OUTPUT

```
NORTHEAST TERRITORY 03 FEB 1987

Page 36
```

After a heading is set, it is printed at the top of every page until it is disabled by the command

```
\HEADING OFF
```

There are no headings from here on unless a complete new heading is set.

FOOTINGS

The footing instruction prints a footing at the bottom of each page that follows the command. Normally it is placed below the heading instruction at the beginning of the item. If there is no heading instruction, the footing command follows the opening Ruler. All footings start with

```
\FOOTING    or
\footing    or
\f
```

The rules and options for footings are exactly the same as those for headings. The last line of the footing is also always

 *

To disable a footing use

 \FOOTING OFF

A JET item can have both heading and footing commands, just as the ACCESS sentences in Chapter 6.2. For example

INSTRUCTION

```
    \heading
                    Parts Inventory as of 'T'
    \*
    \FOOTING
                    Page 'PN'
    \*
```

OUTPUT

```
                    Parts Inventory as of 14:31:18 03 FEB 1987
        .
        .
        .

                    Page 9
```

To leave space between the last line of text on the page and the footing, use as many blank lines as necessary in the footing instruction. For example,

INSTRUCTION

```
    \FOOTING
    <
    <
            Page 'PN'
    \*
```

OUTPUT follows.

.
.
.
(last line of text)

Page 9

8.8.3 NEW PAGE

At some point you may want to interrupt the continuous printing of the item and start on a new page. Page numbering, if used, remains sequential. The command is placed immediately before the text for the new page:

    \BP   or
    \bp   or
    \beginpage   or
    \begin

If you wish to isolate the material, repeat the new page instruction at the end of the special section. Do not use the new page command at the beginning of the item.

8.8.4 SPACING

Within the body of the document up to 4 lines can be specified as spacing between printed lines; this is similar to the spacing control on a typewriter. The text can be entered in the item single spaced and adjusted at output: if there is 1 blank line between lines in the item and the spacing instruction is for double spacing, there will be 3 blank lines between the lines when they are printed. The system defaults to single spacing which is 1. *Default* is action that is taken by the system unless it is otherwise instructed. If there is no spacing command, the output is single spaced. 2 outputs double spacing; 3, triple; and 4, quadruple or 4 lines between the lines of print. The command format is

    \spacing   or
    \sp

followed by 1 or 2 or 3 or 4.

Thus to double space set

>   \spacing 2

A typical application is to use \sp 2 to print the rough draft of the item; comments and corrections can be written in between the lines. After the alterations are made, either delete \sp 2 or change it to \sp 1 and the final printing will be single spaced.

Spacing can also be changed within the item. For example, single space up to a particular block of text; no spacing instruction is necessary for the default condition. Immediately before the block to be, for example, triple spaced insert

>   \sp 3

At the end of block return to single spacing with

>   \sp 1

8.8.5 JUSTIFICATION

Text that is justified has all full lines aligned with the Left and Right margins and looks like a box with straight sides as in most books and newspapers. In JET the Left margin on the Ruler fixes the beginning of the line and the Right margin the end of the line. Justification occurs at output time because the system inserts extra spaces between words to fill out the line when the text was entered with automatic word wrap.

The opposite of justification is non-justification where the text is "ragged" or uneven at the Right margin, as with most typewriters.

The default condition for output is justification, which means you have nothing to do when you want justified text. However justification can be disabled so that extra spaces are not added between words and all the lines do not end in the same column. The command is

>   \nojustify   or
>   \nj

To return to justification enter the following within the item:

>   \justify   or

\j

As mentioned text is automatically justified by default therefore \j is needed only after \nj.

Read the sample text below and note the position of the commands.

```
10                                                                    70
L                                                                      R
```

> This first block illustrates the default condition where text is justified or aligned with both margins. The system adds extra spaces between words to make the print lines the same length across the page.
>
> \nojustify
> The backslash line to disable justification is included only to show its relative position in the item; backslash lines are never printed in the output. This section of text is not justified and so the Right margin is ragged. No extra spaces are placed between words and therefore each line is a slightly different length.
>
> \justify
> Return to justified text. The text that follows \justify looks like the first block above as it aligns with the Right margin.

The item MOVE will look more like a hand typed letter if the text is not justified. From Insert mode add a blank line if necessary below the opening Ruler. Position the cursor at the Left margin and type in the backslash line:

> \nojustify

Note how the backslash moves to the left edge of the line. No other characters are allowed on the line. Press ESC to go to Command mode.

8.8.6 INDENT

The indent instruction shifts output toward the right a specified number of columns. The format is

> \indent n

where n is the number of columns to indent from the Left margin. If L is at 10 and the indent instruction is

    \indent 10

printing starts at column 20 (the Left margin 10 plus the indent 10) and all text in addition to the Left margin is shifted accordingly. Whatever fits on the line is printed; text that extends beyond the Right margin is not output because it does not wrap to the next line. Therefore you must be sure that the material will fit in the narrower space.

When used with a negative number, indent shifts text a limited distance to the left. NEVER specify a minus number to indent that will place text to the left of column 2. For example if the Left margin is at 10, the most you can indent is -8. If you go beyond the limit, some systems abort (halt the operation) and enter the system debugger with the ! prompt. In this case, type in END <return> which returns you to TCL. JET-IN to the item and correct the \indent instruction.

Disable the indent with

    \indent

Below is sample output to illustrate the results of the indent instruction which is included only to show where it is set and then where it is disabled.

```
          10        20                                            70
          L                                                        R
          Here the text starts as it normally does at the Left margin.
          Name
          Address
          Phone

     \indent 10
                    The text shifts to column 20.
                    Name
                    Address
                    Phone

     \indent
          After the indent is disabled the text returns to the Left margin.
```

8.8.7 HILITE

Add emphasis to an area on the page by using the hilite command to print a user specified character outside one or both margins. (Note that "The Works" version has added options.) The backslash line has three parts starting with

1. The hilite command:

    \hilite   or
    \hl

and is followed by:

2. The character chosen by the user such as:

    *   the asterisk or
    | the line

and ends with

3. The margin(s) at which the character is to be printed:

    L   (Left) or
    R   (Right) or
    B   (Both)

A sample hilite command to print an asterisk outside the Left margin is

    \hilite * L

The hilite is printed until it is disabled by

    \hilite OFF

In the example below, the hilite commands are inserted to show their position in the text; they are not printed in the output.

    \hilite * L

```
* A typical application of the hilite flags a change in
* documentation since the last printing. Note that blank
* lines are hilited until the command is disabled.

\hilite OFF
```

Set and disable the hilite after end of line indicators.

For greater emphasis, we can enclose text in a box by printing a row of characters for the top and bottom, and using the hilite command to print the sides. To frame a block of text by a broken line use the dash for the top and bottom, and the | for the sides. On the screen the item looks like

```
         ------------------------------------------------------
\hilite | B
         This section illustrates output that is enclosed in a box.
         The block to be enclosed can be as large as necessary.
         ------------------------------------------------------
\hilite OFF
```

The output is

```
         ------------------------------------------------------
       | This section illustrates output that is enclosed in a box. |
       | The block to be enclosed can be as large as necessary.     |
         ------------------------------------------------------
```

The example above is not filled in to the corners because the hilite character is printed outside the L and R margins. It is possible to output the hilite characters beyond the margins and up to the hilite. Normally text cannot extend past the margins. However the C tab overrides this limitation. Tab to C at column 40. Enter the hilite character so that it extends two characters beyond L and R as shown below.

```
         ------------------------------------------------------
\hilite | B
         In this box we close the corners by tabbing to C and extend-
         ing the dashes beyond the margins.
         ------------------------------------------------------
\hilite OFF
```

The output is

```
------------------------------------------------------------
| In this box we close the corners by tabbing to C and extend- |
| ing the dashes beyond the margins.                          |
------------------------------------------------------------
```

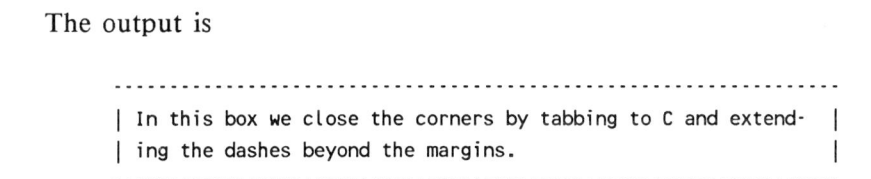

The asterisk * is also popular for hiliting text.

TILDE AND CONTROL COMMANDS

8.8.8 UNDERLINE

The backslash lines in the preceding sections apply to one or more lines of text and the command itself is on a line without any other text. In comparison, the underline and boldface instructions are used with one or more characters; the commands are set and disabled within the text immediately before and after the character(s) affected. Both the underline and the boldface have formats that start with either the tilde ~ or the <control> key. Note that some versions of JET may have other formats, particularly "The Works"; consult your users' manual. If you want a tilde in the text, type in two of them i.e. ~~ and one will be output.

Underline and boldface instructions are entered from Insert mode and executed when the item is printed, but not necessarily when it is displayed on the screen with O.

Consider both underline and boldface as commands with two parts: set and disable. When entering or deleting an instruction, remember to deal with both parts. Note that JET automatically disables underline and boldface at the end of a paragraph.

An underline can be added by a typewriter and placed below a character. JET-IN can handle only one character in each column (position). Therefore, the underline instruction must be inserted in the item to be carried out at output time. There are two types of underline: the continuous underline which prints under words or groups of characters and also the spaces between them, and the broken underline which prints only below words. The terms "continuous" and "broken" refer to the scope of the underline rather than the actual character, which is the same in both cases. Your system may accept the tilde and/or the control key commands which follow. Set all instructions immediately before the first character and disable immediately after the last character with no space between instruction and character.

THE BROKEN UNDERLINE

This underlines words only and not spaces.

>Set with ~UW or ~uw
>Disable with ~UX or ~ux

Note that either upper or lower case letters are permitted; the set and disable parts of the command need not be the same case. Text with the underline instruction looks like this on the screen:

>This illustrates ~uwthe broken underline~ux in the item.

The output is

>This illustrates the broken underline in the item.

When you are using the Spelling checker and have a tilde command joined with a word, JET cannot find a match and asks if the word is spelled correctly. Type in Y (for Yes) and then N (No, do not enter the word in the file) and continue.

Some versions of JET take the control key and a letter pressed together as the command. For the broken underline:

>Set with <control> W
>Disable with <control> X

These commands are also entered from Insert mode. The screen displays either the underline itself as specified or the square brackets [ ] around the underlined text, depending on your terminal.

THE CONTINUOUS UNDERLINE

Here, both the words and the spaces are underlined. The tilde commands are

>Set with ~UL or ~ul
>Disable with ~UX or ~ux

Sample text is

> This is how ~ulthe continuous underline~ux shows in the text.

The output is

> This is how the continuous underline shows in the text.

On some systems you may have a problem when there is a tab stop within the underline instruction ~ul and ~ux. The tab space is also underlined such as

> Start the underline here ~uland continue the text
>   at the tab on the next line ending the underline here~ux.

The output may look like this:

> Start the underline here and continue the text
>   at the tab on the next line ending the underline here.

To eliminate the underline where there is no text either

1. Change to the broken underline ~uw which does not underline spaces or
2. Use ~ul and disable the underline with ~ux at the end of the line. Press <return> to go to a new line and then tab to reach the position you want. Then set the underline again with ~ul and disable it where necessary.

Using the latter, the revised item now is

> In this example we start here ~uland go to the end of the line~ux
>   ~ula new underline is set and ends here~ux.

The output is

> In this example we start here and go to the end of the line
>   a new underline is set and ends here.

The control key command for the continuous underline is

Set with <control> V
Disable with <control> X

The screen display depends upon your terminal as with the other control key underline.

8.8.9 BOLDFACE

The ultimate result of the boldface command is on paper: specified characters are printed darker so that they stand out from the rest of the text providing that your printer has the capability. If it does not, the command has no effect. When the item is printed to the screen, the boldface characters may be brighter or in reverse video (the colors of the characters and the background are switched).

Like the underline, boldface has a pair of tilde commands and a pair of control key commands, all of which are entered from Insert mode. The Spelling checker reacts the same as it does with the tilde underline.

Set with ~BF
Disable with ~BX

The commands as they look inside an item are:

This illustrates ~BFthe boldface command~BX.

If your printer can perform boldfacing, your output will look like

This illustrates **the boldface command**.

The control key command is

Set with <control> B
Disable with <control> D

When the commands are inserted in the text, the display of boldface characters on the screen may be brighter or in reverse video or enclosed in curved brackets { } or angle brackets < >. On some systems the display starts when the command is set and continues to the end of the line. After the boldface is disabled the display is confined to the specified characters and the balance of the line, if any, reverts to normal.

SUMMARY: FINISHING TOUCHES

FUNCTION	SET	DISABLE

BACKSLASH LINES

Headings and Footings	\HEADING or \heading or \h \FOOTING or \footing or \f text line(s) options with text or alone: 'T' Time 'D' Date 'PN' or 'P' Page number 'I' Item-id *	\HEADING OFF \FOOTING OFF
New Page	\BP or \bp or \beginpage or \begin	
Spacing (the default is single space)	\spacing or \sp 1 or 2 or 3 or 4	
Justification	because the default is justified text \justify or \j is necessary only after \nojustify	\nojustify or \nj
Indent	\indent n	\indent
Hilite	\hilite or \hl character L or R or B	\hilite OFF

TILDE and CONTROL KEY COMMANDS

Underline (broken)	~uw or <control> W	~ux <control> X
(continuous)	~ul or <control> V	~ux <control> X
Boldface	~BF or <control> B	~BX or <control> D

8.9 PRINT THE ITEM

The verb JET-IN has taken us to the item where we performed a variety of operations to prepare it for output. Although the command O executes and displays the results of some of the output instructions, you must use the JET output command to see the finished document. The verb is

    JET-OUT

Output can be directed either to the screen or to the printer. The command format to output to the screen is

    >JET-OUT filename item-id

Using the test data the command is

    >JET-OUT LETTERS MOVE <return>

This allows you to check the final form of the item and make the necessary corrections before sending it to the printer. When an item requires more than one screen, press <return> to continue. To leave the display before the end of the item press <control> X together.

As mentioned in Chapter 4 there are many models of printers. You must consult your manual in order to load the paper, start up the printer, and, when finished, release the paper. Do not attempt to use a printer until you are thoroughly familiar with its operating procedures.

To route output to the printer add two options to the end of the JET-OUT command

    (FP

Note that the opening parenthesis is required; the closing parenthesis is optional

    (FP)

F is almost always used with P and starts each item on a new page. If F is omitted, an item might begin in mid-page. This is particularly important if there is an explicit item list with the JET-OUT command as follows:

    JET-OUT filename item-id1 item-id2 item-id3 etc.

Without F all the items would run together. When output is directed to the screen, a new page is generally not necessary; however (F or (F) can be added at the end of the JET-OUT command when P is not used.

P sends the output to the printer. Without the new page instruction it is

    (P   or (P)

The complete command to output to the printer is

    >JET-OUT filename item-id (FP

or for our example

    >JET-OUT LETTERS MOVE (FP <return>

F and P are the most commonly used options with JET-OUT and probably serve your needs. Consult your users' manual for other options that are called for less frequently.

The SPOOLER software utility, which manages printed output, is mentioned in Chapter 1 and is part of the Pick Operating System. Management is essential because users at more than one terminal might all try to use the same printer at one time. Without control their output would be interspersed and therefore worthless. Transparent to the user, the SPOOLER intercepts output headed for the printer and holds it until the printer is available. After you enter a JET-OUT command routing output to the printer, you know that the SPOOLER is working from the message

    ENTRY #n

n is a number automatically assigned to each print job. For example the message might be

    ENTRY #6

Whether the printer is in use at the moment or not, the SPOOLER takes over. When the SPOOLER has finished, the TCL prompt is displayed on the screen. You may work at the terminal on any of the tasks we have covered while the printer is operating.

If there should be a malfunction, you can stop the printing by a command from TCL. Refer to Volume II Chapter 13 of this series for instructions on how to use the SPOOLER.

In Section 8.6.1 we noted that an item larger than the maximum 32,267 bytes must be broken into as many smaller and separate items as necessary to keep each within the size limit. When you are ready to output the items that make up the whole piece, you can link them together and print them to screen or printer as one continuous document.

The command is the backslash line

    \CHAIN filename item-id

It is placed at the end of an item and directs JET to link that item to the one specified in the \CHAIN command. In this way multiple items can be linked: the first to the second, the second to the third, and so on. The last item does not have \CHAIN because it is the end of the chain. For example, output item-id1, item-id2, and item-id3 together. The first CHAIN is from item-id1 to item-id2. On the last line of item-id1 enter

    \CHAIN filename item-id2

Next we must link item-id2 and item-id3. On the last line of item-id2 enter

    \CHAIN filename item-id3

item-id3 is the last link and has no CHAIN. The output command is

    JET-OUT filename item-id1

JET outputs item-id1, is instructed by CHAIN to go to item-id2, and outputs item-id2. The next CHAIN sends JET to item-id3 for output. The CHAINed output is then complete.

The other command to link output works differently.

    \READ filename item-id   or
    \read filename item-id   or
    \r filename item-id

This not only instructs JET to link the item specified, but also to return to the item containing the \READ after the link is completed. Suppose you want to output item-id1 and include item-id2 within it. At the appropriate place in item-id1 enter

```
\READ filename item-id2
```

When you

```
JET-OUT filename item-id1
```

JET goes to item-id1 and outputs it up to the \READ, goes to item-id2 and outputs it, then returns to item-id1 and completes the output.

A practical application is to set up text that will be used repeatedly as an item and link it to another item by a \READ.

8.10 JOIN THE DATABASE WITH THE ITEM

Did you ever wonder how junk mail seems to be written just for you? Personal facts like your birthdate, name, and street address are inserted as if by magic into what is obviously a form letter. This is exactly what has been done but without any magic. First the form letter is designed and it includes the places to be filled in with the particulars. At output time the data values are retrieved from a file and inserted in the appropriate spots. The result looks like a personal letter to each recipient, but was only a routine operation for the computer.

For our exercise, the first step is to alter the item MOVE so that it can be used as a basic form letter. In order to retrieve the individual facts to insert in the letter, we must have a data file. Therefore we work with the VENDOR Data File and take some of the data values from it to put into the letter; we confine ourselves to one data file. If you do not want to use the VENDOR file, adapt what is available to you but do _not_ experiment with live data. Always use only test data to learn an operation.

In its present form MOVE is a general letter without personal details and could be sent to all of the suppliers. By revising it slightly to make places for several attributes, we can produce letters that will look as if each one were typed especially for the vendor who receives it, yet the main body of the text is the same for all.

A sample of the new version of MOVE is below; to it we have added data values for item-id TOPS.55 in the VENDOR file. This is not ready to be typed in yet but illustrates how we work backwards from the final presentation.

```
03 FEB 1987


Tops In Gadgets
Janet Lane
Charles Neck, MA 67890


Dear Ms. Ellen Van:

Thanks to reliable suppliers like you folks at Tops In
Gadgets our business has grown substantially over the last
five years.

On September 19th we are moving to larger quarters to
facilitate our expanded operations.

The new address is

    123 Tain Street
    Aceville, NY 34567

As our major vendor in Charles Neck, you can be assured of
our continued loyalty.

Cordially,

F. Gundelfinger
President
```

Do not attempt to output the item until you have followed all of the preliminary instructions and reached the JET-OUT command.

First, JET-IN LETTERS MOVE. Then add four blank lines after the \nojustify backslash line at the beginning of the item. Now that we have the form for the letter, we replace the data values as shown in the letter above with the names of the attributes and also add new text as follows:

```
\nojustify
    CO.NAME<
    STREET<
    CITY, STATE ZIP<
    <
    <
    Dear CONTACT:<
    <
    Thanks to reliable suppliers like you folks at CO.NAME our
    business has grown substantially over the last five years.<
    <
    On September 19th we are moving to larger quarters to
    facilitate our expanded operations.<
    <
    The new address is<
    <
        123 Tain Street<
        Aceville, NY 34567<
    <
    As our major vendor in CITY, you can be assured of our con-
    tinued loyalty.<
    <
    Cordially,<
    <
    F. Gundelfinger<
    President<
```

This is not enough for JET to retrieve the data values. As you would expect if you were to JET OUT the item as it stands, all of the output would be exactly as it appears above. JET must be given a specific command and also the name of the file along with the names of the attributes to be able to fetch each data value.

The command is

```
~INSERT filename attributename
```

At output time JET inserts the specified data from the file in place of the command. Do not confuse this with Insert mode.

The ~INSERT (or ~I) command is delimited by the tilde ~ at the beginning, and by a space at the end (unless there is no additional text adjacent).

When there is no space between the text and the tilde as in

    Dear~INSERT VENDOR CONTACT

output for the test data is

    DearMS. ELLEN VAN

When there is a space before the tilde

    Dear ~INSERT VENDOR CONTACT

the output is

    Dear MS. ELLEN VAN

In comparison, the delimiting space that follows the ~INSERT command is <u>not</u> output. Therefore,

    Dear ~INSERT VENDOR CONTACT :

outputs

    Dear MS. ELLEN VAN:

If you do not have a space to delimit the end of the command, JET cannot differentiate between the attributename and whatever follows. For example, suppose the JET item contains

    Dear ~INSERT VENDOR CONTACT:

At JET-OUT time JET outputs the item until it reaches the ~INSERT with no delimiter. It displays the error message

    [24] THE WORD "CONTACT:" CANNOT BE IDENTIFIED

and stops output. You must add a space between CONTACT and the colon.

To output a space after the attributename use 2 spaces, such as

Word Processing with JET

```
    Dear ~INSERT VENDOR CONTACT  :
```

for

```
    Dear MS. ELLEN VAN :
```

Below is the item with the ~INSERT commands. Note that ~D has been added at the top of the item to output the current date. The command to disable justification remains in the item.

```
    \nojustify<
       ~D<
       <
       <
       <
       ~INSERT VENDOR CO.NAME<
       ~INSERT VENDOR STREET<
       ~INSERT VENDOR CITY , ~INSERT VENDOR STATE  ~INSERT VENDOR ZIP<
       <
       <
       Dear ~INSERT VENDOR CONTACT :<
       <
       Thanks to reliable suppliers like you folks at ~INSERT VENDOR
       CO.NAME  our business has grown substantially over the last five
       years.<
       <
       On September 19th we are moving to larger quarters to
       facilitate our expanded operations.<
       <
       The new address is<
       <
            123 Tain Street<
            Aceville, NY 34567<
       <
       As our major vendor in ~INSERT VENDOR CITY , you can be assured of
       our continued loyalty.<
       <
       Cordially,<
       <
       F. Gundelfinger<
       President<
```

As you recall, the alphabetic characters for the VENDOR file data values were entered as upper case letters; the system outputs them as capitals unless otherwise instructed. All correlatives can be applied when data is ~INSERTed into a JET item. Therefore we can use MCT to output upper and lower case letters in order to make the data values consistent with the rest of the text. Without MCT code a sample letter would have

    Dear MS. ELLEN VAN:

With the MCT code as a correlative in the Descriptor for CONTACT the output is

    Dear Ms. Ellen Van:

The second version looks much more like a personal letter to Ms. Van.

Update the following Descriptors as shown below:

```
             CO.NAME   STREET   CITY   CONTACT
   line
   001       A         A        A      A
   002       8         4        5      7
   003 through 007 null values for all the Descriptors
   008       MCT       MCT      MCT    MCT
   009       L         L        L      L
   010       35        30       20     35
```

Two Descriptors referenced by ~INSERT do not require MCT code: STATE because the values are conventionally shown as two capital letters, and ZIP because the values are numeric. Check that both Descriptors conform to those below.

```
          STATE  ZIP
   line
   001    A      A
   002    2      3
   003 through 007 null values for both Descriptors
   009    L      R
   010    2      5
```

The date is printed in caps by JET and cannot be changed by code.

Although it seems that we are ready to print we have one more step before we can use the JET-OUT command. If you used it now you would see only one copy of MOVE as last shown with the ~INSERT commands. Before the data can be joined to the item, the file must be prepared. At TCL the verb

    SELECT

places the item-ids in the workspace and sets a flag which instructs the system to use these items for the next command. The format is

    >SELECT filename

It SELECTs the items in their internally stored order like the LIST verb. But here you do not see any output, only the response

    [404] the number of ITEMS SELECTED.

In this exercise the command is

    >SELECT VENDOR <return>

Response

    [404] 6 ITEMS SELECTED.

The response to the SELECT command must be followed immediately by the JET-OUT command, here

    >JET-OUT LETTERS MOVE (FP <return>

Omit P for output to the screen.

The individualized letters to each VENDOR in the file are output in the same sequence as the items are stored. The first sample letter for TOPS.55 at the beginning of this Section is the final version of MOVE joined with the data values. When you compare the output letters, you will find that the space reserved for the values to be inserted does not depend on the length of the command itself as written in the item. When the value is placed in the text, the balance is shifted according to the amount of space required for the value; for example, "The Summit for Housewares" takes far more room than "Zenith". And so all the output will probably not be exactly the same because in one letter a line may contract, in another it may wrap.

The name and address at the top of the letter can be positioned to fit in a window envelope. Printing address labels is covered in Volume II of this series.

You may want the items output in a particular order as we have done with the SORT verb and Sort keys in Chapter 5.6. To place the items in the workspace in Sorted order use the verb

    SSELECT filename

with BY attributename for each Sort key. The format is

    >SSELECT filename BY attributename (BY attributename}

For example our item could be output sorted by CO.NAME.

    >SSELECT VENDOR BY CO.NAME <return>
    >JET-OUT LETTERS MOVE (FP <return>

At times you may not want to output the entire file but only those items that meet certain requirements. Use selection criteria with SELECT and SSELECT just as we do with LIST and SORT. For example print the MOVE letter only for VENDORs in SC:

    >SELECT VENDOR WITH STATE "SC" <return>

Response

    [404] 1 ITEMS SELECTED.

The next command is

    >JET-OUT LETTERS MOVE (FP <return>

Only one item - SUMMIT.33 - has STATE equal to SC. SELECT brings it to the workspace. When the JET-OUT command is executed, the data for the one item is all that is available and so only one MOVE letter is output.

The selection criteria can just as easily contain an attribute that is not inserted, such as PHONE. For example output in ascending order of PHONE values only those suppliers with area code 516:

    >SSELECT VENDOR WITH PHONE "516-^^^-^^^^" BY PHONE <return>

Response

    [404] 3 ITEMS SELECTED.

This is followed by

    >JET-OUT LETTERS MOVE (FP <return>

There are three VENDORs with area code 516: ACME.66, ACF.88, and SUMMIT.33. Having met the selection criteria, the values for PHONE are then Sorted in ascending order and their item-ids are placed in that sequence in the workspace. The MOVE letters are output in the same order for the three items that were SELECTed.

8.11 ERROR EXAMPLES

TCL Command: >CREATE-FILE LETTERS
RESPONSE: [416] RANGE ERROR IN MODULO OR SEPARATION PARAMETER.
COMMENT: The dict.mod and data.mod are omitted from the command sentence.

TCL Command: >JET-IN filename item-id
RESPONSE: [201] 'FILENAME' IS NOT A FILENAME
COMMENT: The name of the file in the command does not exist: either it is spelled incorrectly or has not been created

---

JET: Command mode
PRESS: The cursor positioning keys to move along the Ruler but without the desired results.
COMMENT: You must be in Ruler mode to control cursor movement along the Ruler.

JET:	Command mode
PRESS:	G (intending to Get a Saved Ruler)
RESPONSE:	Go To which line #
COMMENT:	You must be in Ruler mode to Get a Saved Ruler.

TCL Command:	>LISTFILES JET-IN
RESPONSE:	[10] FILE NAME MISSING
COMMENT:	Two commands have been mixed together here. They should be either:

      1. LISTFILES to output the names of the files or
      2. JET-IN filename item-id to enter the JET item

JET	Item has on a line alone: /bp
OUTPUT:	/bp appears in the text as shown
COMMENT:	The backslash command for a new page is \bp not /bp

JET item:	\HEADING SALES REPORT 'D'
OUTPUT:	there is no heading on the page
COMMENT:	The heading backslash line must be alone on the line; the actual heading text should be on the line(s) below.

TCL Command:	>JET-IN PASTE*00*8
RESPONSE:	[201] 'PASTE*00*8' IS NOT A FILE NAME
COMMENT:	The Paste number is an item-id, it must be preceded by the name of the file.

JET item:	as shown below with an indent backslash line. Note the margins on the Ruler, the text, the position of the indent backslash line, and the resulting output.

```
\nj
   10                        45                    70
```

```
                                                         R
```
This example illustrates a full line of text from the Left
margin to the Right margin. The same text is shown below
after the indent backslash line is inserted to start the
output 35 columns from the Left margin.

\indent 35

                                This example illustrates
                                margin to the Right marg
                                after the indent backsla
                                output 35 columns from t

COMMENT: Every line is shifted to the right without regard to the edge of the paper. There is no wrapping, so whatever extends past the Right margin is not output. You must anticipate the results of indenting.

TCL Command: >JET-OUT LETTERS MOVE (FP
JET ITEM: Dear ~INSERT VENDOR CONTACT :
OUTPUT: Dear ~INSERT VENDOR CONTACT :
COMMENT: SELECT VENDOR was not given before the JET-OUT command.

8.12 REVIEW QUESTIONS

1. Describe two types of Searches.
2. What commands enable us to find the names of our JET files and items?
3. What are the functions of backslash lines? Give four examples.
4. How do you get to a JET item? How do you leave it?
5. Compare the Merge and Cut/Paste procedures: their similarities and differences.
6. How is a database joined to a JET item for output?
7. How is a JET item started?
8. What is word wrap?

9. How is a JET item output to the screen? To the printer?
10. What is the purpose of a Ruler? How many can there be in one item?
11. Describe the differences between a typewriter and a word processor.
12. Give three examples of status lines and explain their functions.
13. Name the three JET modes and when each is used.
14. Why must the size of an item be considered?
15. What are the advantages and disadvantages of the Spelling checker?

Glondex

* (EDITOR): EDIT all the items in the file. 81, 98, 104
. EDITOR prompt 41
<control> <shift> _ <return> Continue the command sentence on the next line. 72, 177
<control> R Re-display the screen. 34
<control> X Terminates a multi-screen display at the end of the current screen. 69, 318, 342, 354
<control>] Delimiter to separate multiple instructions in a Tag, Conversion, and Correlative Codes. 198, 257
<return> The key pressed to indicate the end of the input. Also used to continue a multiscreen display. 28, 29, 286
> TCL prompt

A: Abbreviation for Attribute Definition Item in a Descriptor.
A Code: Arithmetic and Concatenation. Perform calculations on numeric data; also concatenate user supplied text and/or the results of processing. 239-253
ACCESS: A processor and also a data retrieval language. 10, 111, Summary: Sentence format 146-7, 153
Account: A user-oriented collection of files and commands: a Master Dictionary, Dictionaries, and Data Files. 24, 30
Address: The specific location on the disk of a frame by which the data in it can be retrieved. 23
ADI: Attribute Definition Item; see Descriptor
AI, Artificial Intelligence: The science of making computers more powerful by attempting to duplicate human intelligence. 4
Alphabetic: Data consisting of letters.
Alphanumeric: Data made up of letters and numbers.
AMC: see Attribute Mark Count
Analog: A continuous quantity which represents another such as mercury in a thermometer for temperature or a signal on a telephone wire for sound.
AND 115-6, 127
ASCII, American Standard Code for Information Interchange: The standard code for characters; used on most mini and microcomputers. 2
Attribute: A property of an item; analogous to a field in other systems. 15
Attribute Definition Item, ADI: See Descriptor
Attribute Mark Count, AMC: The number of the attribute. 38-9

Attributename constraints 20

Auxiliary Storage, Secondary storage: Data and instructions stored outside the computer and brought in as necessary for processing. Disk and tape are frequently used. 8

Backslash lines (JET): Output formatting instructions that are inserted in an item and start with the \ backslash. 354-69

Backup: Duplicating data on another medium, usually magnetic tape, for storage outside the computer. 8

BASE: The disk address of the first frame of a file. 35-6, 287

BASIC: Beginners All-Purpose Symbolic Instruction Code; a high level programming language. 6, 259-61

Beginpage Command (JET) 359

Binary: A two state numbering system wherein, for example, data is represented by 1's (ON) and 0's (OFF). 2

Bit: Abbreviation for Binary digit; either 0 or 1. 2

Boldface Command (JET) 368

Booting, Boot, Bootstrap: The process which loads the operating system into main memory and makes the computer ready to use. 9

BREAK-ON modifier (ACCESS): The instruction for control breaks, used with SORT. 166-178, Summary 178

Buffer: A temporary work area for data. 96

BY: BY is followed by the name of the attribute to be used as Sort Key for an ascending SORT. 135-6

BY-DSND: BY-DSND is followed by the attribute to be used as Sort Key in a descending SORT. 139

Byte: Eight bits, usually one character. 2

C Code: Concatenation. Join and output attribute values with or without user supplied text. 220-9, 241-2

C modifier option (ACCESS): Center text. 159

C option (ACCESS), COL-HDR-SUPP: Suppress heading, column headings, and summary line. 156

Call: To use the results of an Arithmetic Code in one Descriptor for another Code that is in a different Descriptor. 241,248

CHAIN Command (JET) 372

COL-HDR-SUPP modifier (ACCESS), C option (ACCESS): Suppress heading, column headings, and summary line. 155

Command line limit: 148 characters 72

Command mode (EDITOR): Used for editing operations except for inputting text. 41

Command mode (JET): The base mode for general editing. 288
Computer: An electrically powered device that stores data and processing instructions to produce information. 1
Concatenation: see A Code, C Code
Control Break: A subdivision of sorted output based on a change in the value of the Sort Key. 166-178
Conversion: An instruction code on line 7 in the Descriptor (normally processed after line 8) that changes the output form of the data. 200-278
Correlative: An instruction code on line 8 in the Descriptor (normally processed before line 7) that changes the output form of the data. 200-278
COUNT 117-8, 122-3
CPU, Central Processing Unit: The heart of the computer system; it controls all operations. 7
CREATE-ACCOUNT 30
CREATE-FILE 31, 35-6, 286-7
CRT, Cathode Ray Terminal: A user terminal consisting of a screen and keyboard.
Cursor: The symbol on the screen that shows the position of the next typed character. 28, 284
Cursor positioning (JET) Command mode 292-5, Summary 294-5
Cursor positioning (JET) Ruler mode 307
Cut and Paste Commands (JET), [] P: Cut text from an item; delete the cut or save it as a Paste item for copying. 338-345

D modifier option (ACCESS): Date 157-8
Data: "Facts" for computer processing.
Data File: A collection of facts about related items such as employee personnel records. 24, 33-4, 55-60, Summary: Create 59-60
Database: A collection of related data files organized for efficiency. 22
DATE: A utility program on some systems that changes date values from external to internal format and vice versa. Also a BASIC program to perform the same operations. 258-262
Date Conversion Code, D: Change date values from internal to external format for output. 258-263, Summary 263, 266, 271, 275-278
DE Command (EDITOR), DElete line(s) 93-6
Default: An action taken or value used by the system unless otherwise instructed. 36, 134, 136, 138-9, 153, 176, 179, 181, 192-3, 213
Delete an item: see FD Command (EDITOR)
DELETE-FILE 107

Delimiter: A character that separates data elements. 44, 198-9, 228, 230, 232

Descriptor, Attribute Definition Item: A Dictionary item that describes the format and relative position of an attribute within an item. 37-54, Summary: Create 52-4, 189

Dictionary, File Dictionary: A directory to the location and format of a Data File. 24, 33-4, Summary: Create 52-4,

Digital: Data in the form of individual units such as the electronic impulses common to most computers. 2

Direct Access, Random Access: The means of retrieving an item based on its item-id without processing through the entire file. 23

Disk: A flat plate with a magnetic coating for data storage. 8, 23

Diskette, Floppy (disk): A small, removable, flexible disk.

EBCDIC: Extended Binary Coded Decimal Interchange Code: a character code used on most mainframe computers.

ED, EDIT: Verb to invoke the EDITOR. 41

Edit text (JET) 295-302, Summary 302, 322-45

EDITOR: The system processor used for creating and modifying text. 10, 41, 74-5, Summary: Terms 107-8, 285

ENIAC, Electronic Numerical Integrator and Calculator: The first large scale electronic calculator (1946). 6

EOI, End Of Item: Message displayed by the EDITOR at the last line in an item. 46

EX Command (EDITOR): EXit the item; discard changes if any. 96-7, 104

EXK Command (EDITOR): EXit the current item, discard changes (if any), and leave the EDITOR. 98

Explicit Attribute List: Descriptor names specified in an ACCESS sentence for output. 179, 181-2

Explicit Item List: One or more item-ids specified in a command sentence. 72, 84, 98, 179, 319

External format (Date): The conventional expression of Date in month, day, and year. 258

F Command (EDITOR): Flip the contents of the secondary buffer onto the primary buffer. 96, 103

F option (JET): Start output of each item on a new page. 370

FD Command (EDITOR): Delete the item. 99, 100

FD Command (JET): Delete the item. 303

FI Command (EDITOR): FIle the item. 48, 96, 103

FI Command (JET): FIle the item. 291, 302-3

FIK Command (EDITOR): FIle the current item, leave the EDITOR. 98

File: A collection of related items. 13, 18, 24-5, 36, 286, 317, Summary (JET) 346

File Dictionary: see Dictionary

Filename constraints 18-9

Fill character: Output an * or space in each unused position of numeric data to fill a specified number of places. 233, 235-7

Finishing touches (JET): 353-69, Summary 369

FK Command (JET): Exit the item, discard changes (if any), leave JET. 319

Floppy (disk): see Diskette

Fold: see Wrap

FOOTING Command (JET) 357-9

FOOTING modifier (ACCESS) 159-161, Summary 161

Frame: The smallest unit of storage space on the disk. 23, 192

FS Command (EDITOR): File the current version of the item, remain in the item, and in the EDITOR. 85-6, 96, 103

FS Command (JET): File the current version of the item, remain in the item, and in JET. 291, 303

Functions of the keys in JET 286, Summary 351-3

G Code: Group Extraction. Output part(s) of a data value where the elements are separated by a non-numeric character. 212-5, 218-9, 251, 257

G Command (JET Ruler mode): Get a saved ruler. 312-3

General Purpose Descriptor: See Synonym Descriptor

GRAND-TOTAL modifier (ACCESS): Specifies user supplied text for output at the end of TOTAL instead of *** default. 163-5, Summary 165, 195

Group: The vertical dimension of a file: one or more frames linked together. 23

H option (ACCESS), HDR-SUPP: Suppress heading and summary line. 156

Hardware: The physical components of a computer. 7-8

Hashing: A calculation performed by the system to generate the storage location for an item. 23

HDR-SUPP modifier (ACCESS), H option (ACCESS): Suppress heading and summary line. 154

HEADING Command (JET) 354-7
HEADING modifier (ACCESS) 157-9, Summary 161
High level language: A people-oriented programming language wherein one statement can generate many machine level instructions. 6
Hilite Command (JET) 363-5

I Command (EDITOR): Enter Input mode. 41
I Command (JET): Enter Insert mode. 324-5
I option (ACCESS), ID-SUPP: Suppress item-ids. 156
I/O devices: see Peripherals
ID-SUPP modifier (ACCESS), I option (ACCESS): Suppress item-ids. 155
Implicit Attribute List: Sequentially numbered attributes output by default when no explicit attributes are specified in an ACCESS sentence. 179-183, 200
Indent Command (JET) 361-2
Input: Data and instructions that are entered into the computer. 3
Input mode (EDITOR) 41-2, 77
INSERT Command (JET) 375-8
Insert mode (JET): Enter new text. 288
Integer: A whole number without a fraction or decimal portion.
Interface: Contact between two entities such as a person and a computer. 8
Intermediate Control Break: A control break that occurs where the value of the Secondary Sort Key changes. 175
Internal format (Date): Date expressed as an integer. 258
Item: A data entity in a file; each item consists of an item-id (and attributes). Comparable to a record in non-Pick systems. 15
Item size (maximum): 32,267 bytes (characters)
ITEM-ID, ITEM ID: The unique identifier or key by which an item is stored and retrieved. 15, 288
Item-id constraints 20

JET: The word processing software routinely installed with the Pick Operating System. 10, 283-4
JET modes 285, Summary 347-51
JET-IN: Invoke the word processor. 285, 287
JET-OUT: Output JET item(s). 285, 370-2, 379-80
Justification: The direction from which characters proceed: L (left) for letters and combinations of letters and numbers; and R (right) for numbers. T is used with alphabetic data to wrap (if such occurs)

between words. In JET, justification refers to text aligned with both margins. 39, 129-131, 137, 191-6, 215, 217
Justify Command (JET) 360-1

K suffix (EDITOR) 98, 106
K, KB, Kilobyte: 1,024 bytes (characters). 7
Keyboard 27-8, 284

L Command (JET): Enter Insert mode and start text on a new line. 325-6
L modifier option (ACCESS): New line. 160-1
Leading zero: Zero(s) at the left end of a numeric string; they do not affect the value. 42
Length (output): The number of characters specified on line 10 of the Descriptor is one factor that determines the amount of space allocated for output. 39, 172, 190-2, 196-7
Line continuation: <control> <shift> _ <return> 72, 177, 250
LIST 67, Summary 73-4, 116, 122-3, 200, 318
LIST ONLY 68, 182-3
LIST-ITEM 69-70
LISTFILES 66, 317-8
Literal value: A value which remains fixed during processing; it is enclosed in double quotes. 113, 145
Logging Off: See OFF.
Logging On: Entering the account name by which an authorized user gains access to the system. 29, 31-3
Logical file structure: The conceptual organization of data such as in a two dimensional table. 15-7, 22
LPTR option, (P): Route the output to a printer. 66

Machine Language: The low level instructions in binary code executed by the hardware. 6
Major Control Break: A control break that occurs where the value of the Primary Sort Key changes. 174-5
Master Dictionary, MD: The vocabulary and file pointers of an account. 24-5
MC Codes: Mask character. Change case or block character type(s) in the output. 203-8, Summary 208, 266, 271, 274
MC/A Code: Output characters that are not alphabetic. 207-8
MC/N Code: Output characters that are not numeric. 208
MCA Code: Output alphabetic characters only. 205-6

MCL Code: Output lower case. 203-4
MCN Code: Output numeric characters only. 206-7
MCT Code: Output upper and lower case. 204-5, 227-8, 378
MCU Code: Output upper case. 205
Megabyte, MB: 1,048,576 bytes (characters).
Memory, Main memory: The work area in the CPU that holds currently used data and instructions. 7
Merge Command (JET), M: Copy text into the current location from another; the source text is retained. 326-331, 341
Merge, and Cut and Paste Comparison (JET) 345
Minor Control Break: A control break that occurs at the smallest subdivision produced by a Sort Key. 174
MOD: see Modulo
Modifier: An optional part of an ACCESS sentence which acts on the verb and thus affects the output. 153-6
Modifier options: Options used with modifiers in an ACCESS sentence. 157-9
Modulo, MOD: The horizontal dimension of a disk storage area specified in number of frames. 23, 36, 286-7
Moving Around in JET Diagram 316
Moving Around in JET Summary 317
MR Code: Punctuate numeric data at output. 233-239, 266, 271, 274-5

N notation: The means of referencing other Descriptors in an A (Arithmetic) code. 241, 251
NOJUSTIFY Command (JET), \nj 360-1
Null: No value. 44
Numeric: Data consisting of numbers with or without a decimal point.

O Command (JET): Display Output; does not execute all instructions. 353
OFF, Logging Off: Terminating the user's session on the system. 61
Operating System, OS: The software which controls the hardware and performs utility functions. 9
Option: An optional part of an ACCESS sentence which acts on the verb and thus affects the output. 156
OR (implied): A Throwaway word that may be used in a command but is not required. 114, 139, 142
OS: see Operating System
Output: Information produced by a computer. 3
Over-write: To replace either stored data or output.

P Code: Pattern. Output data values that match the specified number and type of characters. 209-212, 272-3

P Command (EDITOR): Print the current version of the item to the screen. 46-7, 96, 103

P modifier option (ACCESS): Page number (right justified). 160

P option: Route the output to a printer. 66

P option (JET) 370-1

Parameter: A limiting value. 229-30

Password: A security safeguard which permits the authorized user to log on. 31

Paste Command (JET), P: Copy text that has been saved as a Cut. 339-45

Peripherals, I/O devices: Equipment outside of the CPU by which the computer communicates with the external world. 7-8

Physical file structure: The way in which the computer stores data on a medium such as a magnetic disk. 22-3

Pick Operating System: The unique software designed by Richard Pick. 9, 10, 284, 317

Pick, Richard: Author of the Pick Operating System 9

Placeholder: A caret ^ indicating that any character is acceptable in this position in a string comparison. 145

PN modifier option (ACCESS): Page number (left justified). 159

Pointer: Address information that provides a link for the system to find data. 23

Port: A connection on the computer, typically for a terminal or a printer. 342-3

Primary sort 132, 141

Privilege level: A security feature that limits the activities of an account. 22

Program: see Software

Prompt: A special character displayed on the screen indicating the computer's readiness to accept input. 28

R Code: Range. Output item-ids but only those attribute values that fall within the specified parameter(s). 229-232

R Command (EDITOR): Replace 44-5, 90-1, 199

RAM, Random Access Memory: Volatile memory used as a scratch pad for processing. 7

Random Access: see Direct Access

Random Access Memory: see RAM

Re-display a blank screen: <control> R 34

READ Command (JET) 372-3
Read Only Memory: see ROM
Relational operators: Letters or symbols which define the comparison to be made between two values. 113, 126-8, Summary 129, 144, 229, 272, 277
Reserved word: A word that has special meaning to the computer and cannot be used in any other context. 146, 153
ROM, Read Only Memory: Non-volatile memory with unalterable contents, typically used for routines such as booting. 9
Rounding: Adjusting a fractional or decimal number to the desired number of significant places. 247
RU Command (EDITOR): Replace Universal. 90-1
Ruler mode (JET): Manipulate alignment control characters. 288, 304-15, Summary 314-5

Save a Ruler (JET), S 311-2
Screen 28, 285
Search (and Replace) Command (JET), S 331-8, Summaries: 334, 335, 337
Secondary sort 132, 136, 141
Secondary storage: see Auxiliary storage
SELECT 379-80
Selection Criteria: Requirement(s) specified in a command to restrict output to data that passes the test(s). 112-6, 126-8, Summary 147-8, 266-278
SEP, see Separation
Separation, SEP, SEPAR: The vertical dimension of a disk storage area specified in number of frames. 23, 36, 286-7
SIZE Descriptor: Outputs the number of bytes in an item. 320-1
Soft hyphen (JET) 290
Software, Program: The instructions that direct the operation of the computer. 8-9
SORT: To present data for output in a specified sequence without altering its internally stored order. 132-42, 200, 318
Sort Key: The value on which the sequence of the output is arranged. 13-4, 132, 166
Spacing Command (JET) 359-60
Spelling Checker (JET): A comparison of the words in a JET item with those stored in the WORDS file. 322-5
SPOOLER: The software utility (processor) that manages output to be printed. 10, 371-2
SSELECT 380-1

STAT 120-1, 122-3

Status line (JET): A system message displayed across the bottom of the screen. 286, Ruler: 288, Insert: 289, Command: 290

String: A group of characters that represents an entity such as a data value. 143

String search: Selection criteria applied to part of a value. 143-5, Summary 146

SUM 119-20, 122-3

Suppress 153-6

Synonym Descriptor: A Descriptor which is used instead of an A type Descriptor. 130, 140, 179, 201, 220

System Dictionary: The directory of authorized accounts. 25

T Code: Textract, Text extraction. Output the specified numbers of characters (by position) in the data value. 215-20, 252, 264-8

T justification: Used with alphabetic data to wrap (if necessary) between words rather than dividing a word. 191, 219

T modifier option (ACCESS): Output time and date. 158-9

Table: A structure to contain facts. A two dimensionsal table consists of vertical columns and horizontal rows. 17-8

Tag: User supplied text on line 3 of a Descriptor; output as column heading instead of the attributename. 197-200, 231-2, 244

Tape: A linear medium coated with a magnetic surface for auxiliary data storage. 8

TCL, Terminal Control Language: The user-interface processor which invokes all other processors. 10, 33

Terminal: Generally the keyboard and screen that make up a user's work station. 27-8

Terminal Control Language, see TCL

Tfile Code: Translation. An attribute in the original file is used as an item-id in the Translated file. Then an attribute for that item is translated back for output instead of the original value. 253-8, 269-72

Throwaway words: Specific words that are ignored by the computer; they may be added to commands by the user for greater clarity. 116-7

Tilde and Control Commands (JET) 365-9

TOP: Message displayed by the EDITOR at the beginning of an item. 41

TOTAL modifier (ACCESS) 162-5, Summary 165, 168-9, 171-3, 175-8

Truncate: To cut off part of a string. For example, ABCDEFG truncated to 4 characters becomes ABCD if left justified, and DEFG if right justified. 194-5, 238

U Command (JET): Check the spelling of words as they are inserted (toggle). 324-5

U modifier option (ACCESS): Underline; used with GRAND-TOTAL. 164

Underline Command (JET) 365-8

Update: Making changes in data to reflect current conditions. 65, 74, Summaries: Part 1 75-6, Part 2 101-3, Part 3 105-6

V modifier option (ACCESS): Used with TOTAL; replace *** with the name of the value where the control breaks occur. 170-2, 176-7, 190-2

Value: The contents of an attribute which can vary with each item or a fixed string such as a literal.

View (JET): Toggle for display of Ruler(s) and output instructions in the item. 288

WHO 342

WITH: The beginning of a selection criterion phrase. 113

Word Processor: Software with a wide range of options for text creation, storage, manipulation, and output. 283-4

WORDS file (JET) 322

Wrap, Fold: Automatic continuation to the next line. 190, 229, 289

X Command (JET): EXit the item, discard the current version. 303-4, 313

Z Command (JET): Transpose characters. 300-1

| Command (JET): Spelling check existing text from cursor position to end of document. 323

The following additional trademarks are used in this book:

TRADEMARK	COMPANY
Access	Pick Systems
Accu/Plot-II	AccuSoft Enterprises
ADDS	Applied Digital Data Systems
Documentor	Applied Digital Data Systems
English	The Microdata Corporation
IBM	International Business Machines Corporation
Inform	Prime Computer Inc.
JET	Jet Software Inc.
Laser-Jet Pick	Pick Systems
PICK/BASIC	Pick Systems
Recall	The Ultimate Corp.
Ultimate	The Ultimate Corp.
Ulti-word	The Ultimate Corp.
Wordmate	The Microdata Corporation